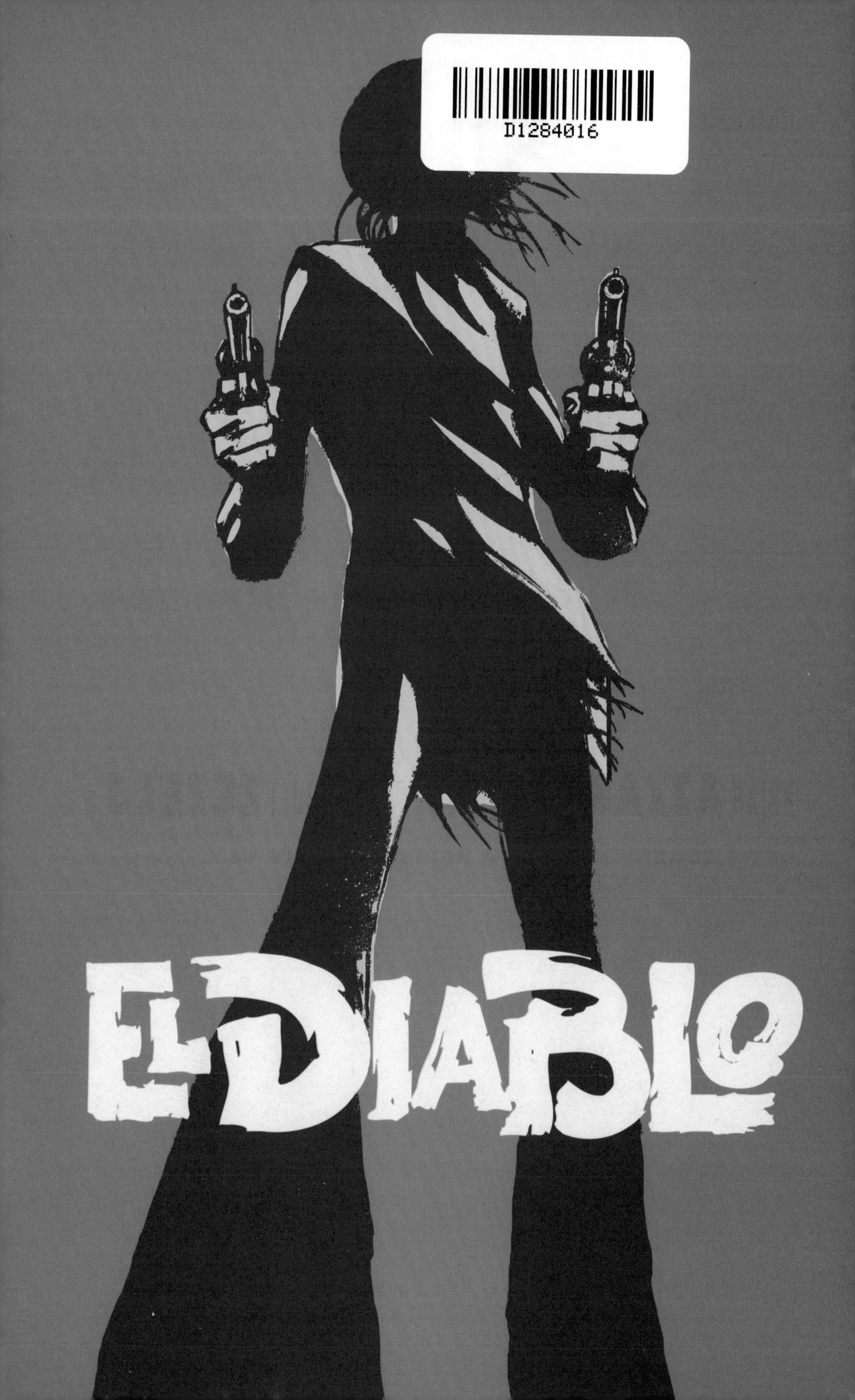
EL DIABLO

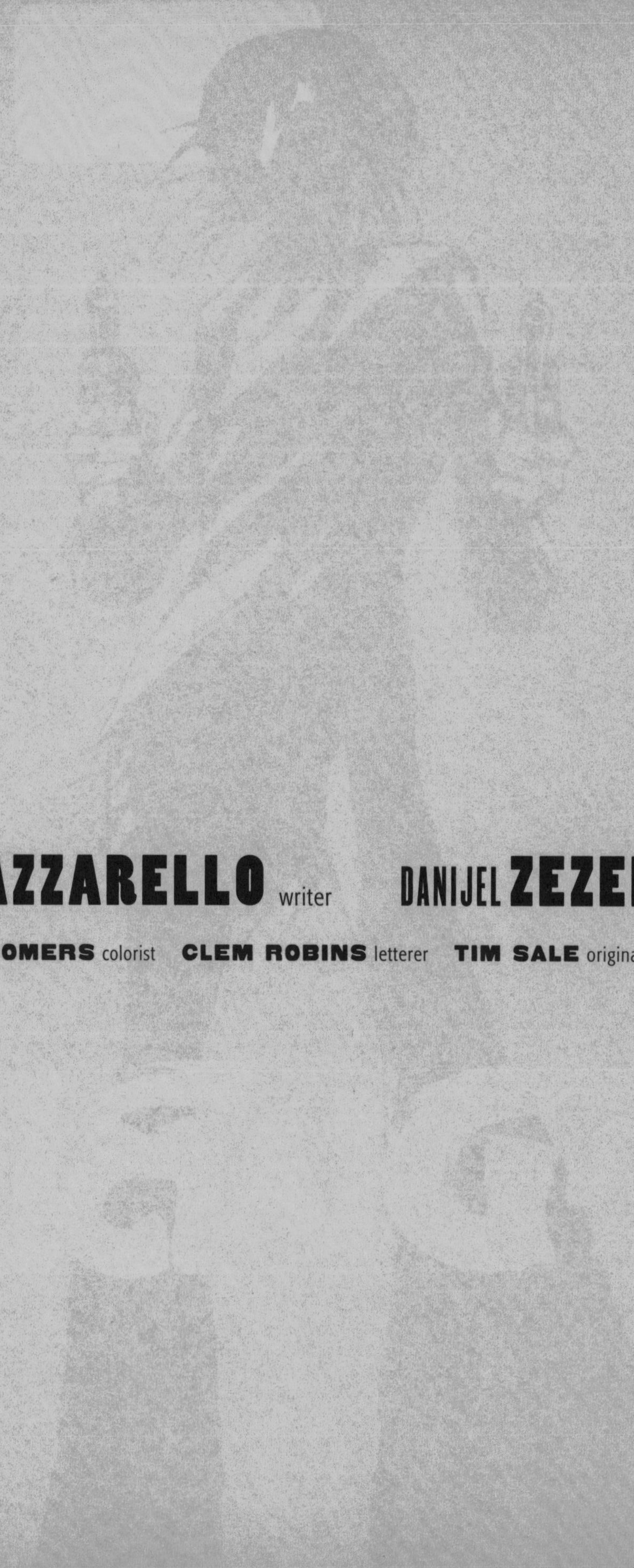

BRIAN AZZARELLO writer **DANIJEL ZEZELJ** artist

KEVIN SOMERS colorist **CLEM ROBINS** letterer **TIM SALE** original series covers

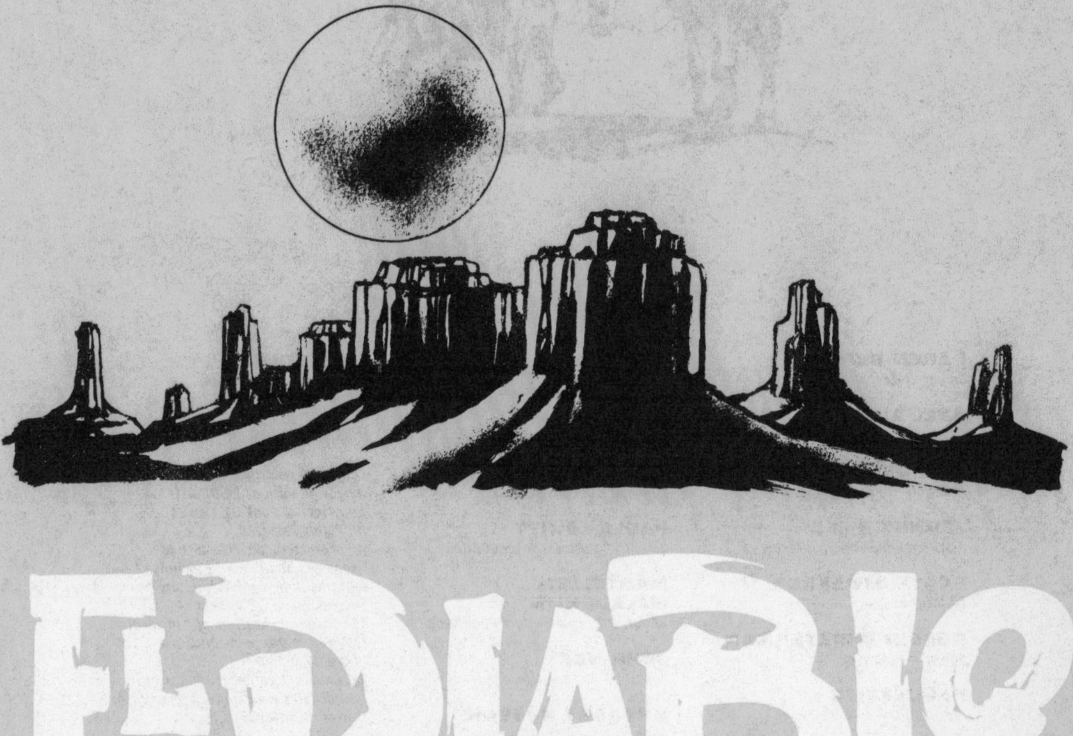

EL DIABLO

KAREN BERGER
Senior VP-Executive Editor

AXEL ALONSO
Editor-original series

WILL DENNIS
Associate Editor-original series

JENNIFER LEE
Assistant Editor-original series

SCOTT NYBAKKEN
Editor-collected edition

ROBBIN BROSTERMAN
Senior Art Director

PAUL LEVITZ
President & Publisher

GEORG BREWER
VP-Design & DC Direct Creative

RICHARD BRUNING
Senior VP-Creative Director

PATRICK CALDON
Executive VP-Finance & Operations

CHRIS CARAMALIS
VP-Finance

JOHN CUNNINGHAM
VP-Marketing

TERRI CUNNINGHAM
VP-Managing Editor

ALISON GILL
VP-Manufacturing

DAVID HYDE
VP-Publicity

HANK KANALZ
VP-General Manager, WildStorm

JIM LEE
Editorial Director-WildStorm

PAULA LOWITT
Senior VP-Business & Legal Affairs

MARYELLEN McLAUGHLIN
VP-Advertising & Custom Publishing

JOHN NEE
Senior VP-Business Development

GREGORY NOVECK
Senior VP-Creative Affairs

SUE POHJA
VP-Book Trade Sales

STEVE ROTTERDAM
Senior VP-Sales & Marketing

CHERYL RUBIN
Senior VP-Brand Management

JEFF TROJAN
VP-Business Development, DC Direct

BOB WAYNE
VP-Sales

Cover illustration by Tim Sale.
Publication design by Amelia Grohman.

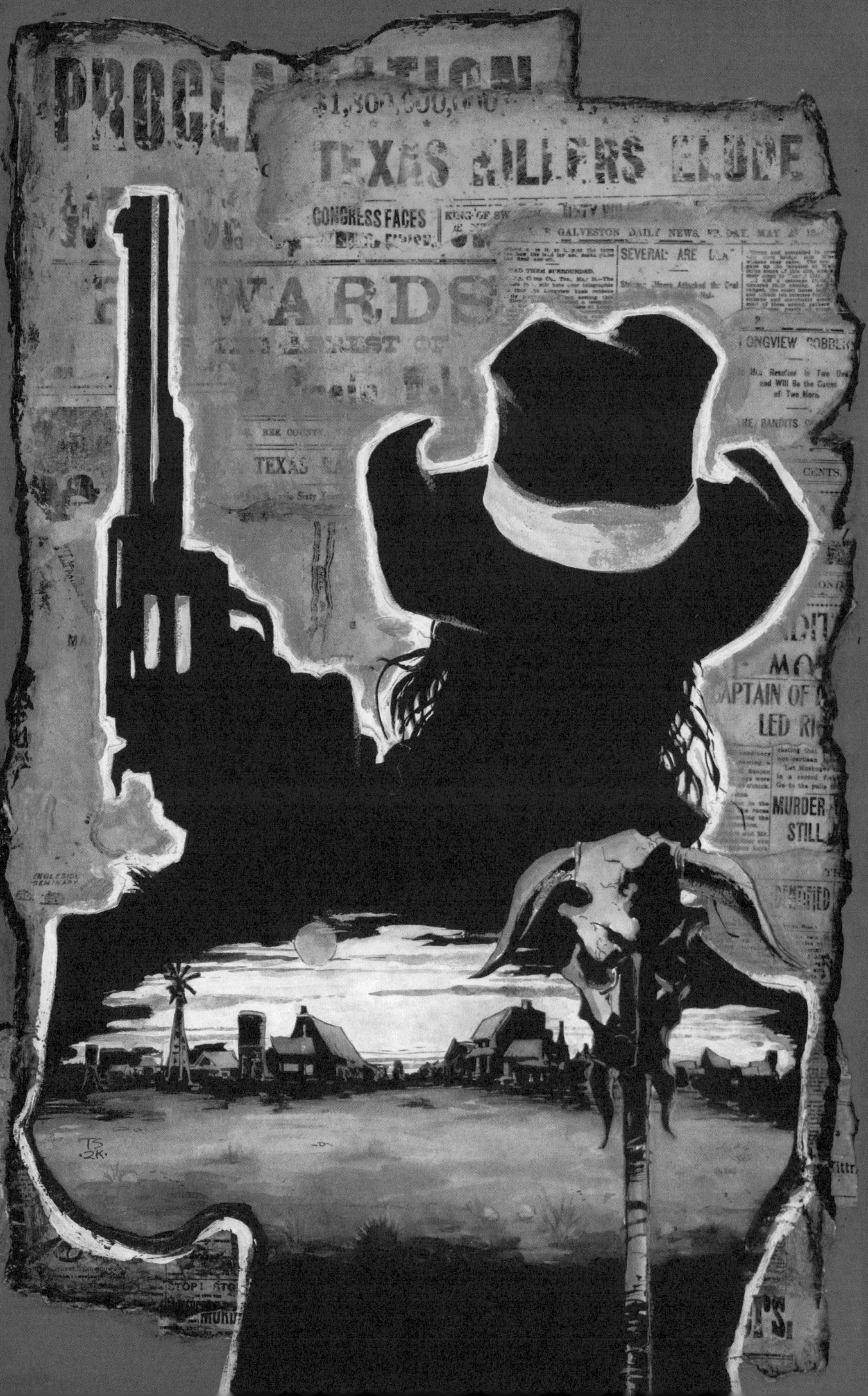

TEXAS
CONGRESS FACES
GALVESTON DAILY NEWS
WARDS
SEVERAL ARE
BEE COUNTY
TEXAS
CAPTAIN OF
MURDER
STILL
STOP!

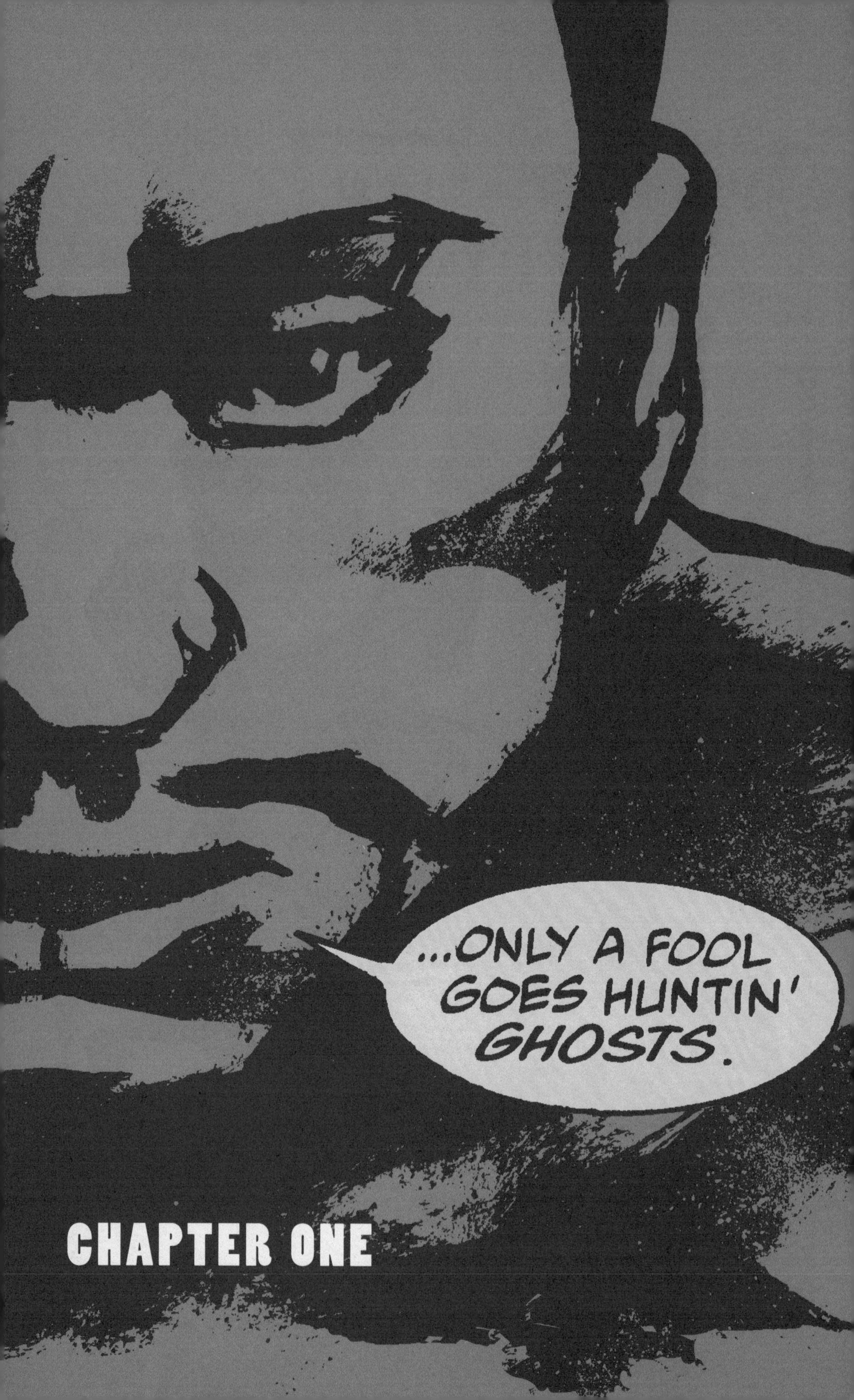
...ONLY A FOOL GOES HUNTIN' GHOSTS.

CHAPTER ONE

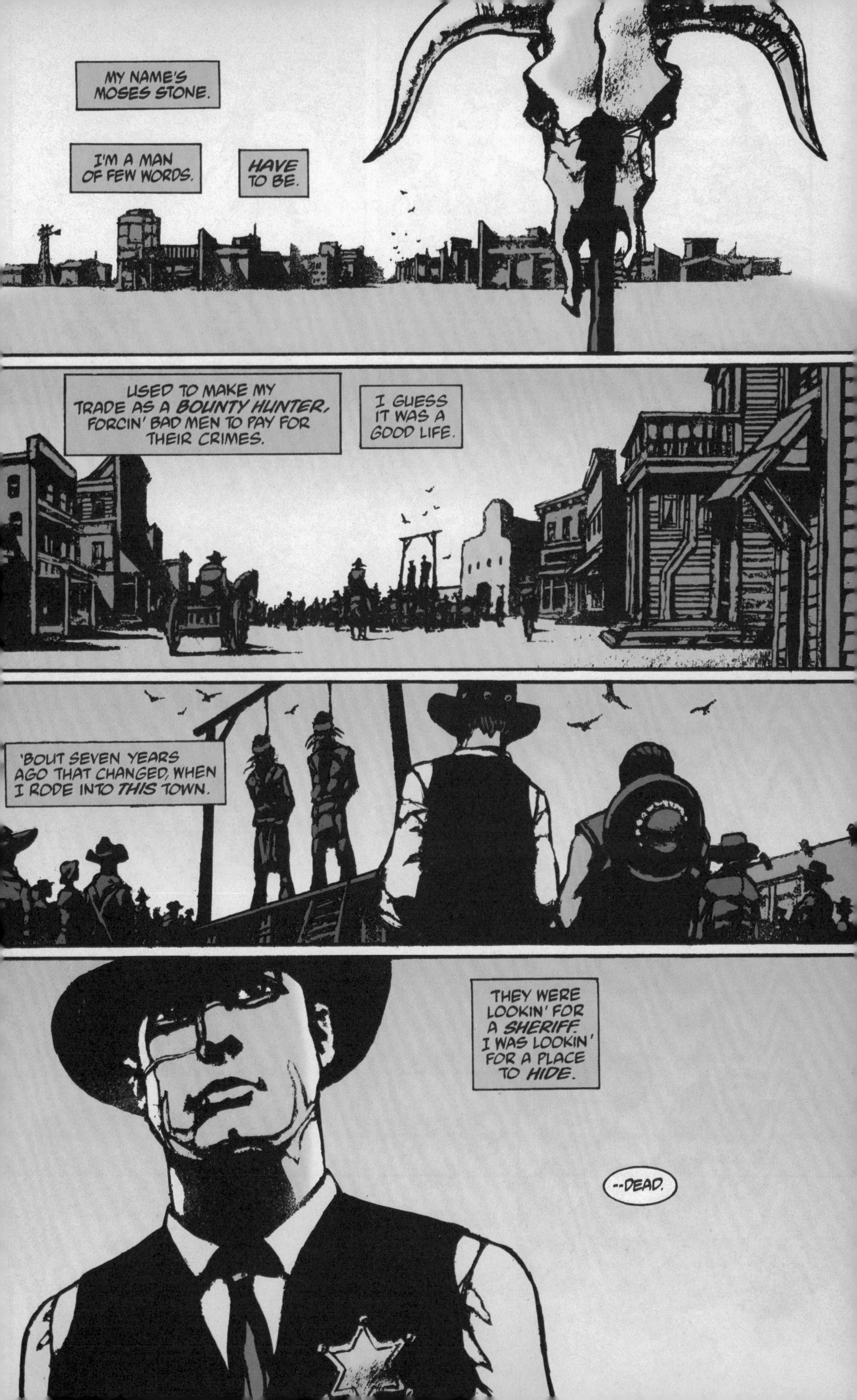
MY NAME'S MOSES STONE.
I'M A MAN OF FEW WORDS.
HAVE TO BE.
USED TO MAKE MY TRADE AS A BOUNTY HUNTER, FORCIN' BAD MEN TO PAY FOR THEIR CRIMES.
I GUESS IT WAS A GOOD LIFE.
'BOUT SEVEN YEARS AGO THAT CHANGED, WHEN I RODE INTO THIS TOWN.
THEY WERE LOOKIN' FOR A SHERIFF. I WAS LOOKIN' FOR A PLACE TO HIDE.
--DEAD.

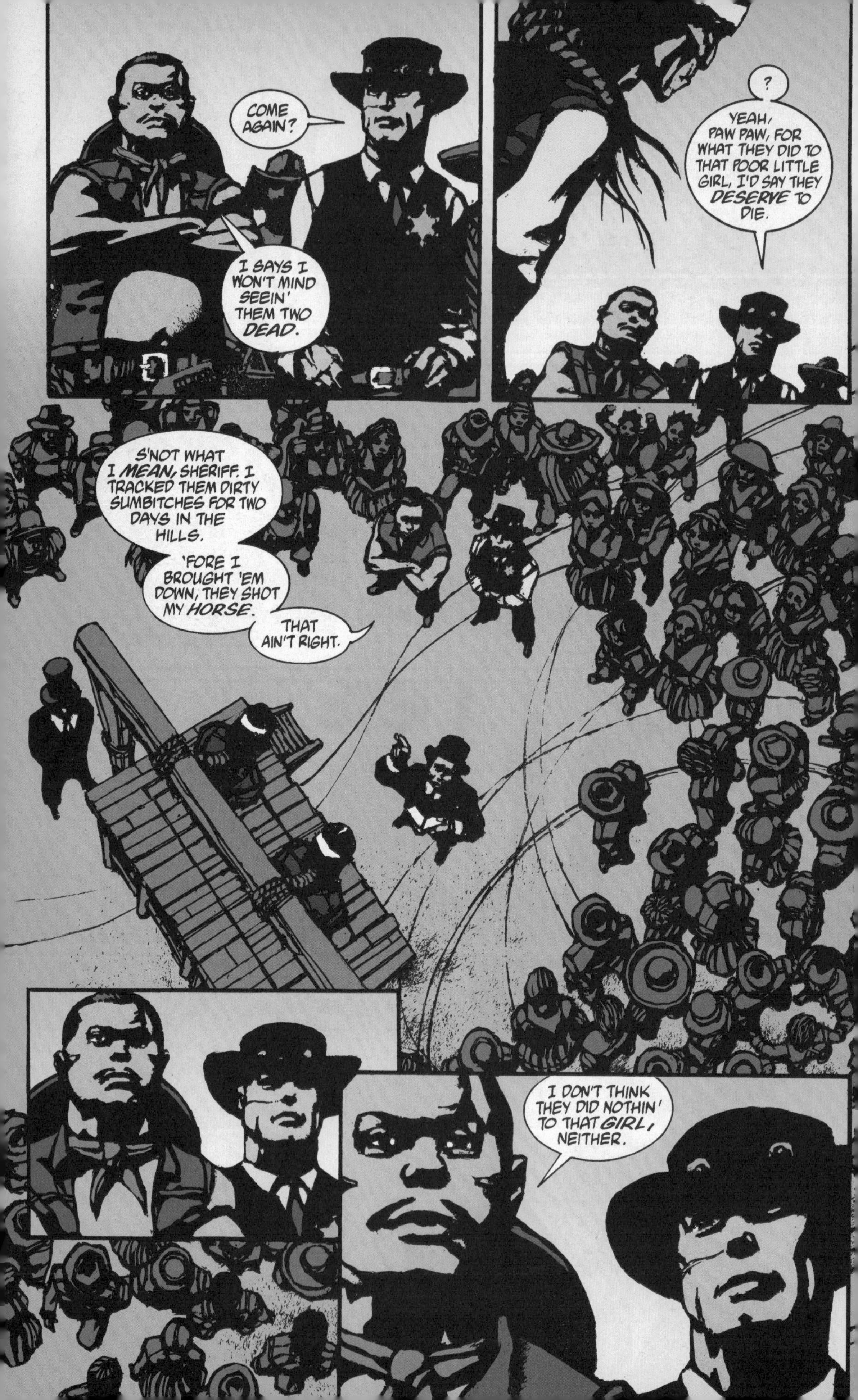
COME AGAIN?
I SAYS I WON'T MIND SEEIN' THEM TWO DEAD.
?
YEAH, PAW PAW, FOR WHAT THEY DID TO THAT POOR LITTLE GIRL, I'D SAY THEY DESERVE TO DIE.
S'NOT WHAT I MEAN, SHERIFF. I TRACKED THEM DIRTY SUMBITCHES FOR TWO DAYS IN THE HILLS.
'FORE I BROUGHT 'EM DOWN, THEY SHOT MY HORSE.
THAT AIN'T RIGHT.
I DON'T THINK THEY DID NOTHIN' TO THAT GIRL, NEITHER.

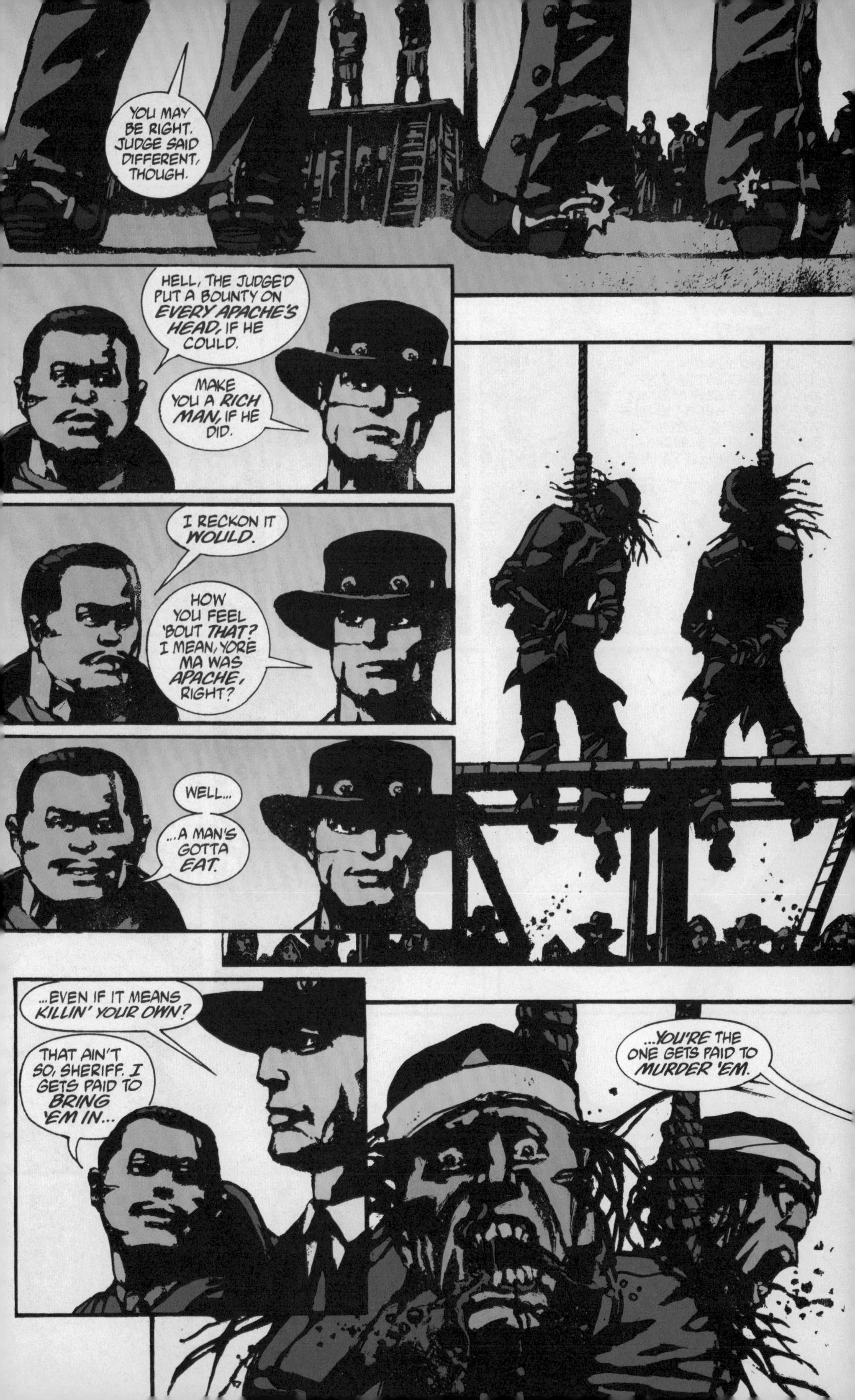
YOU MAY BE RIGHT. JUDGE SAID DIFFERENT, THOUGH.
HELL, THE JUDGE'D PUT A BOUNTY ON EVERY APACHE'S HEAD, IF HE COULD.
MAKE YOU A RICH MAN, IF HE DID.
I RECKON IT WOULD.
HOW YOU FEEL 'BOUT THAT? I MEAN, YO'RE MA WAS APACHE, RIGHT?
WELL...
...A MAN'S GOTTA EAT.
...EVEN IF IT MEANS KILLIN' YOUR OWN?
THAT AIN'T SO, SHERIFF. I GETS PAID TO BRING 'EM IN...
...YOU'RE THE ONE GETS PAID TO MURDER 'EM.

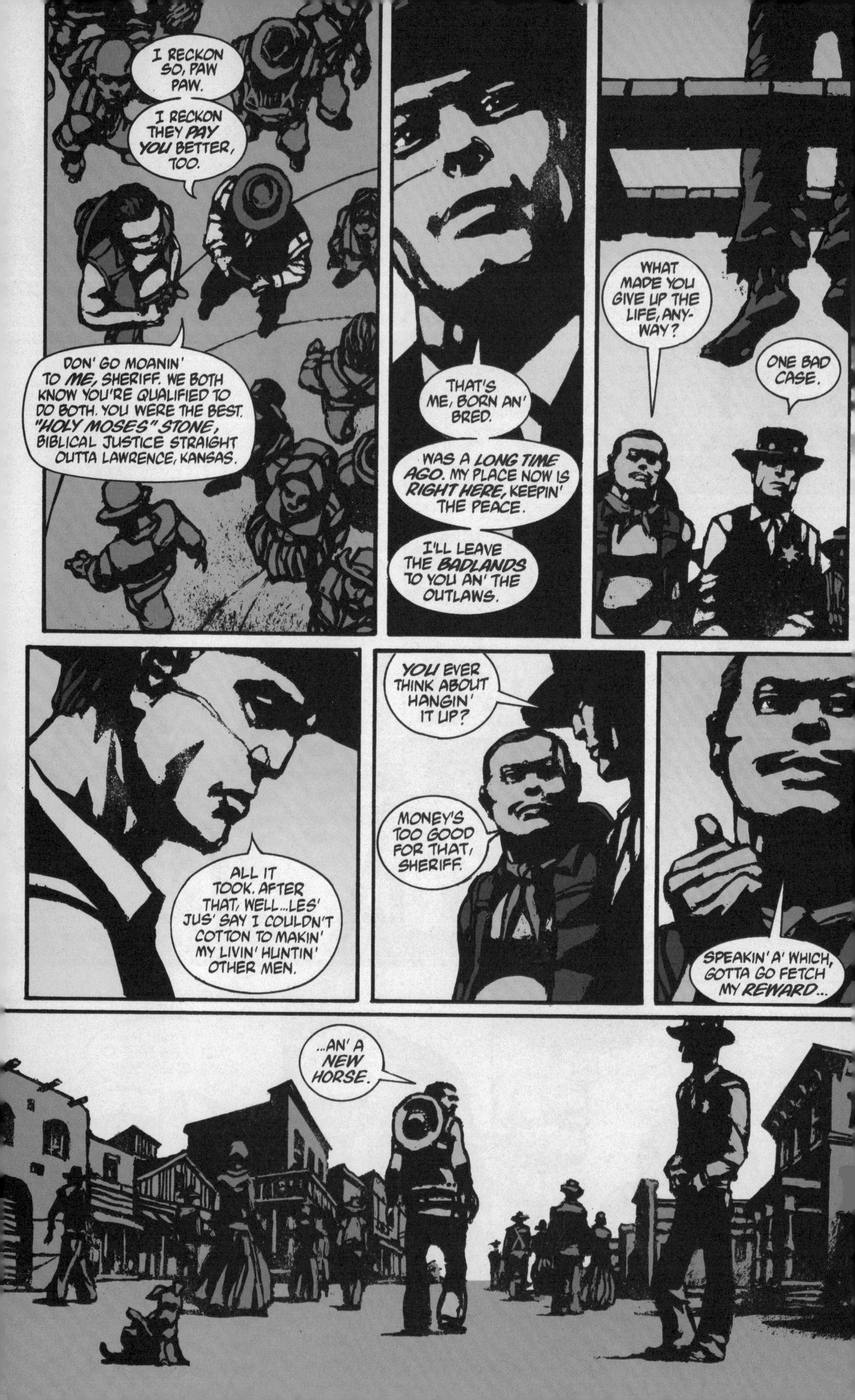
I RECKON SO, PAW PAW.
I RECKON THEY PAY YOU BETTER, TOO.
DON' GO MOANIN' TO ME, SHERIFF. WE BOTH KNOW YOU'RE QUALIFIED TO DO BOTH. YOU WERE THE BEST. "HOLY MOSES" STONE, BIBLICAL JUSTICE STRAIGHT OUTTA LAWRENCE, KANSAS.
THAT'S ME, BORN AN' BRED.
WAS A LONG TIME AGO. MY PLACE NOW IS RIGHT HERE, KEEPIN' THE PEACE.
I'LL LEAVE THE BADLANDS TO YOU AN' THE OUTLAWS.
WHAT MADE YOU GIVE UP THE LIFE, ANYWAY?
ONE BAD CASE.
ALL IT TOOK. AFTER THAT, WELL...LES' JUS' SAY I COULDN'T COTTON TO MAKIN' MY LIVIN' HUNTIN' OTHER MEN.
YOU EVER THINK ABOUT HANGIN' IT UP?
MONEY'S TOO GOOD FOR THAT, SHERIFF.
SPEAKIN' A' WHICH, GOTTA GO FETCH MY REWARD...
...AN' A NEW HORSE.

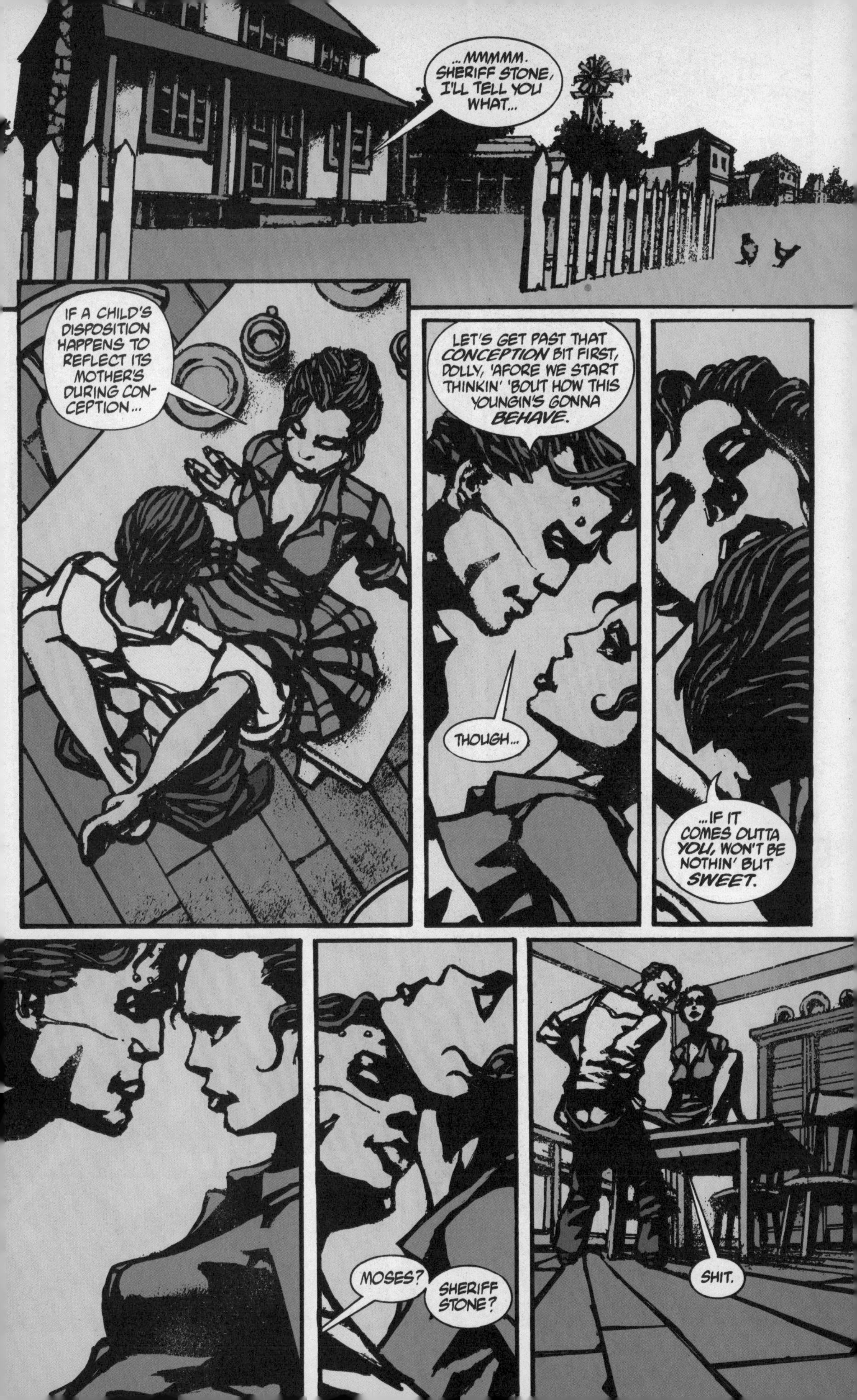
...MMMMM. SHERIFF STONE, I'LL TELL YOU WHAT...
IF A CHILD'S DISPOSITION HAPPENS TO REFLECT ITS MOTHER'S DURING CONCEPTION...
LET'S GET PAST THAT CONCEPTION BIT FIRST, DOLLY, 'AFORE WE START THINKIN' 'BOUT HOW THIS YOUNGIN'S GONNA BEHAVE.
THOUGH...
...IF IT COMES OUTTA YOU, WON'T BE NOTHIN' BUT SWEET.
MOSES?
SHERIFF STONE?
SHIT.

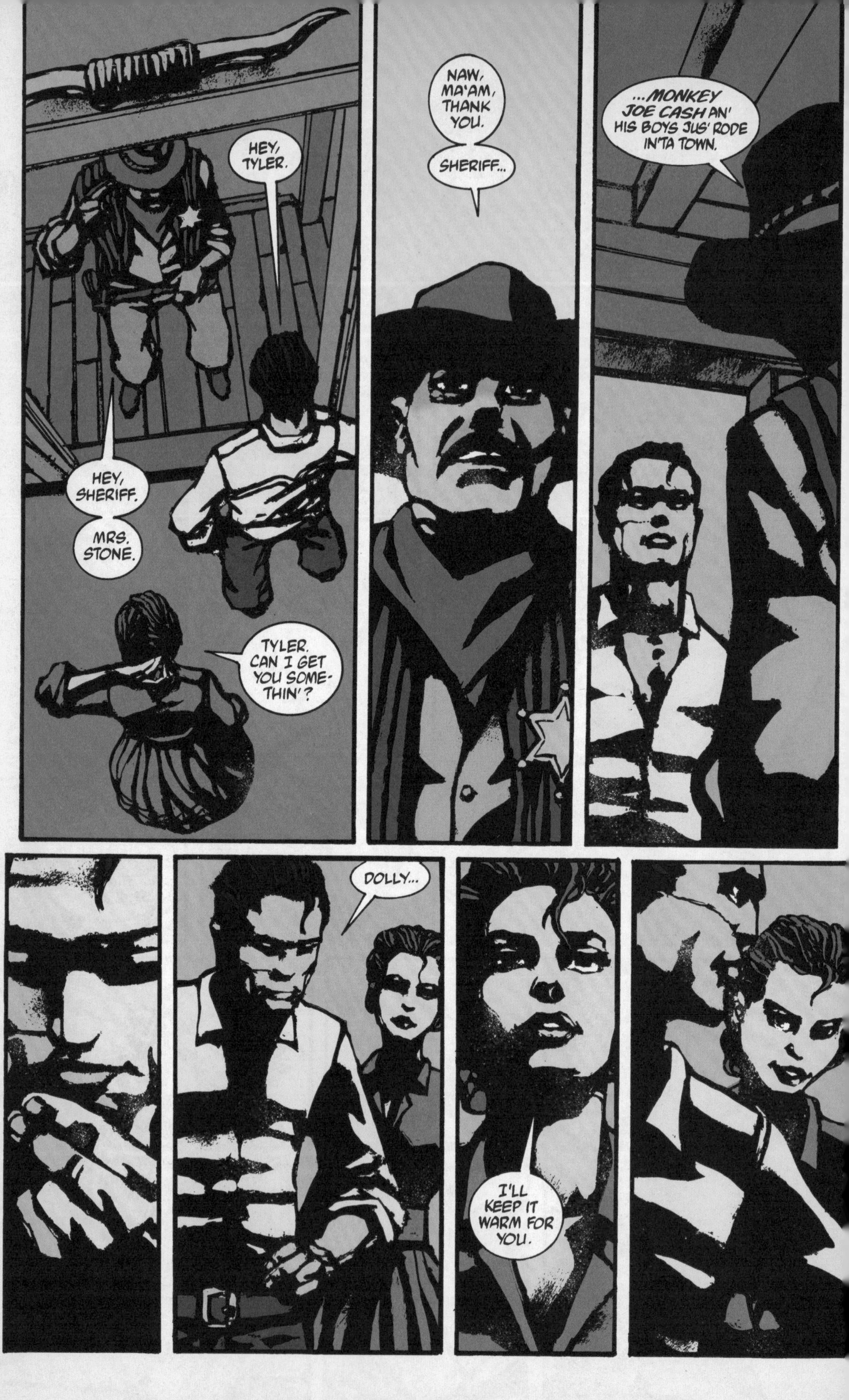
HEY, TYLER.
HEY, SHERIFF.
MRS. STONE.
TYLER. CAN I GET YOU SOMETHIN'?
NAW, MA'AM, THANK YOU.
SHERIFF...
...MONKEY JOE CASH AN' HIS BOYS JUS' RODE IN'TA TOWN.
DOLLY...
I'LL KEEP IT WARM FOR YOU.

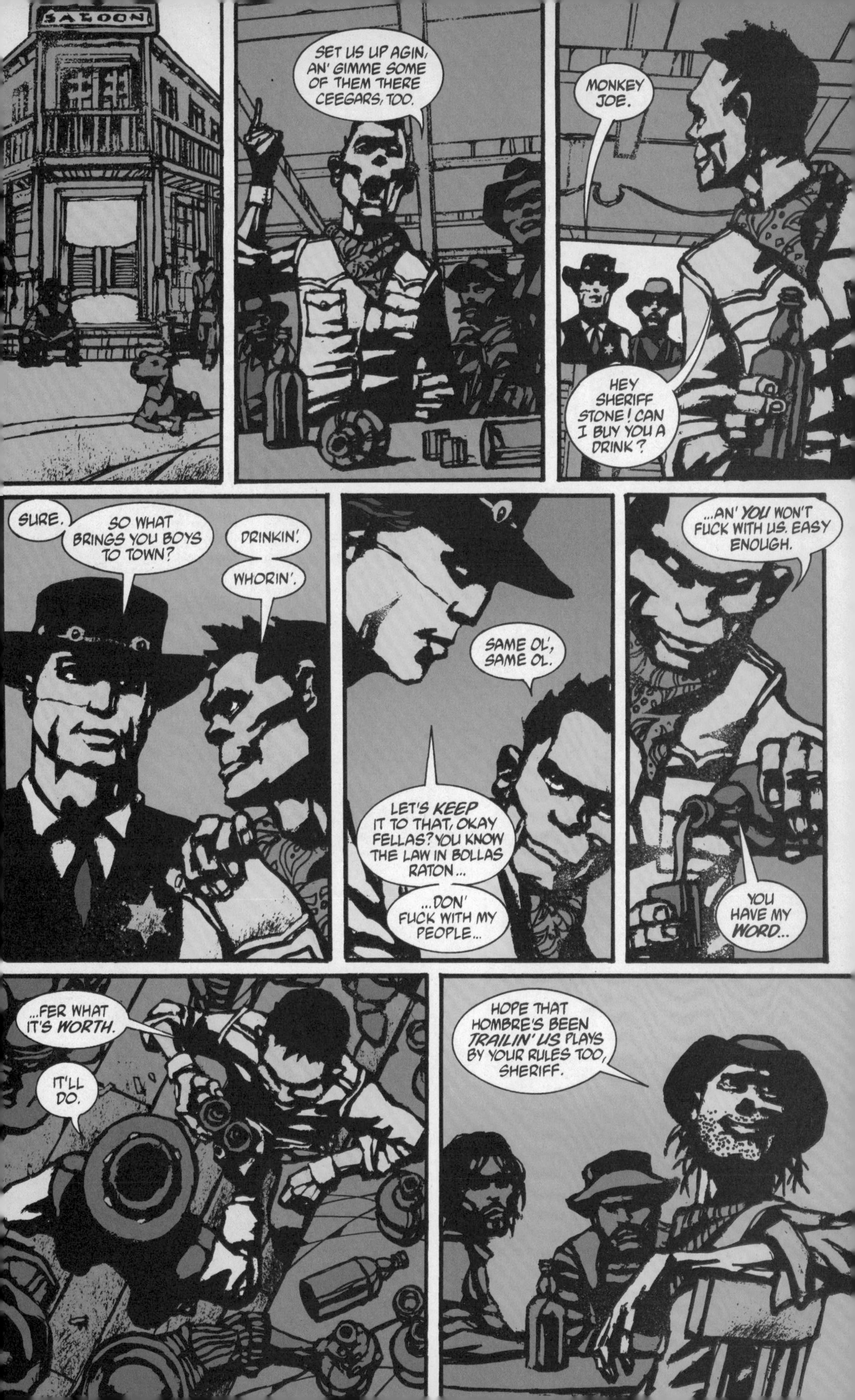
SALOON
SET US UP AGIN, AN' GIMME SOME OF THEM THERE CEEGARS, TOO.
MONKEY JOE.
HEY SHERIFF STONE! CAN I BUY YOU A DRINK?
SURE.
SO WHAT BRINGS YOU BOYS TO TOWN?
DRINKIN'.
WHORIN'.
SAME OL', SAME OL.
LET'S KEEP IT TO THAT, OKAY FELLAS? YOU KNOW THE LAW IN BOLLAS RATON...
...DON' FUCK WITH MY PEOPLE...
...AN' YOU WON'T FUCK WITH US. EASY ENOUGH.
YOU HAVE MY WORD...
...FER WHAT IT'S WORTH.
IT'LL DO.
HOPE THAT HOMBRE'S BEEN TRAILIN' US PLAYS BY YOUR RULES TOO, SHERIFF.

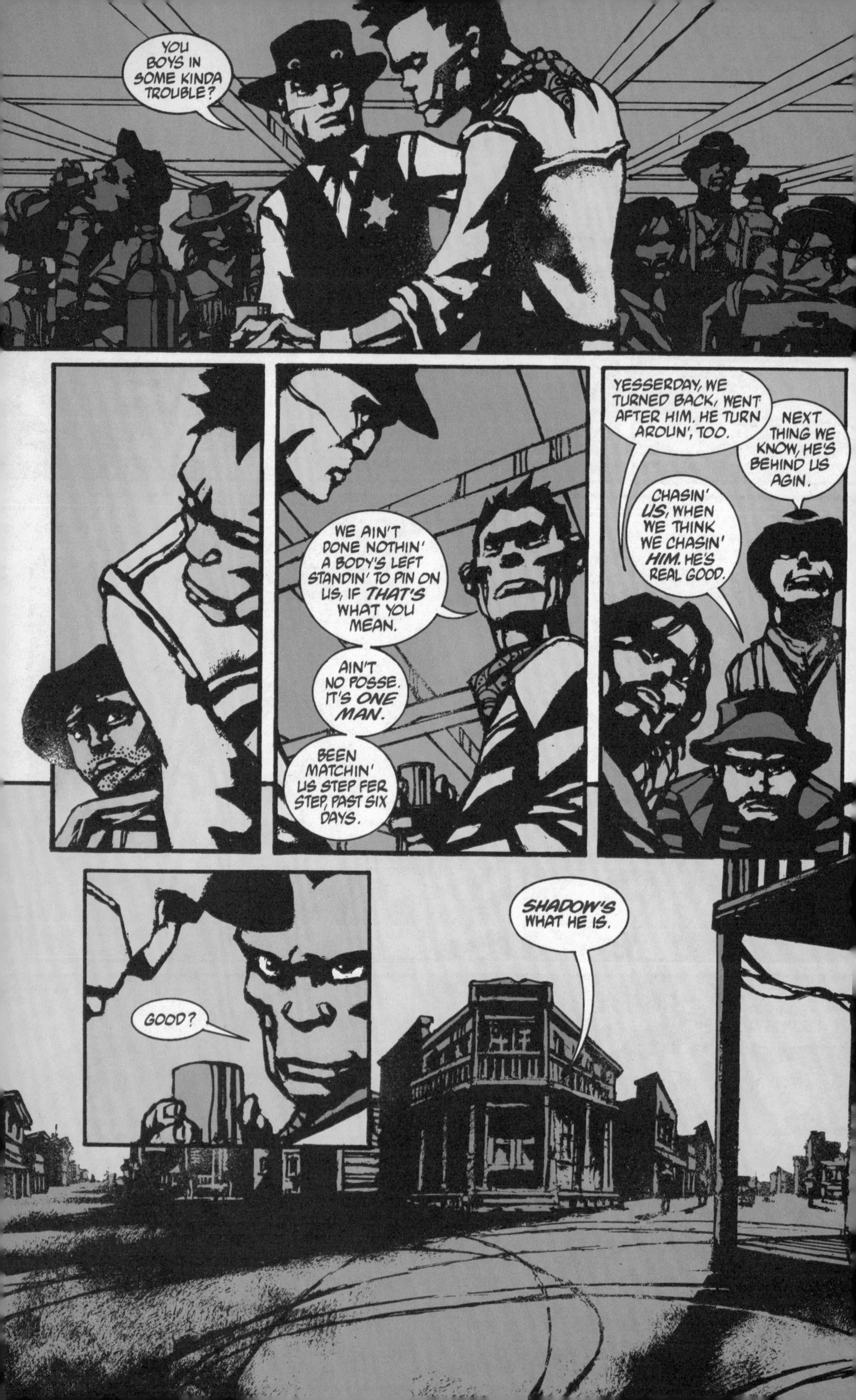
YOU BOYS IN SOME KINDA TROUBLE?
WE AIN'T DONE NOTHIN' A BODY'S LEFT STANDIN' TO PIN ON US, IF THAT'S WHAT YOU MEAN.
AIN'T NO POSSE. IT'S ONE MAN.
BEEN MATCHIN' US STEP FER STEP, PAST SIX DAYS.
YESSERDAY, WE TURNED BACK, WENT AFTER HIM. HE TURN AROUN', TOO.
NEXT THING WE KNOW, HE'S BEHIND US AGIN.
CHASIN' US, WHEN WE THINK WE CHASIN' HIM. HE'S REAL GOOD.
GOOD?
SHADOW'S WHAT HE IS.

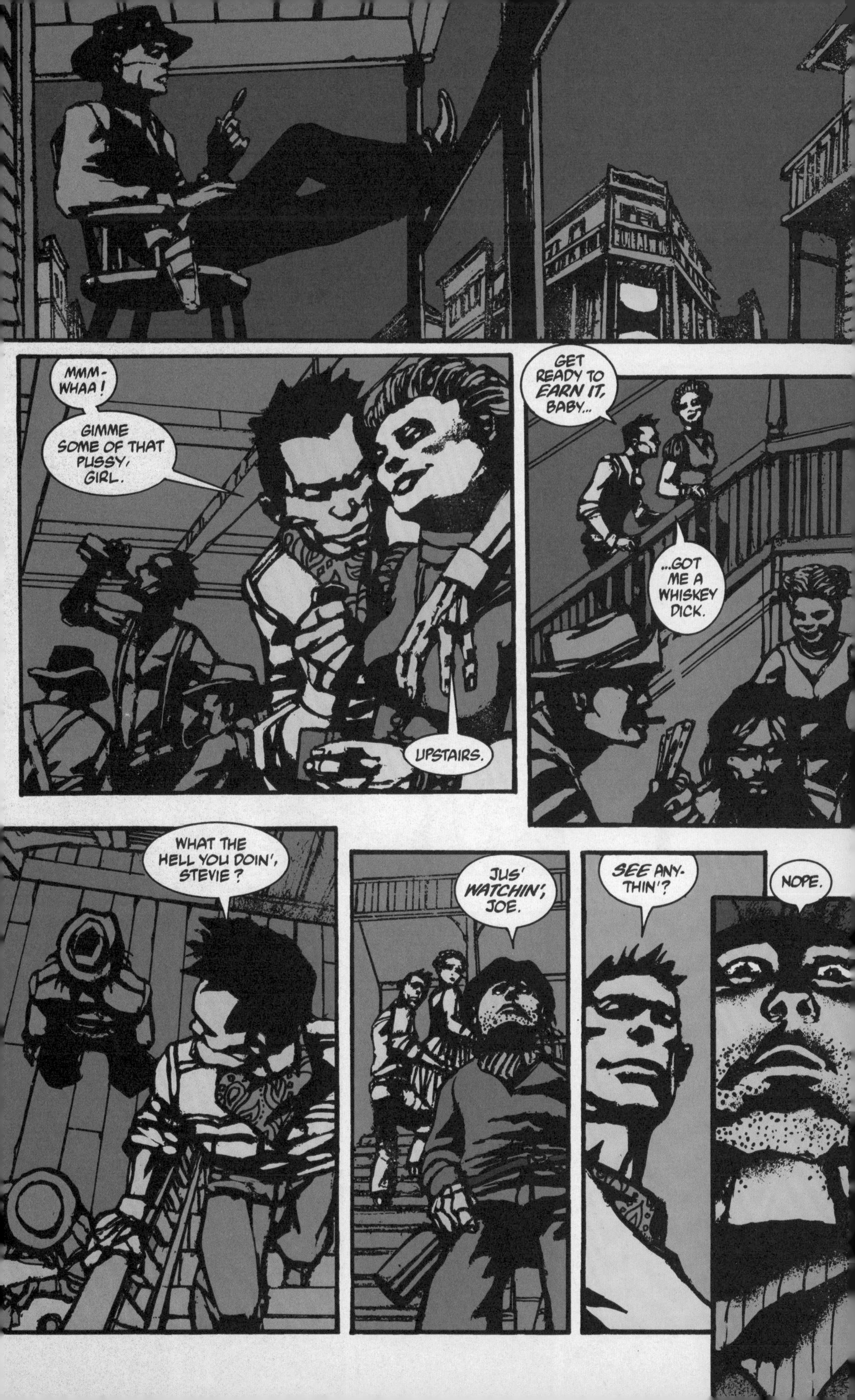
MMM-WHAA!
GIMME SOME OF THAT PUSSY, GIRL.
UPSTAIRS.
GET READY TO EARN IT, BABY...
...GOT ME A WHISKEY DICK.
WHAT THE HELL YOU DOIN', STEVIE?
JUS' WATCHIN', JOE.
SEE ANY-THIN'?
NOPE.

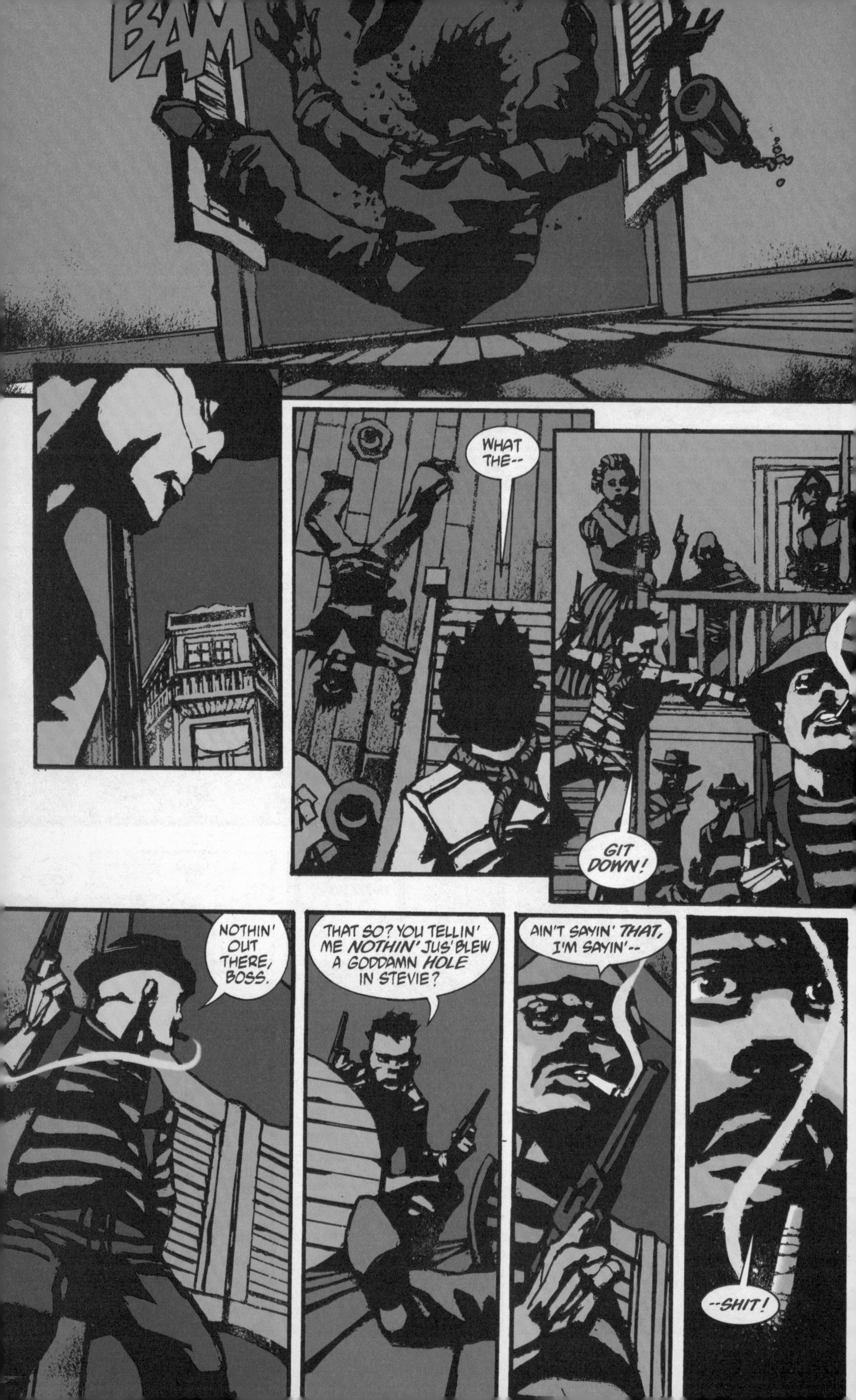
BAM
WHAT THE--
GIT DOWN!
NOTHIN' OUT THERE, BOSS.
THAT SO? YOU TELLIN' ME NOTHIN' JUS'BLEW A GODDAMN HOLE IN STEVIE?
AIN'T SAYIN' THAT, I'M SAYIN'--
--SHIT!

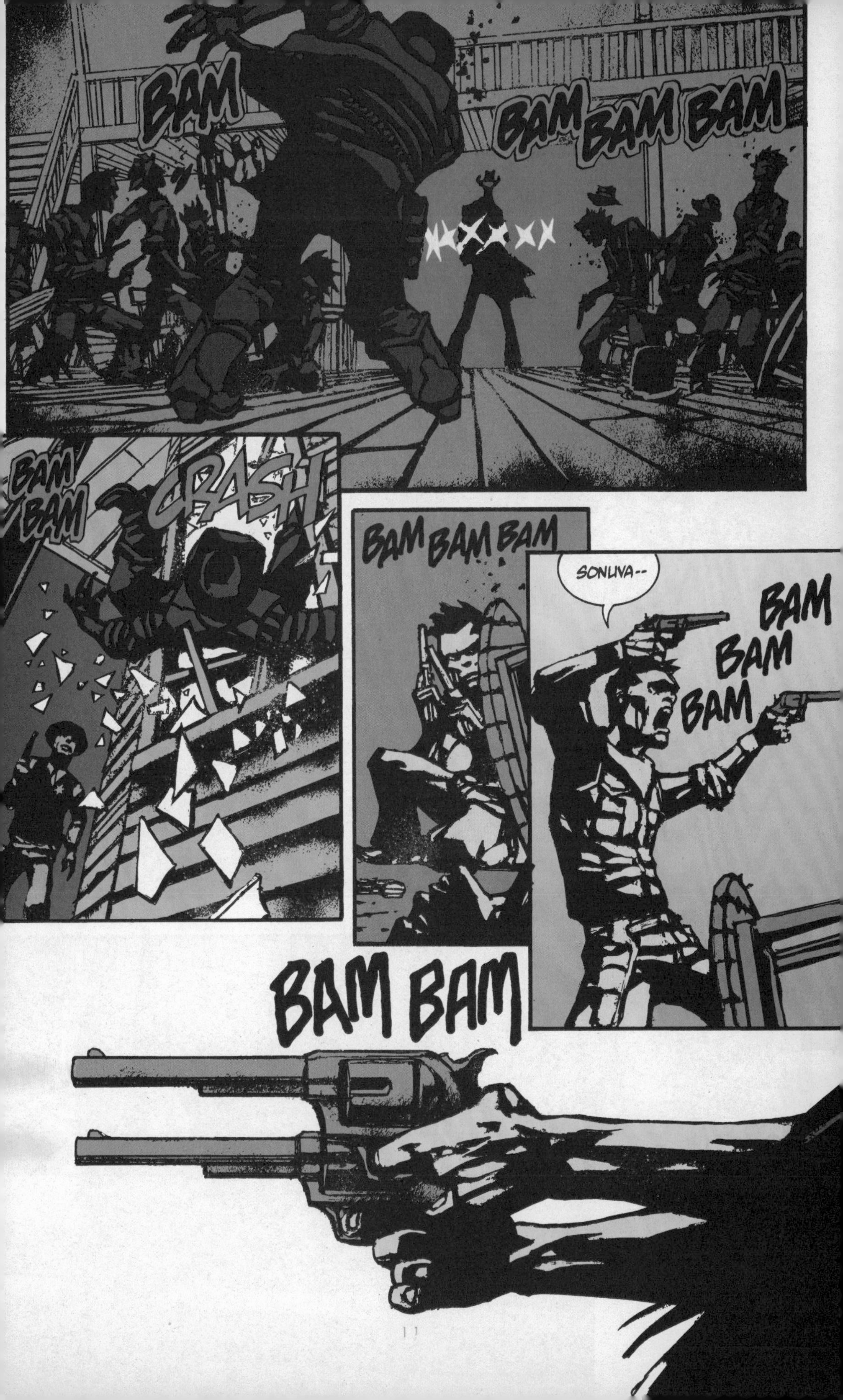
BAM
BAM BAM BAM
BAM BAM
CRASH
BAM BAM BAM
SONUVA--
BAM BAM BAM
BAM BAM

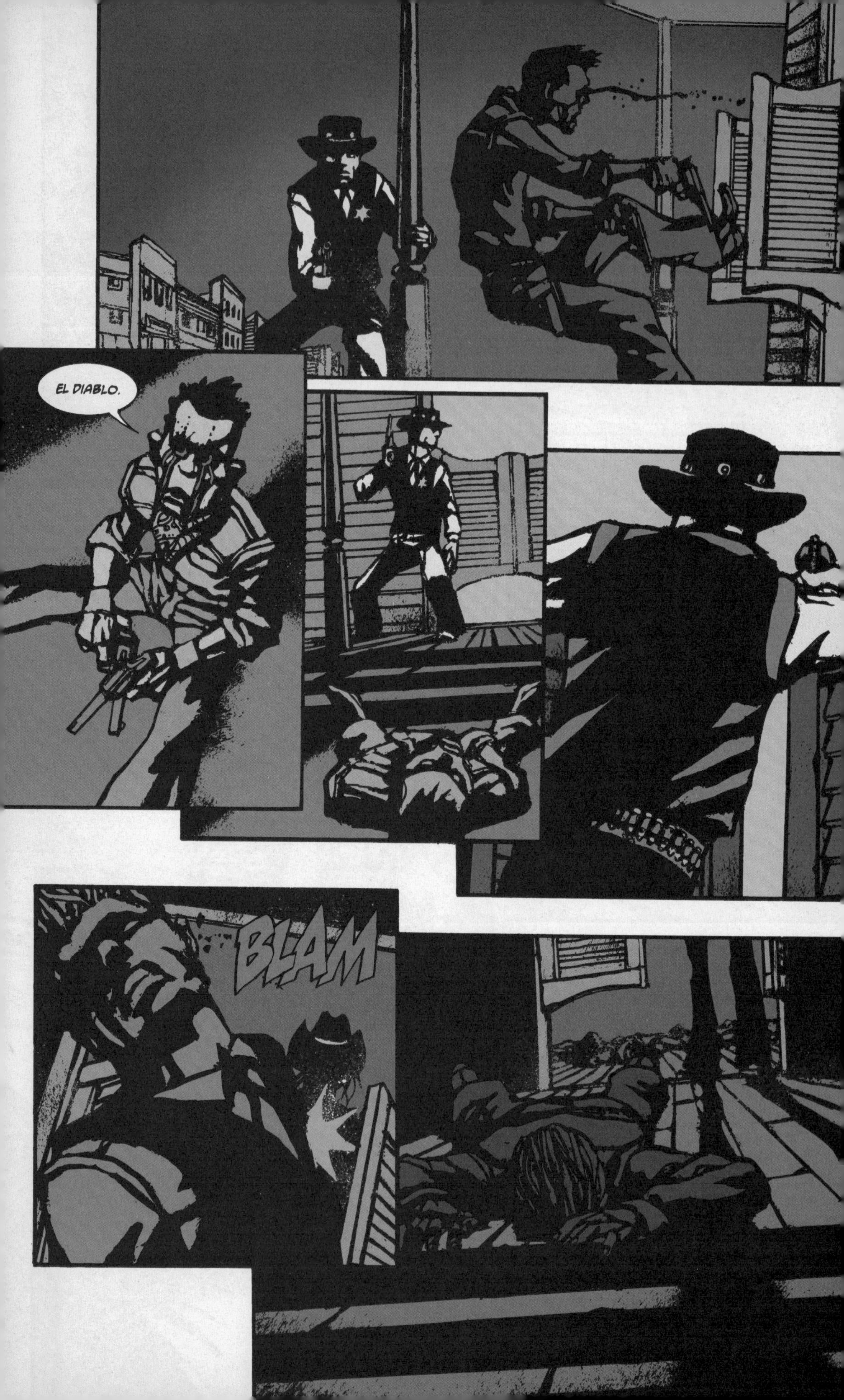
EL DIABLO.
BLAM

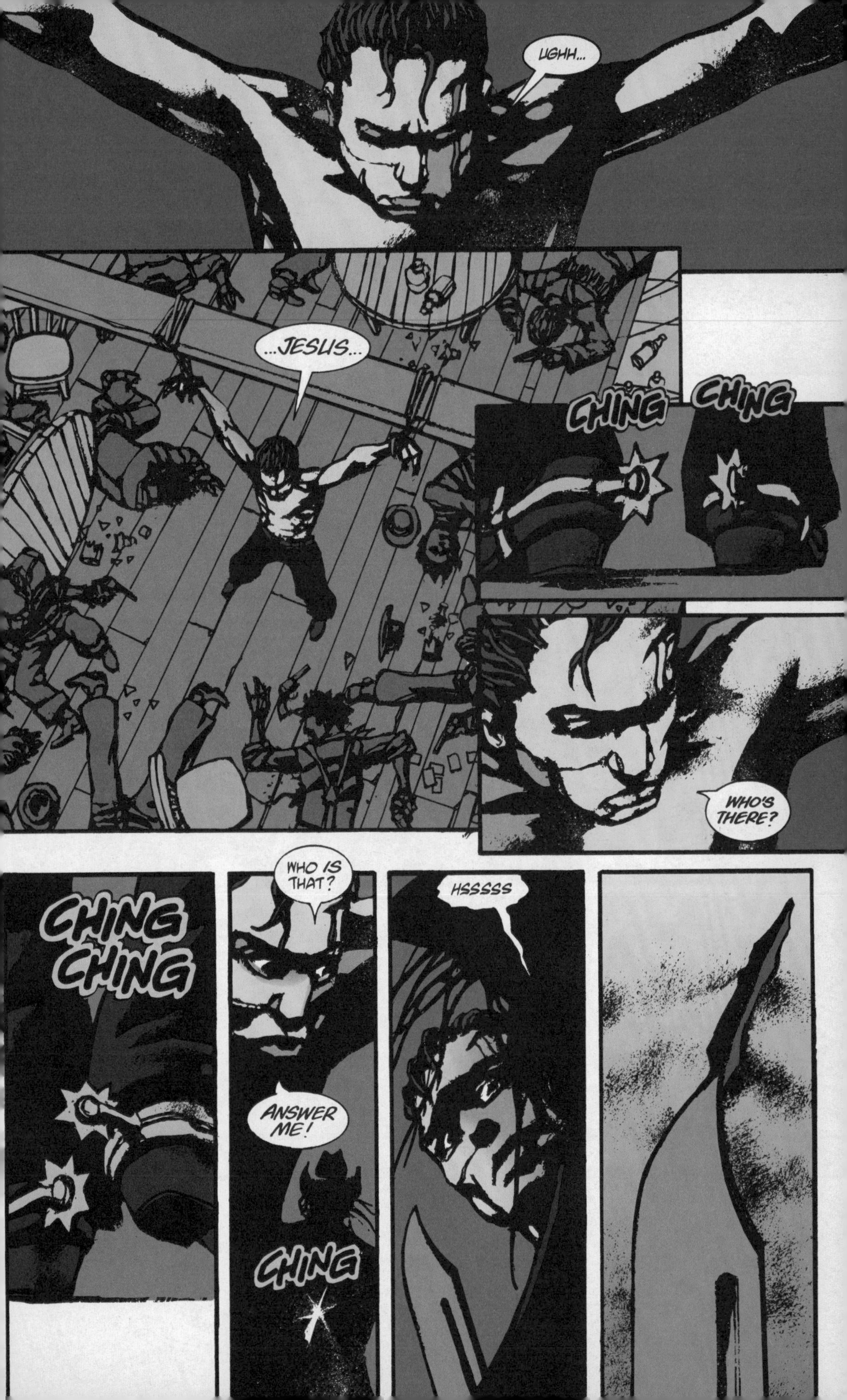
UGHH...
...JESUS...
CHING
CHING
WHO'S THERE?
CHING
CHING
WHO IS THAT?
ANSWER ME!
CHING
HSSSSS

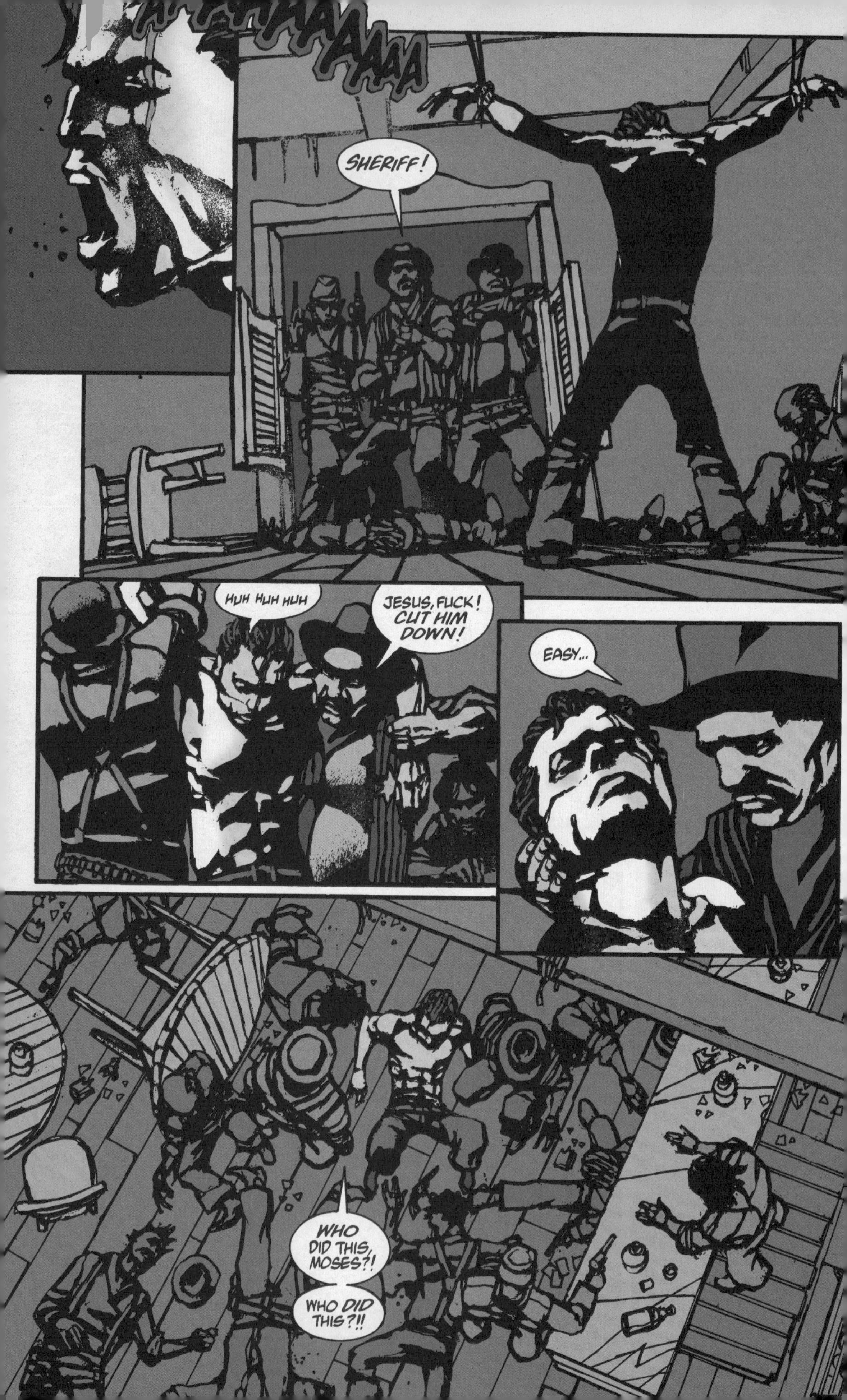
AAAAAAAAAA
SHERIFF!
HUH HUH HUH
JESUS, FUCK! CUT HIM DOWN!
EASY...
WHO DID THIS, MOSES?!
WHO DID THIS?!!

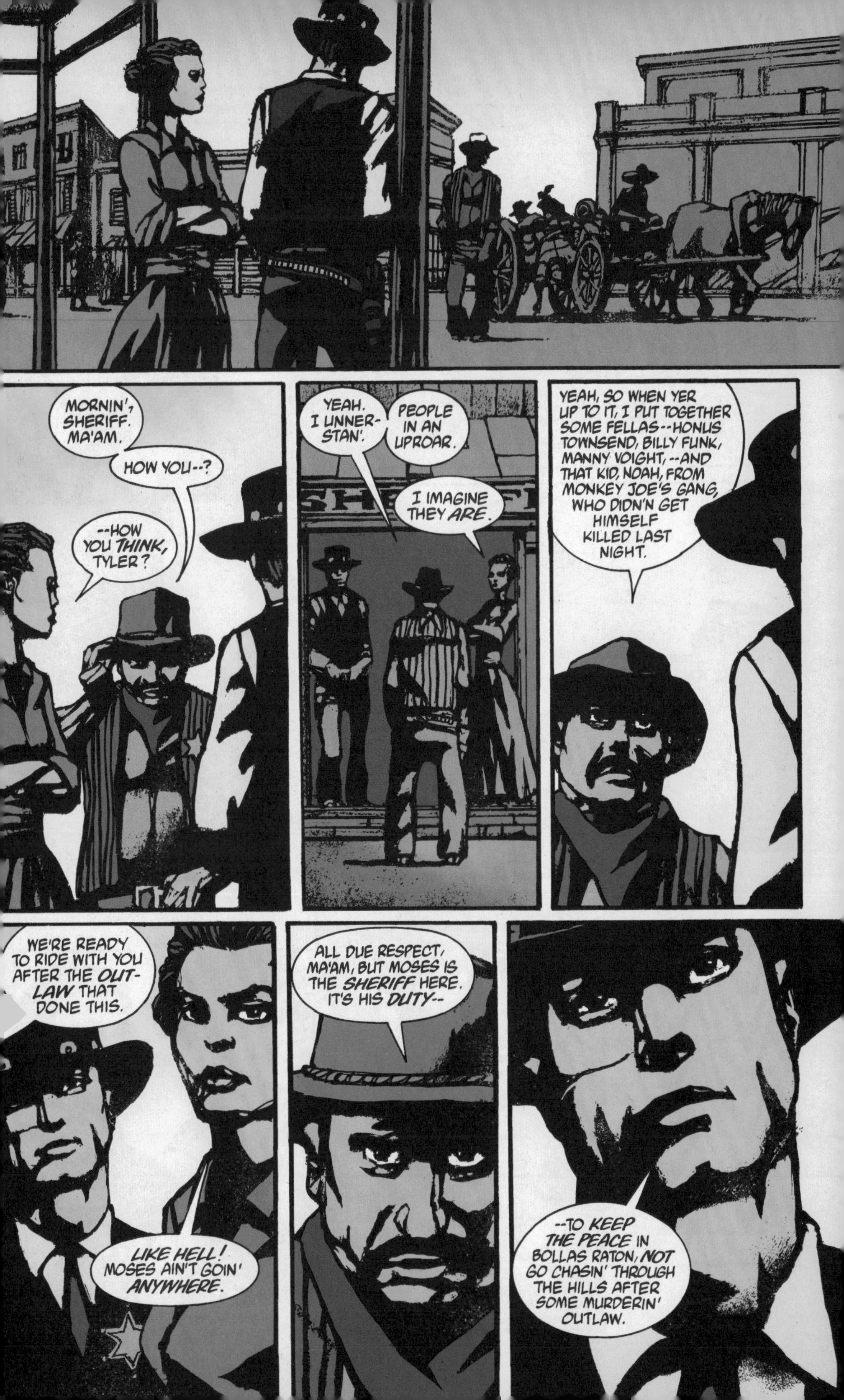
MORNIN', SHERIFF. MA'AM.
HOW YOU--?
--HOW YOU THINK, TYLER?
YEAH. I UNNER-STAN'.
PEOPLE IN AN UPROAR.
SHE
I IMAGINE THEY ARE.
YEAH, SO WHEN YER UP TO IT, I PUT TOGETHER SOME FELLAS--HONUS TOWNSEND, BILLY FUNK, MANNY VOIGHT, --AND THAT KID, NOAH, FROM MONKEY JOE'S GANG, WHO DIDN'N GET HIMSELF KILLED LAST NIGHT.
WE'RE READY TO RIDE WITH YOU AFTER THE OUT-LAW THAT DONE THIS.
LIKE HELL! MOSES AIN'T GOIN' ANYWHERE.
ALL DUE RESPECT, MA'AM, BUT MOSES IS THE SHERIFF HERE. IT'S HIS DUTY--
--TO KEEP THE PEACE IN BOLLAS RATON, NOT GO CHASIN' THROUGH THE HILLS AFTER SOME MURDERIN' OUTLAW.

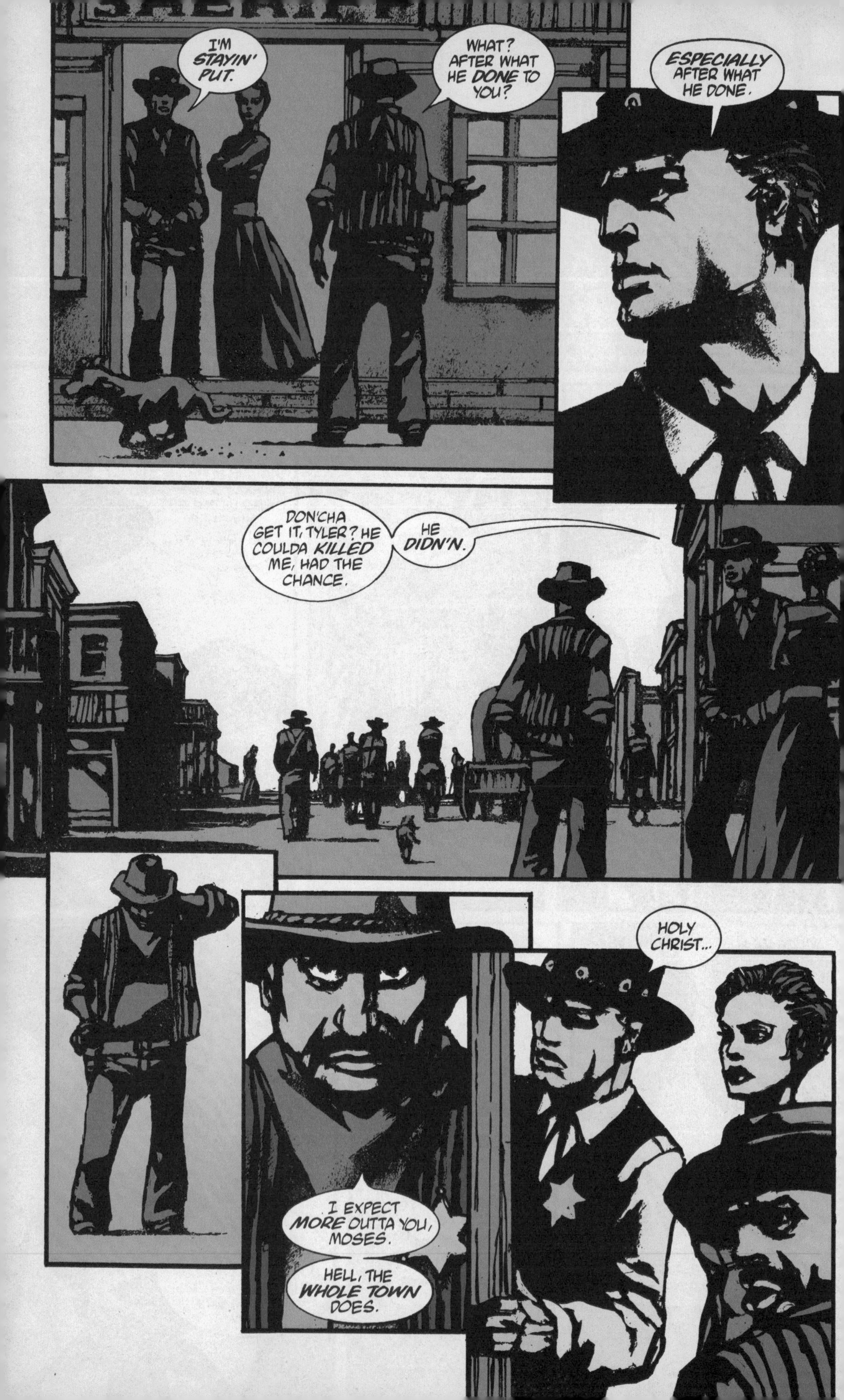
I'M STAYIN' PUT.
WHAT? AFTER WHAT HE DONE TO YOU?
ESPECIALLY AFTER WHAT HE DONE.
DON'CHA GET IT, TYLER? HE COULDA KILLED ME, HAD THE CHANCE.
HE DIDN'N.
HOLY CHRIST...
I EXPECT MORE OUTTA YOU, MOSES.
HELL, THE WHOLE TOWN DOES.

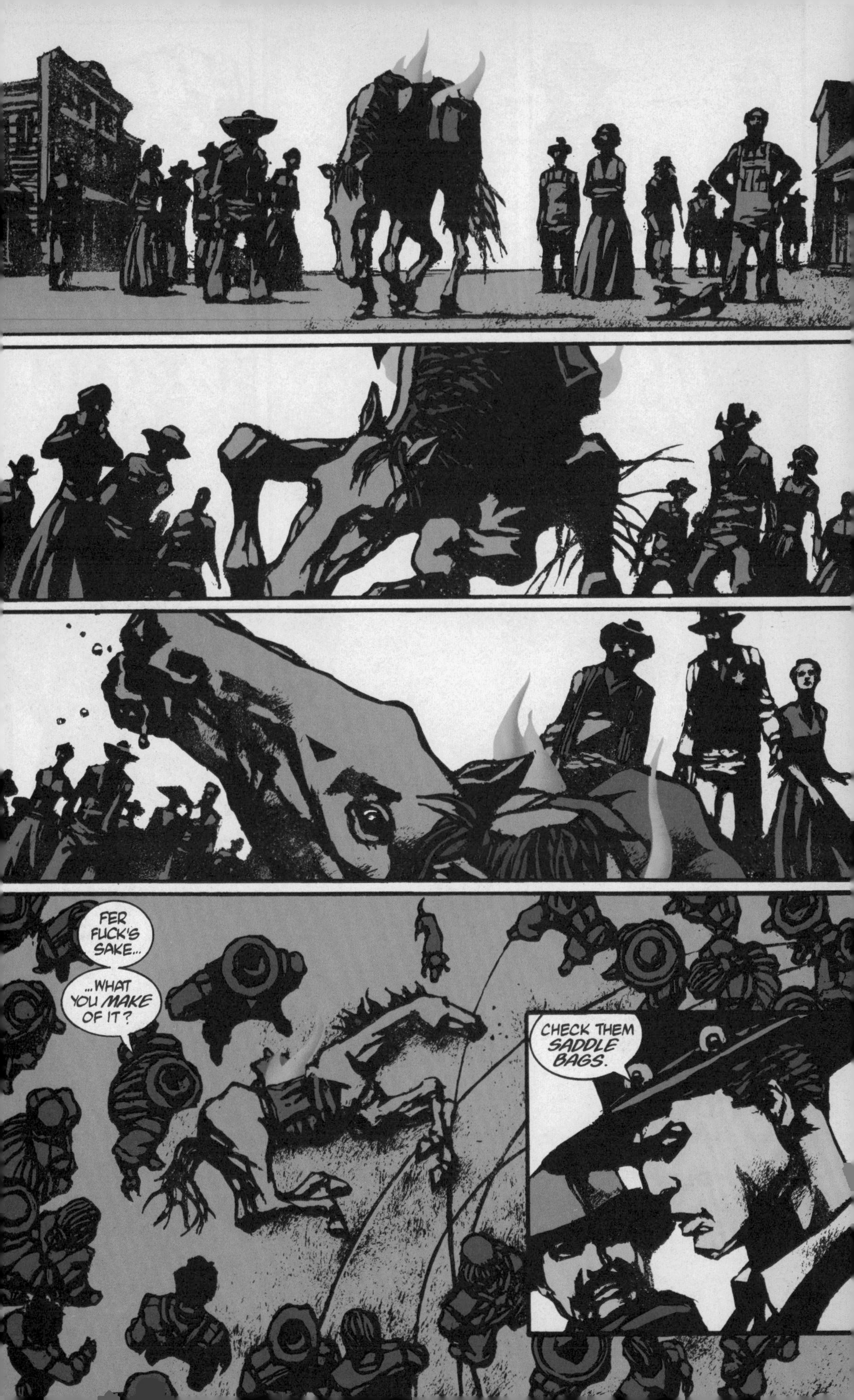
FER FUCK'S SAKE...
...WHAT YOU MAKE OF IT?
CHECK THEM SADDLE BAGS.

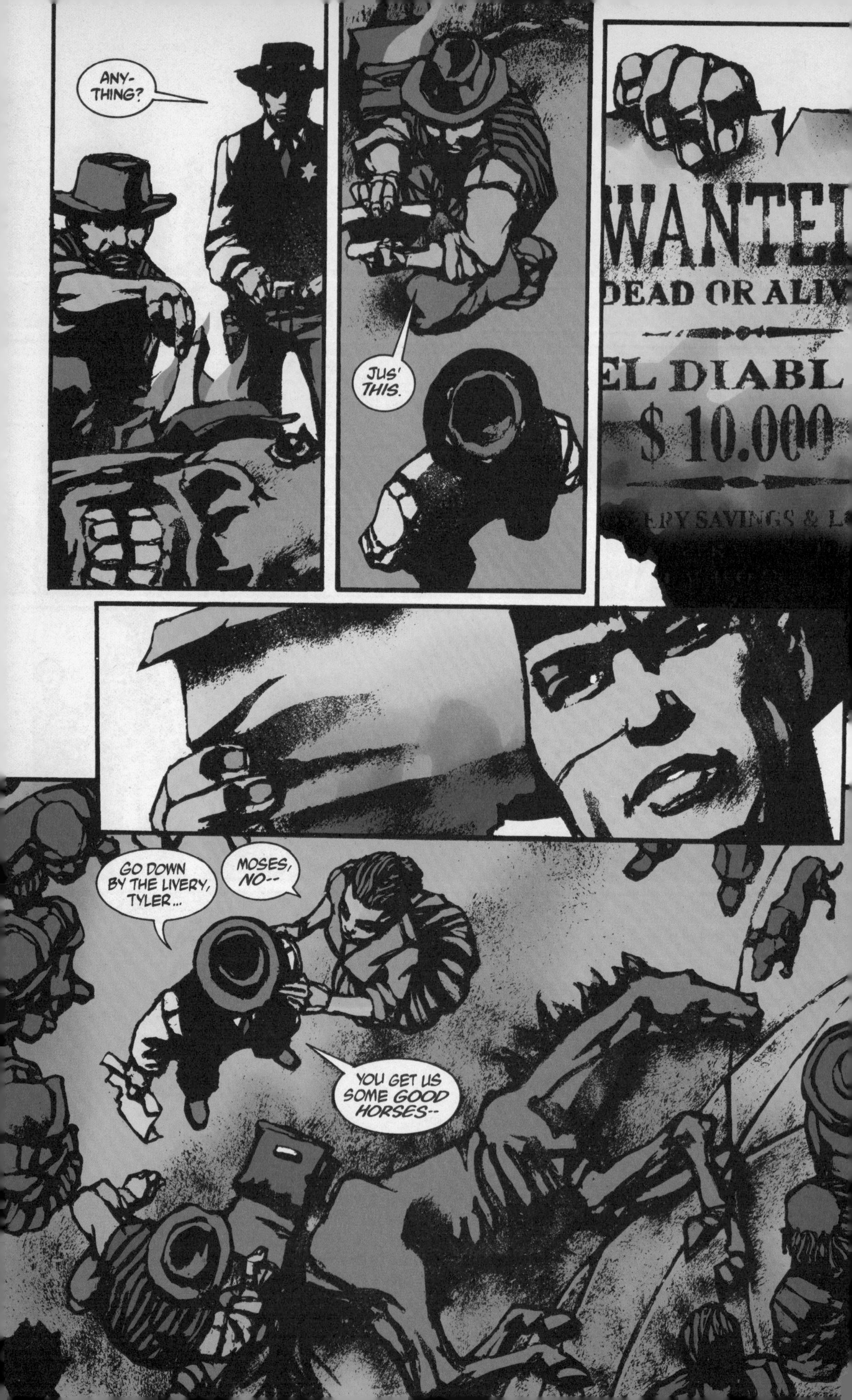
ANY-THING?
JUS' THIS.
WANTEI
DEAD OR ALIV
EL DIABL
$ 10.000
GO DOWN BY THE LIVERY, TYLER...
MOSES, NO--
YOU GET US SOME GOOD HORSES--

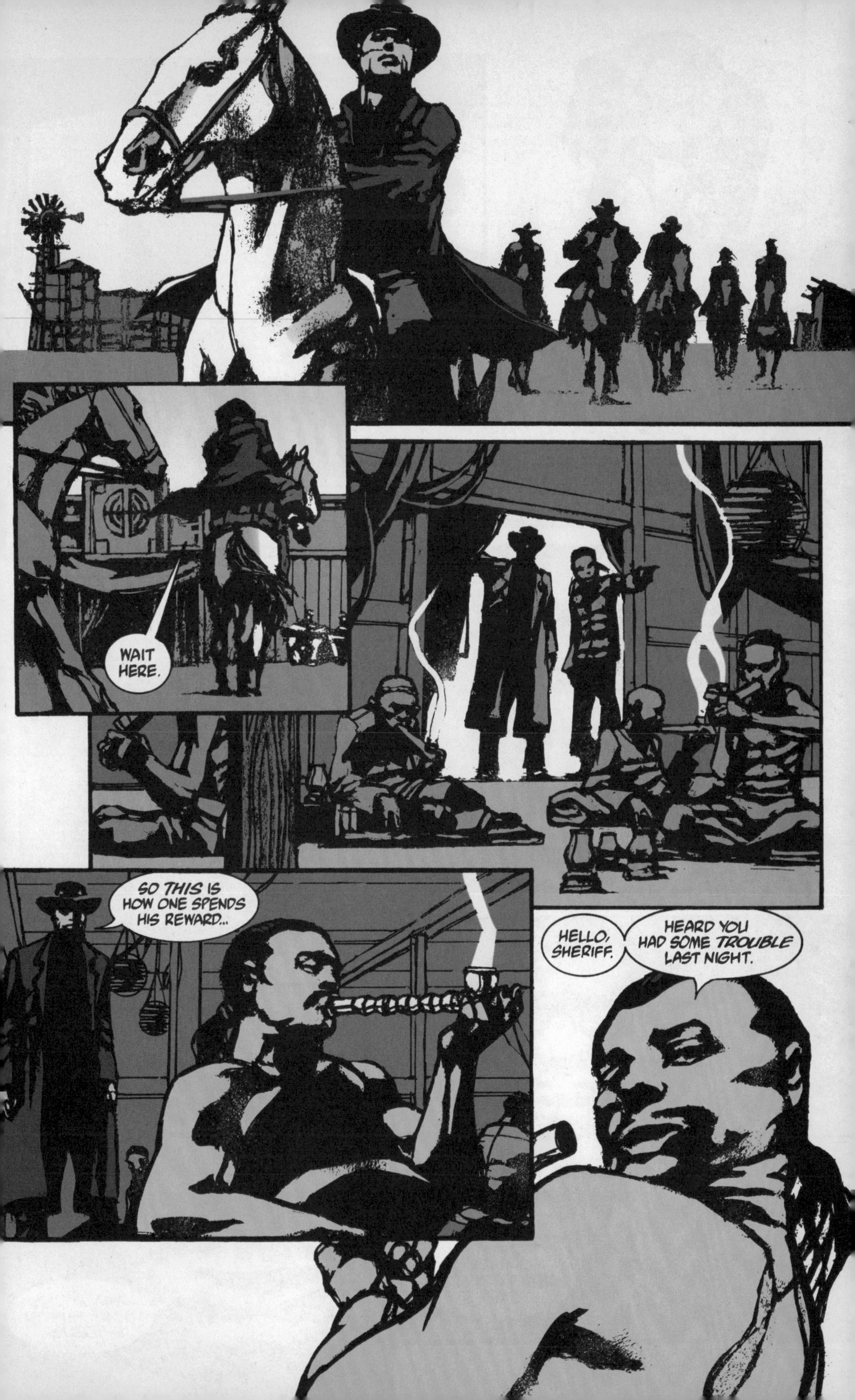
WAIT HERE.
SO *THIS* IS HOW ONE SPENDS HIS REWARD...
HELLO, SHERIFF.
HEARD YOU HAD SOME *TROUBLE* LAST NIGHT.

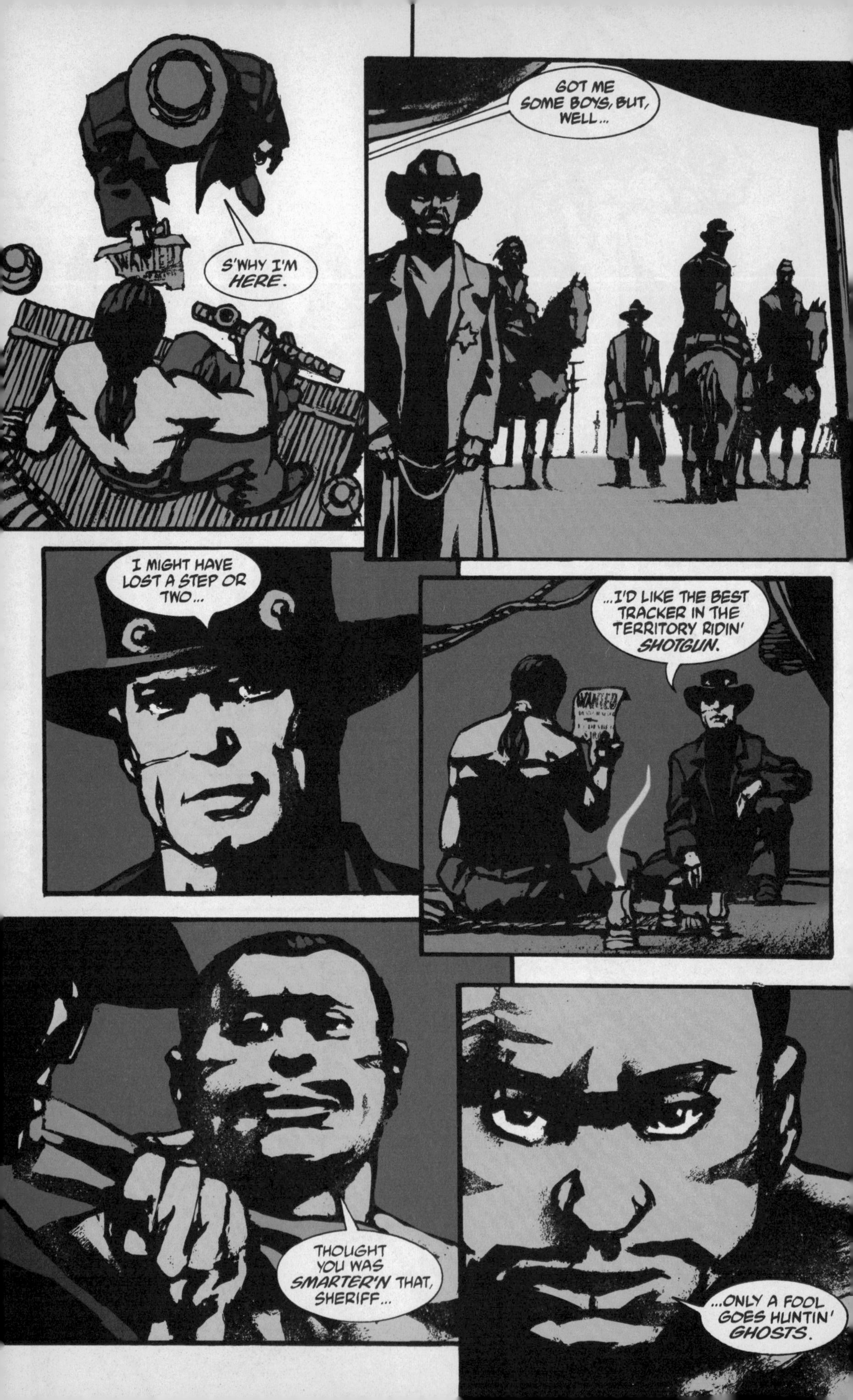
S'WHY I'M HERE.
GOT ME SOME BOYS, BUT, WELL...
I MIGHT HAVE LOST A STEP OR TWO...
...I'D LIKE THE BEST TRACKER IN THE TERRITORY RIDIN' SHOTGUN.
THOUGHT YOU WAS SMARTER'N THAT, SHERIFF...
...ONLY A FOOL GOES HUNTIN' GHOSTS.

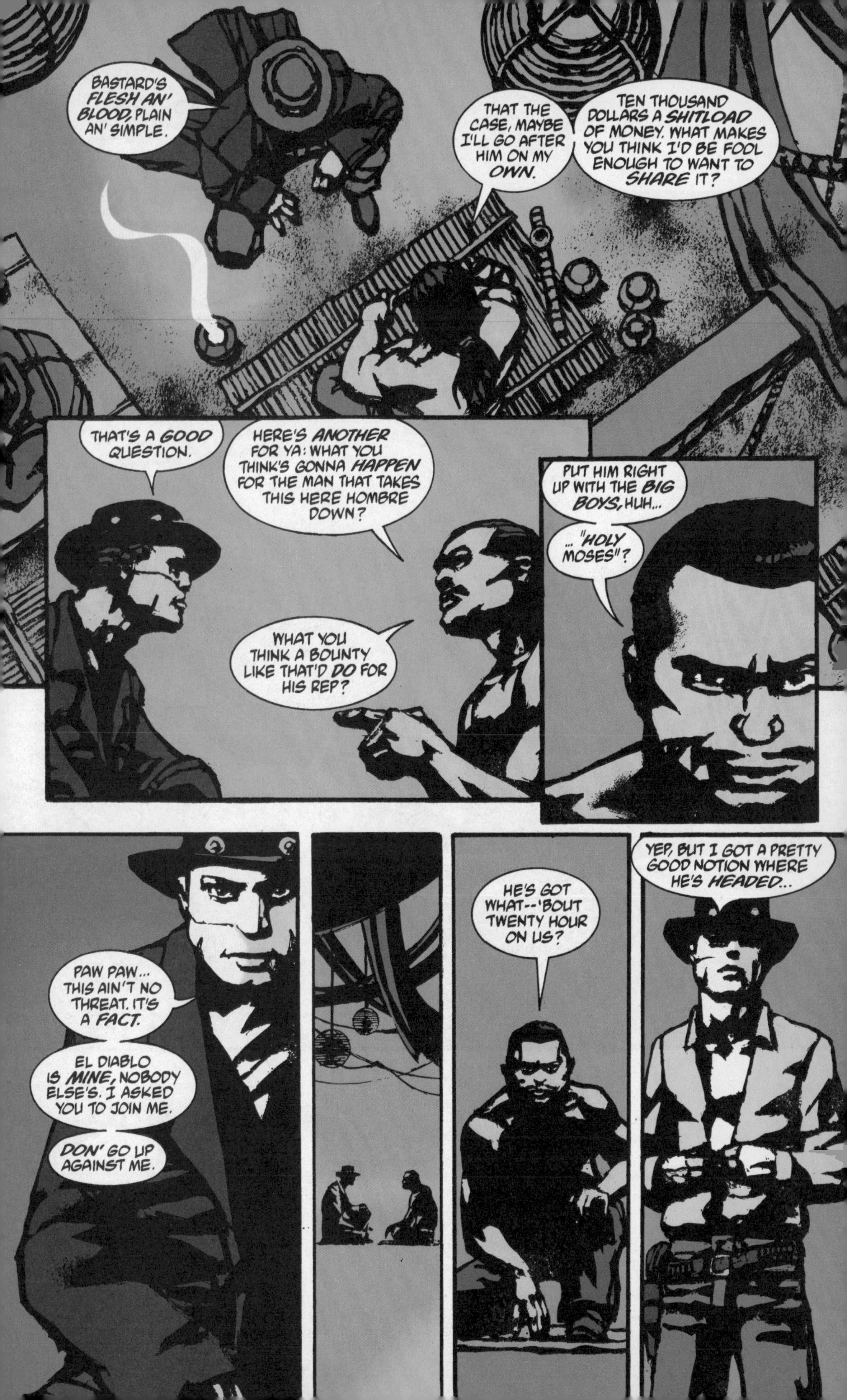
BASTARD'S FLESH AN' BLOOD, PLAIN AN' SIMPLE.
THAT THE CASE, MAYBE I'LL GO AFTER HIM ON MY OWN.
TEN THOUSAND DOLLARS A SHITLOAD OF MONEY. WHAT MAKES YOU THINK I'D BE FOOL ENOUGH TO WANT TO SHARE IT?
THAT'S A GOOD QUESTION.
HERE'S ANOTHER FOR YA: WHAT YOU THINK'S GONNA HAPPEN FOR THE MAN THAT TAKES THIS HERE HOMBRE DOWN?
WHAT YOU THINK A BOUNTY LIKE THAT'D DO FOR HIS REP?
PUT HIM RIGHT UP WITH THE BIG BOYS, HUH...
..."HOLY MOSES"?
PAW PAW... THIS AIN'T NO THREAT. IT'S A FACT.
EL DIABLO IS MINE, NOBODY ELSE'S. I ASKED YOU TO JOIN ME.
DON' GO UP AGAINST ME.
HE'S GOT WHAT--'BOUT TWENTY HOUR ON US?
YEP, BUT I GOT A PRETTY GOOD NOTION WHERE HE'S HEADED...

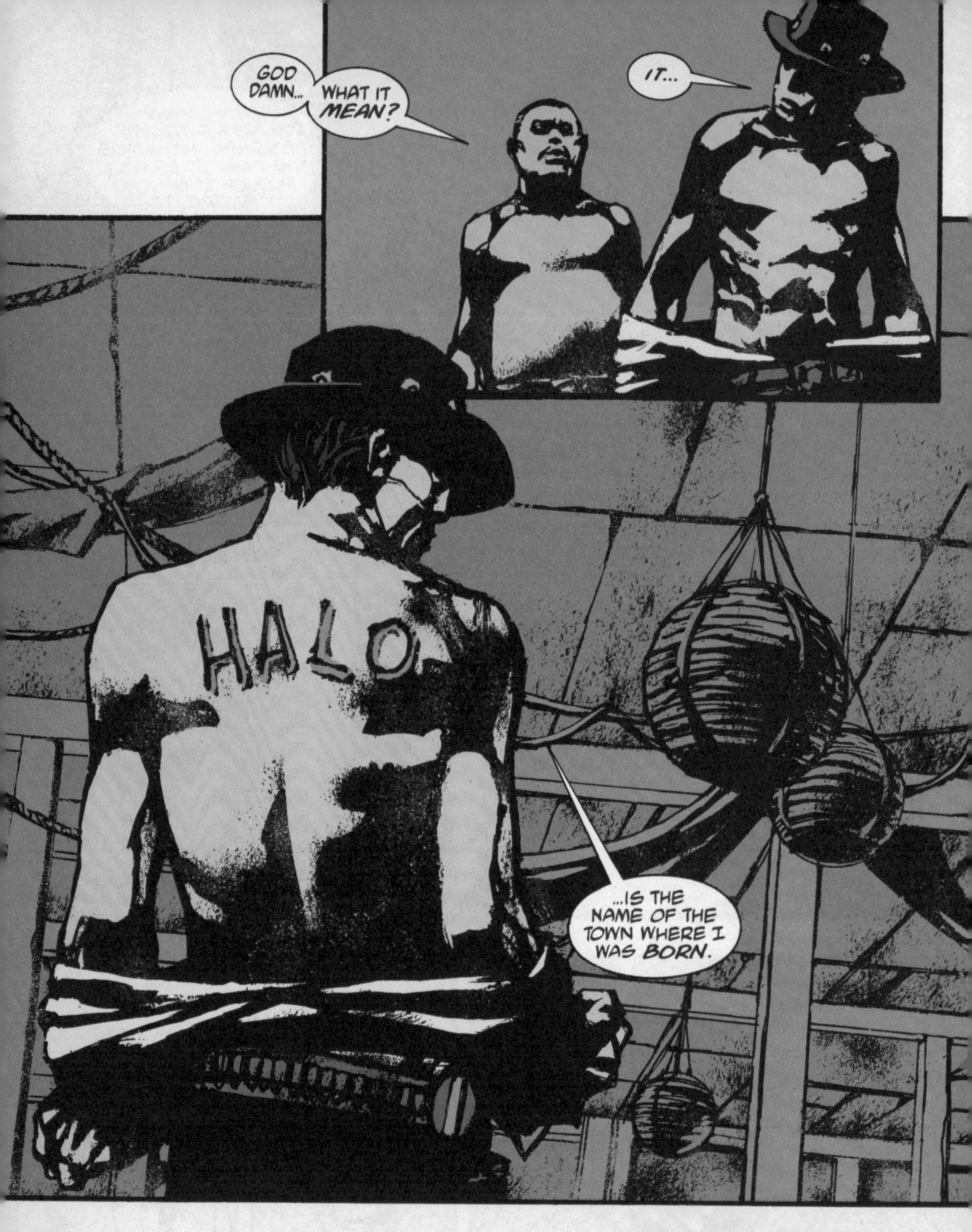
GOD DAMN...
WHAT IT MEAN?
IT...
HALO
...IS THE NAME OF THE TOWN WHERE I WAS BORN.

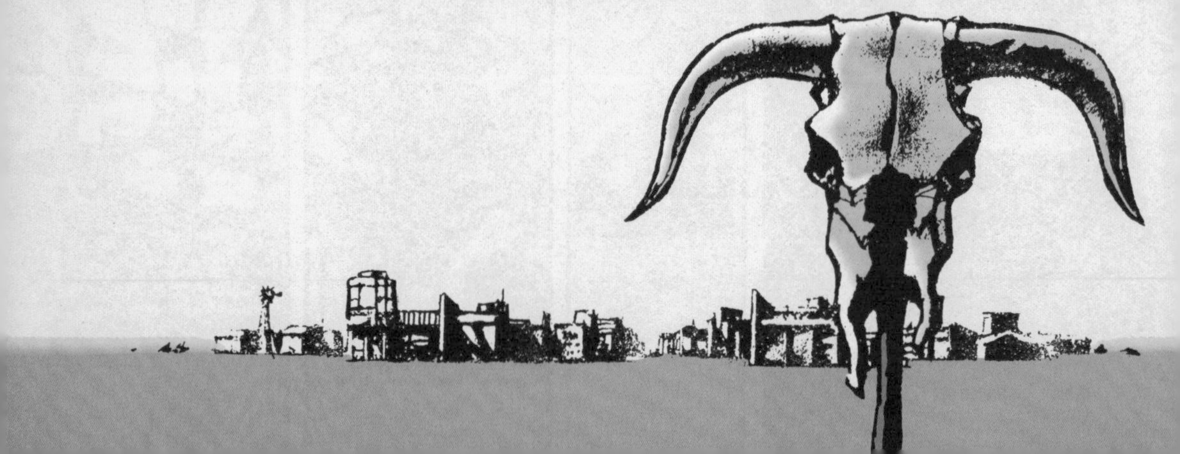

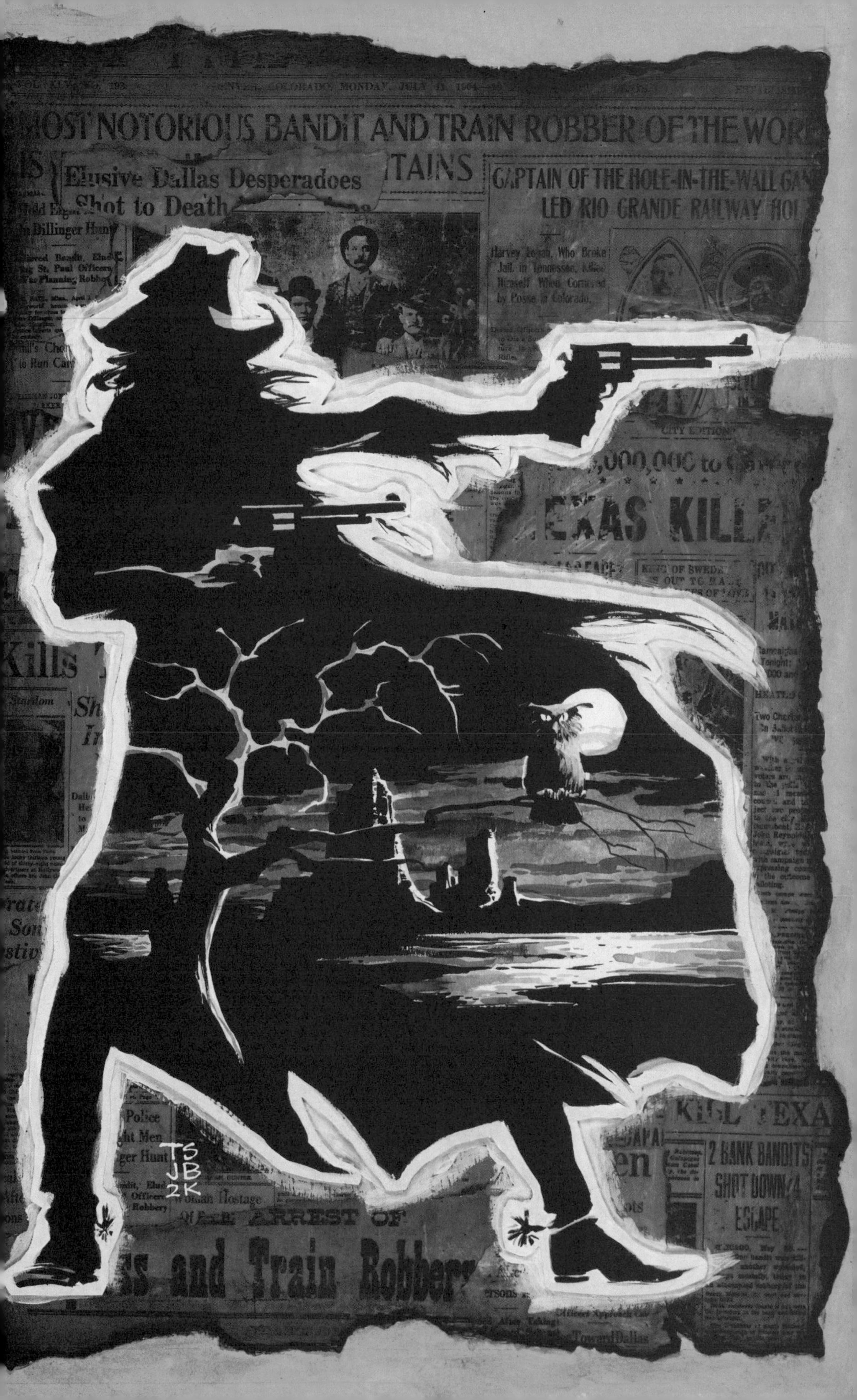
MOST NOTORIOUS BANDIT AND TRAIN ROBBER OF THE WOR
Elusive Dallas Desperadoes
Shot to Death
TAINS
CAPTAIN OF THE HOLE-IN-THE-WALL GAN
LED RIO GRANDE RAILWAY HOL
Jail in Tennessee, Kills
Himself When Cornered
by Posse in Colorado.
CITY EDITION
EXAS KILL
Kills
Stardom
KILL TEXA
Police
Woman Hostage
ARREST OF
and Train Robber
2 BANK BANDITS
SHOT DOWN; 4
ESCAPE
Toward Dallas
TS
JB
2K

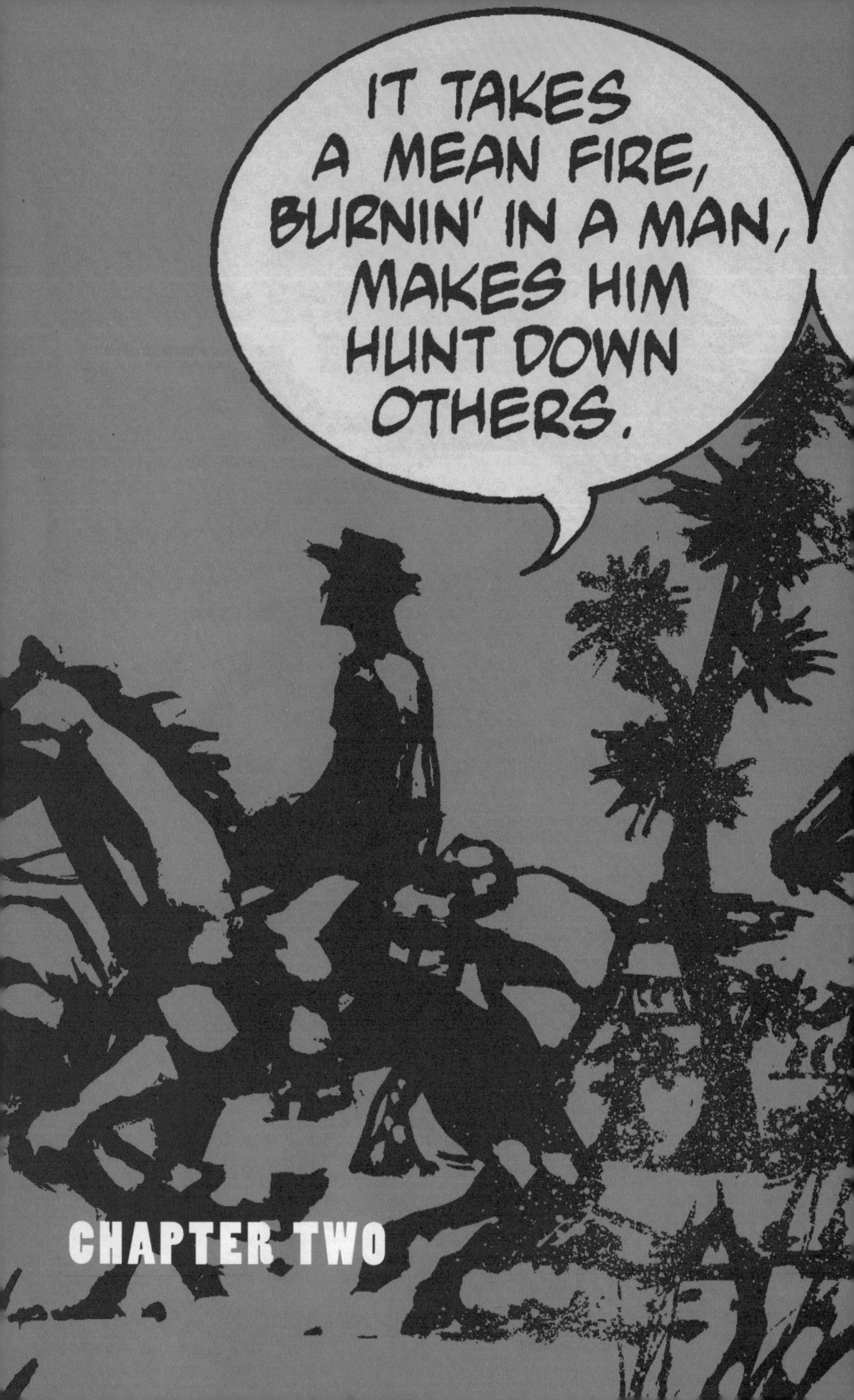
IT TAKES A MEAN FIRE, BURNIN' IN A MAN, MAKES HIM HUNT DOWN OTHERS.
CHAPTER TWO

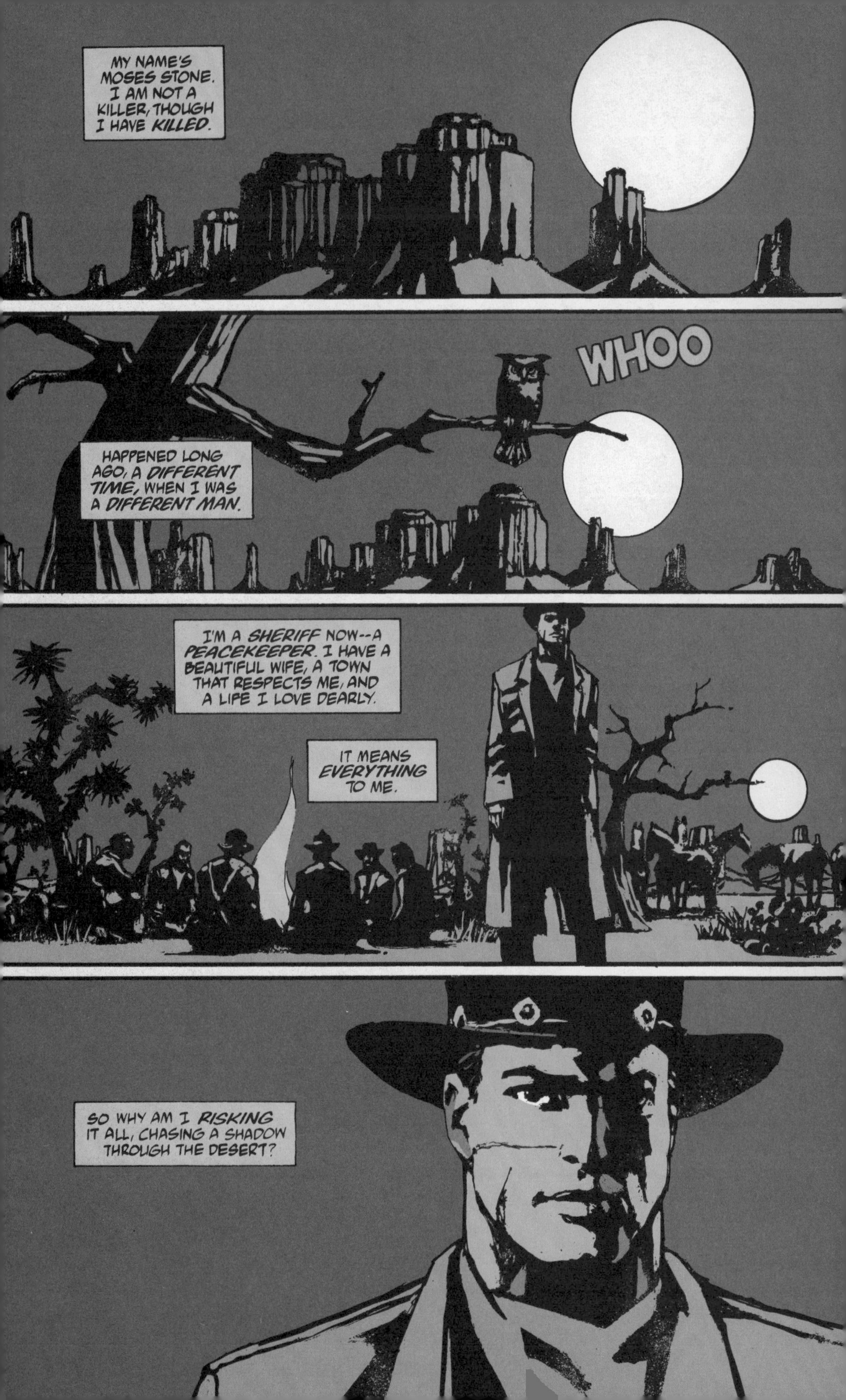
MY NAME'S MOSES STONE. I AM NOT A KILLER, THOUGH I HAVE KILLED.
WHOO
HAPPENED LONG AGO, A DIFFERENT TIME, WHEN I WAS A DIFFERENT MAN.
I'M A SHERIFF NOW--A PEACEKEEPER. I HAVE A BEAUTIFUL WIFE, A TOWN THAT RESPECTS ME, AND A LIFE I LOVE DEARLY.
IT MEANS EVERYTHING TO ME.
SO WHY AM I RISKING IT ALL, CHASING A SHADOW THROUGH THE DESERT?

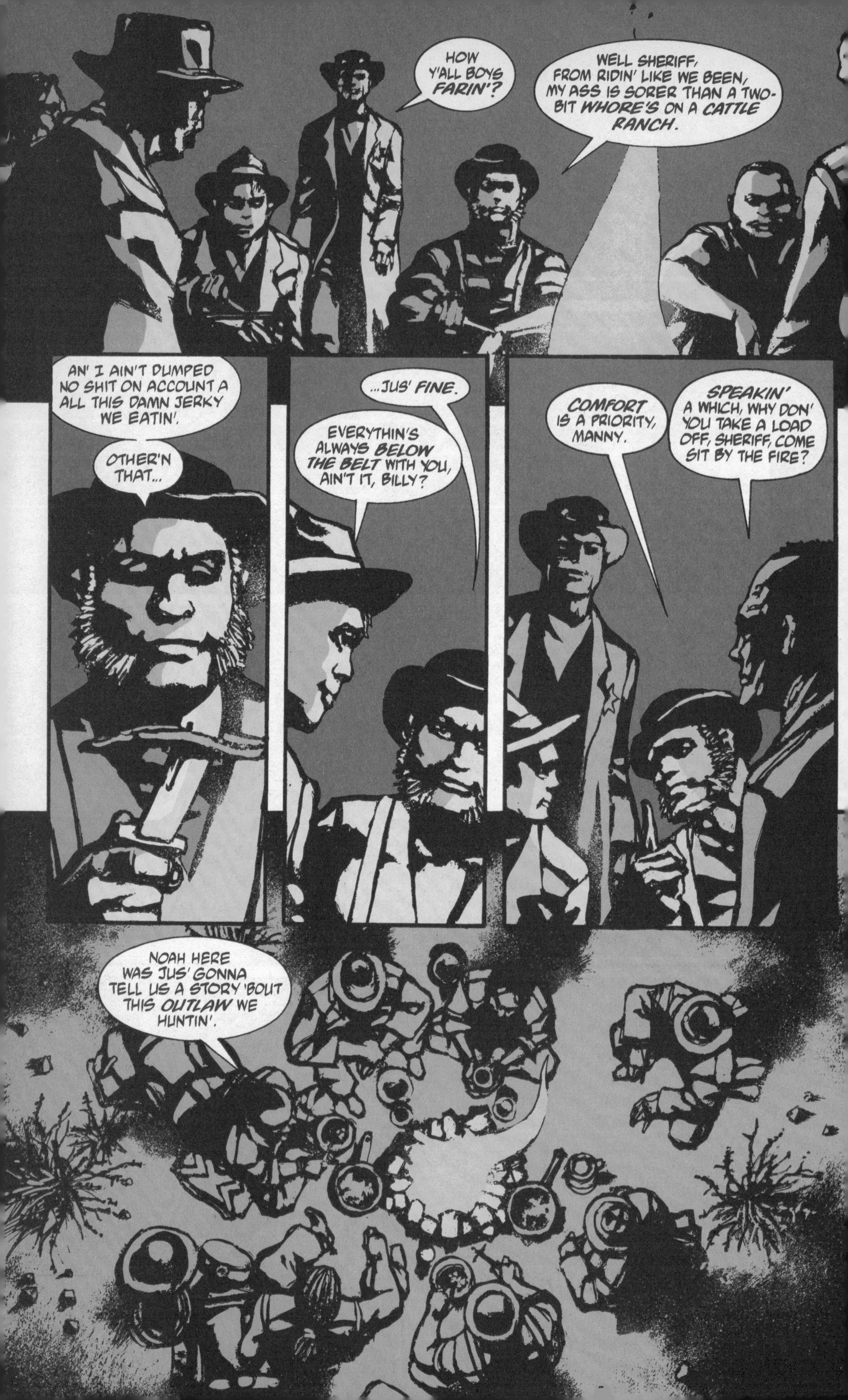
HOW Y'ALL BOYS FARIN'?
WELL SHERIFF, FROM RIDIN' LIKE WE BEEN, MY ASS IS SORER THAN A TWO-BIT WHORE'S ON A CATTLE RANCH.
AN' I AIN'T DUMPED NO SHIT ON ACCOUNT A ALL THIS DAMN JERKY WE EATIN'.
OTHER'N THAT...
...JUS' FINE.
EVERYTHIN'S ALWAYS BELOW THE BELT WITH YOU, AIN'T IT, BILLY?
COMFORT IS A PRIORITY, MANNY.
SPEAKIN' A WHICH, WHY DON' YOU TAKE A LOAD OFF, SHERIFF, COME SIT BY THE FIRE?
NOAH HERE WAS JUS' GONNA TELL US A STORY 'BOUT THIS OUTLAW WE HUNTIN'.

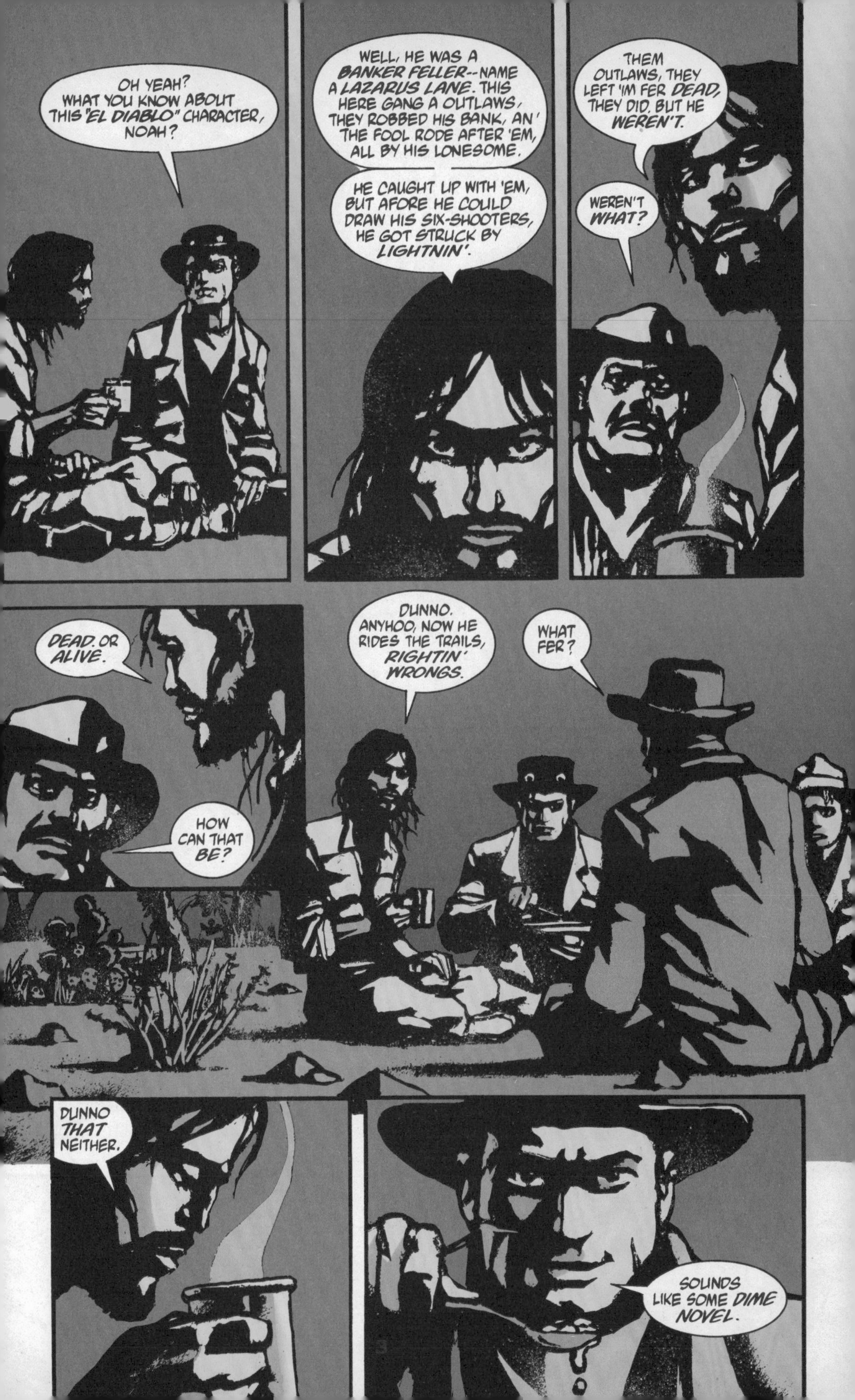
OH YEAH? WHAT YOU KNOW ABOUT THIS "EL DIABLO" CHARACTER, NOAH?
WELL, HE WAS A BANKER FELLER--NAME A LAZARUS LANE. THIS HERE GANG A OUTLAWS, THEY ROBBED HIS BANK, AN' THE FOOL RODE AFTER 'EM, ALL BY HIS LONESOME.
HE CAUGHT UP WITH 'EM, BUT AFORE HE COULD DRAW HIS SIX-SHOOTERS, HE GOT STRUCK BY LIGHTNIN'.
THEM OUTLAWS, THEY LEFT 'IM FER DEAD, THEY DID, BUT HE WEREN'T.
WEREN'T WHAT?
DEAD. OR ALIVE.
HOW CAN THAT BE?
DUNNO. ANYHOO, NOW HE RIDES THE TRAILS, RIGHTIN' WRONGS.
WHAT FER?
DUNNO THAT NEITHER.
SOUNDS LIKE SOME DIME NOVEL.

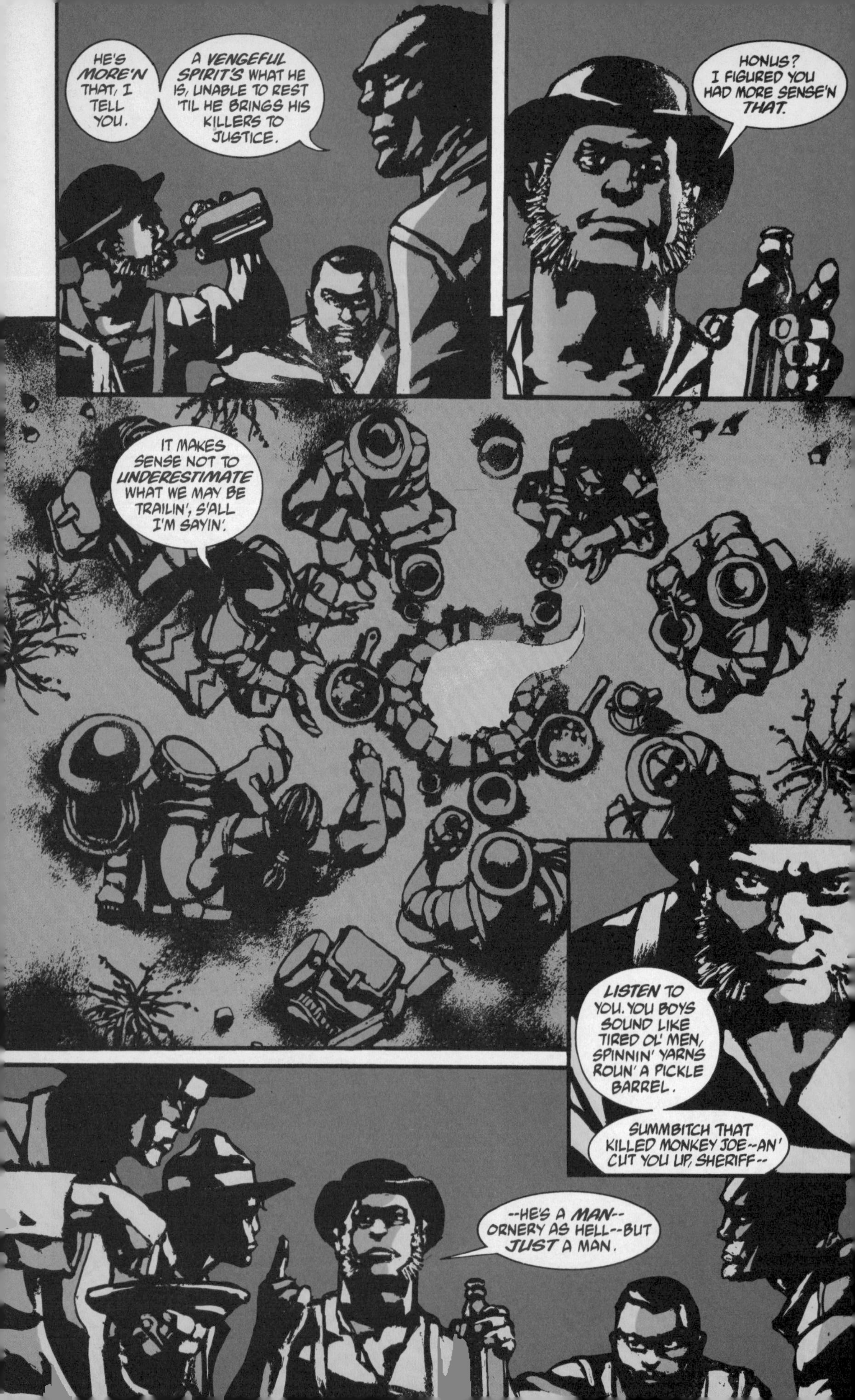
HE'S MORE'N THAT, I TELL YOU.
A VENGEFUL SPIRIT'S WHAT HE IS, UNABLE TO REST 'TIL HE BRINGS HIS KILLERS TO JUSTICE.
HONUS? I FIGURED YOU HAD MORE SENSE'N THAT.
IT MAKES SENSE NOT TO UNDERESTIMATE WHAT WE MAY BE TRAILIN', S'ALL I'M SAYIN'.
LISTEN TO YOU. YOU BOYS SOUND LIKE TIRED OL' MEN, SPINNIN' YARNS ROUN' A PICKLE BARREL.
SUMMBITCH THAT KILLED MONKEY JOE--AN' CUT YOU UP, SHERIFF--
--HE'S A MAN--ORNERY AS HELL--BUT JUST A MAN.

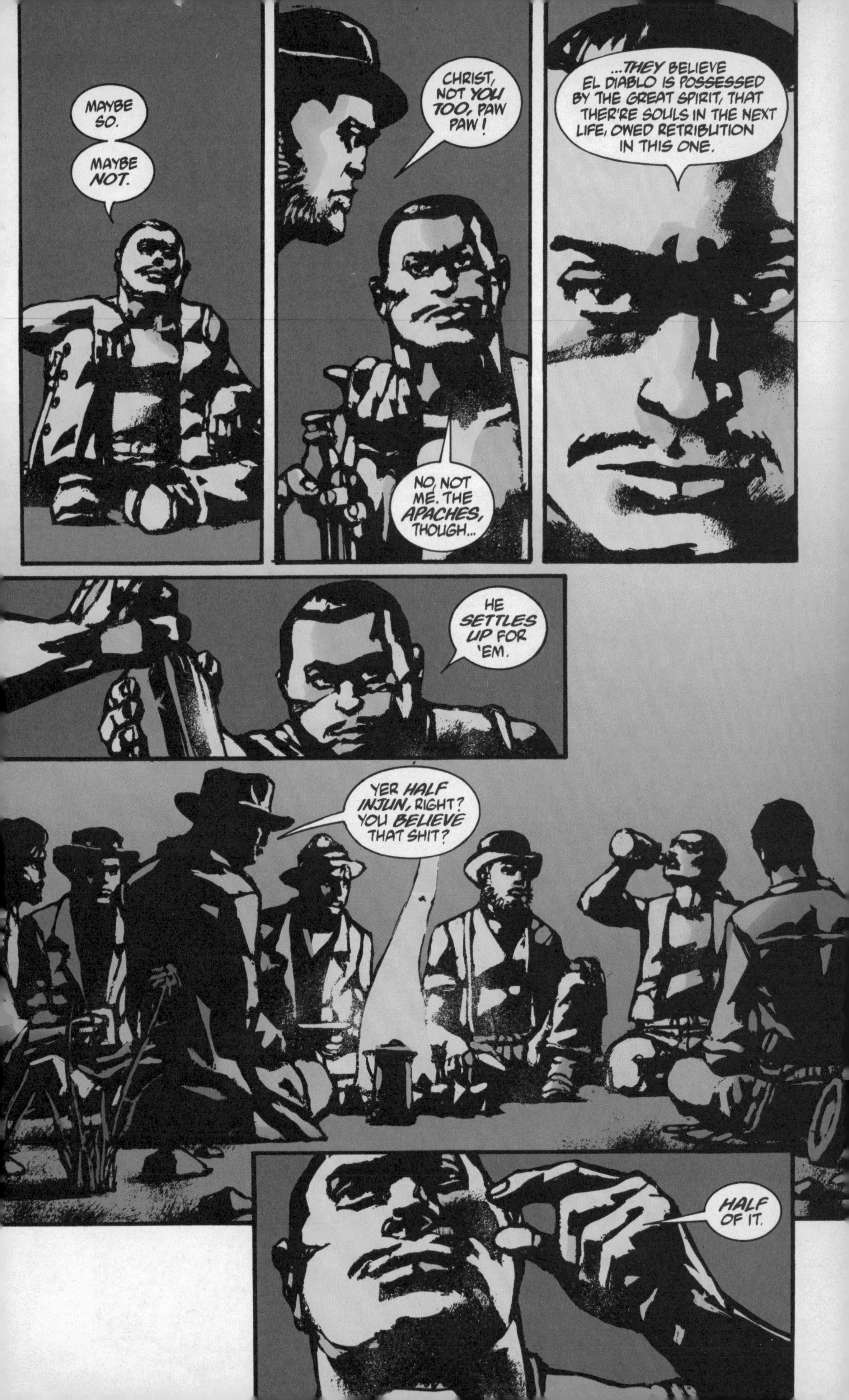
MAYBE SO.
MAYBE NOT.
CHRIST, NOT YOU TOO, PAW PAW!
NO, NOT ME. THE APACHES, THOUGH...
...THEY BELIEVE EL DIABLO IS POSSESSED BY THE GREAT SPIRIT, THAT THER'RE SOULS IN THE NEXT LIFE, OWED RETRIBUTION IN THIS ONE.
HE SETTLES UP FOR 'EM.
YER HALF INJUN, RIGHT? YOU BELIEVE THAT SHIT?
HALF OF IT.

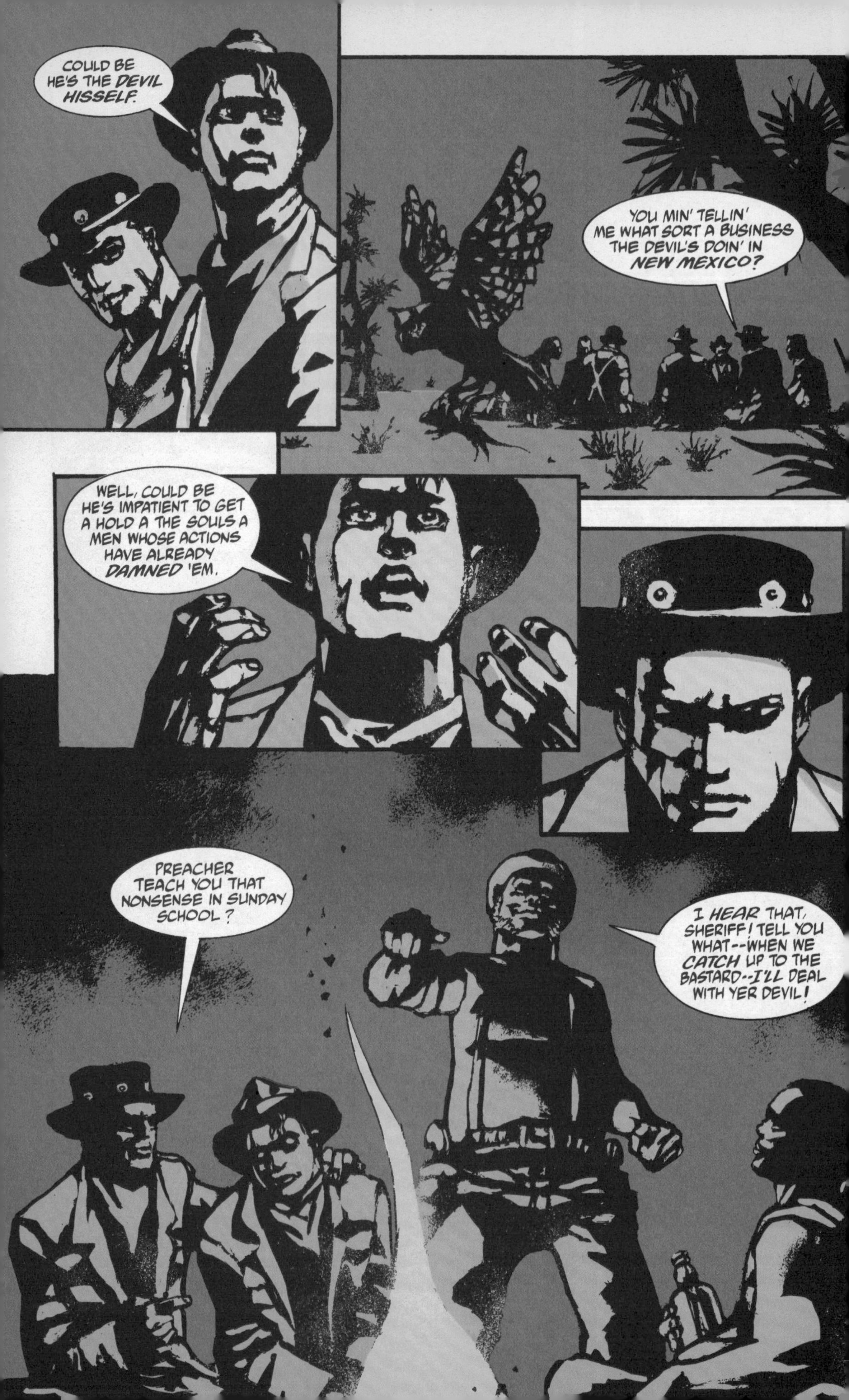
COULD BE HE'S THE DEVIL HISSELF.
YOU MIN' TELLIN' ME WHAT SORT A BUSINESS THE DEVIL'S DOIN' IN NEW MEXICO?
WELL, COULD BE HE'S IMPATIENT TO GET A HOLD A THE SOULS A MEN WHOSE ACTIONS HAVE ALREADY DAMNED 'EM.
PREACHER TEACH YOU THAT NONSENSE IN SUNDAY SCHOOL?
I HEAR THAT, SHERIFF! TELL YOU WHAT--WHEN WE CATCH UP TO THE BASTARD--I'LL DEAL WITH YER DEVIL!

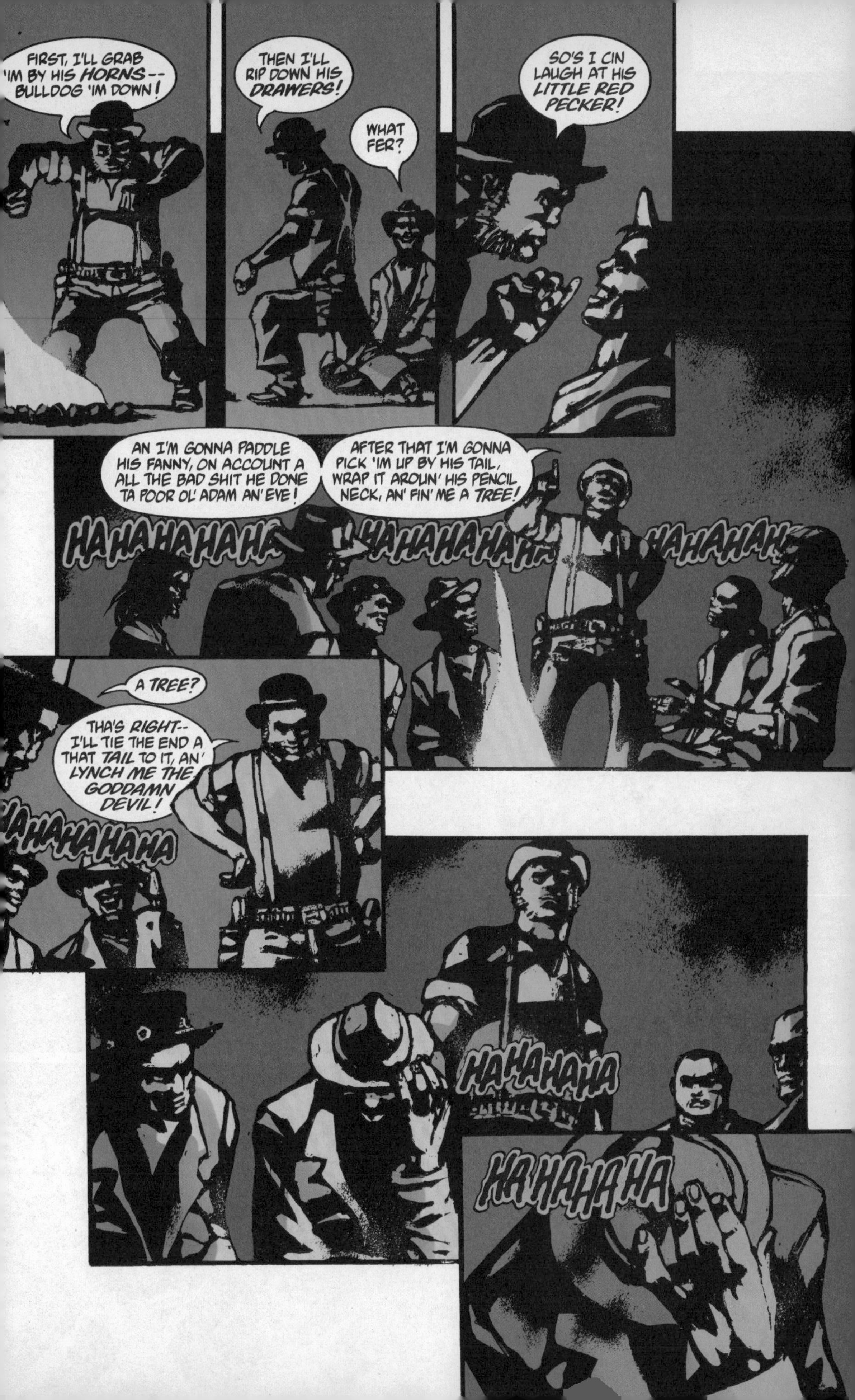
FIRST, I'LL GRAB 'IM BY HIS HORNS-- BULLDOG 'IM DOWN!
THEN I'LL RIP DOWN HIS DRAWERS!
WHAT FER?
SO'S I CIN LAUGH AT HIS LITTLE RED PECKER!
AN I'M GONNA PADDLE HIS FANNY, ON ACCOUNT A ALL THE BAD SHIT HE DONE TA POOR OL' ADAM AN' EVE!
AFTER THAT I'M GONNA PICK 'IM UP BY HIS TAIL, WRAP IT AROUN' HIS PENCIL NECK, AN' FIN' ME A TREE!
HAHAHAHAHA
HAHAHAHAHA
HAHAHAHA
A TREE?
THA'S RIGHT-- I'LL TIE THE END A THAT TAIL TO IT, AN' LYNCH ME THE GODDAMN DEVIL!
HAHAHAHAHA
HAHAHAHA
HAHAHAHAHA

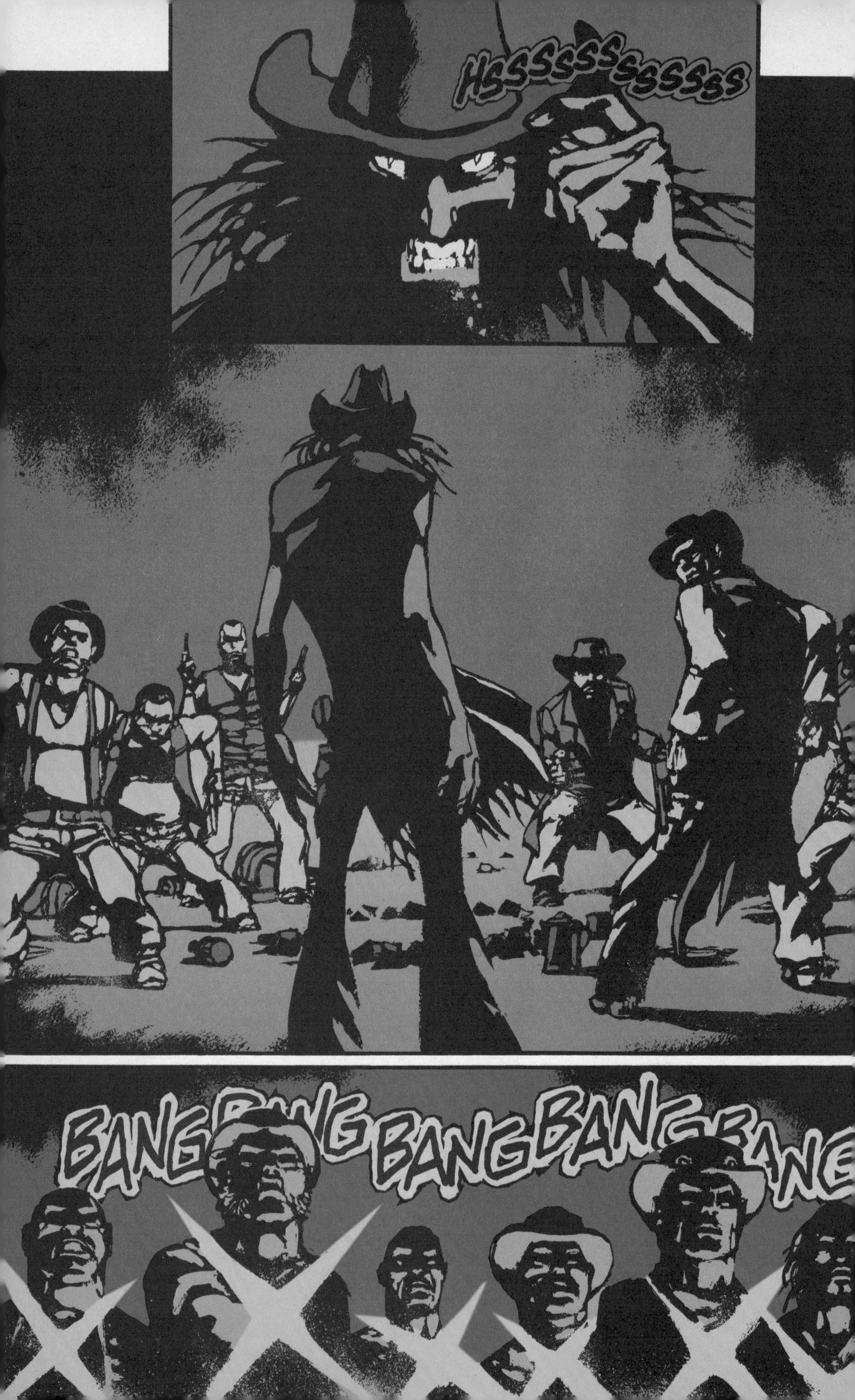
HSSSSSSSSSSSS
BANG
BANG
BAN

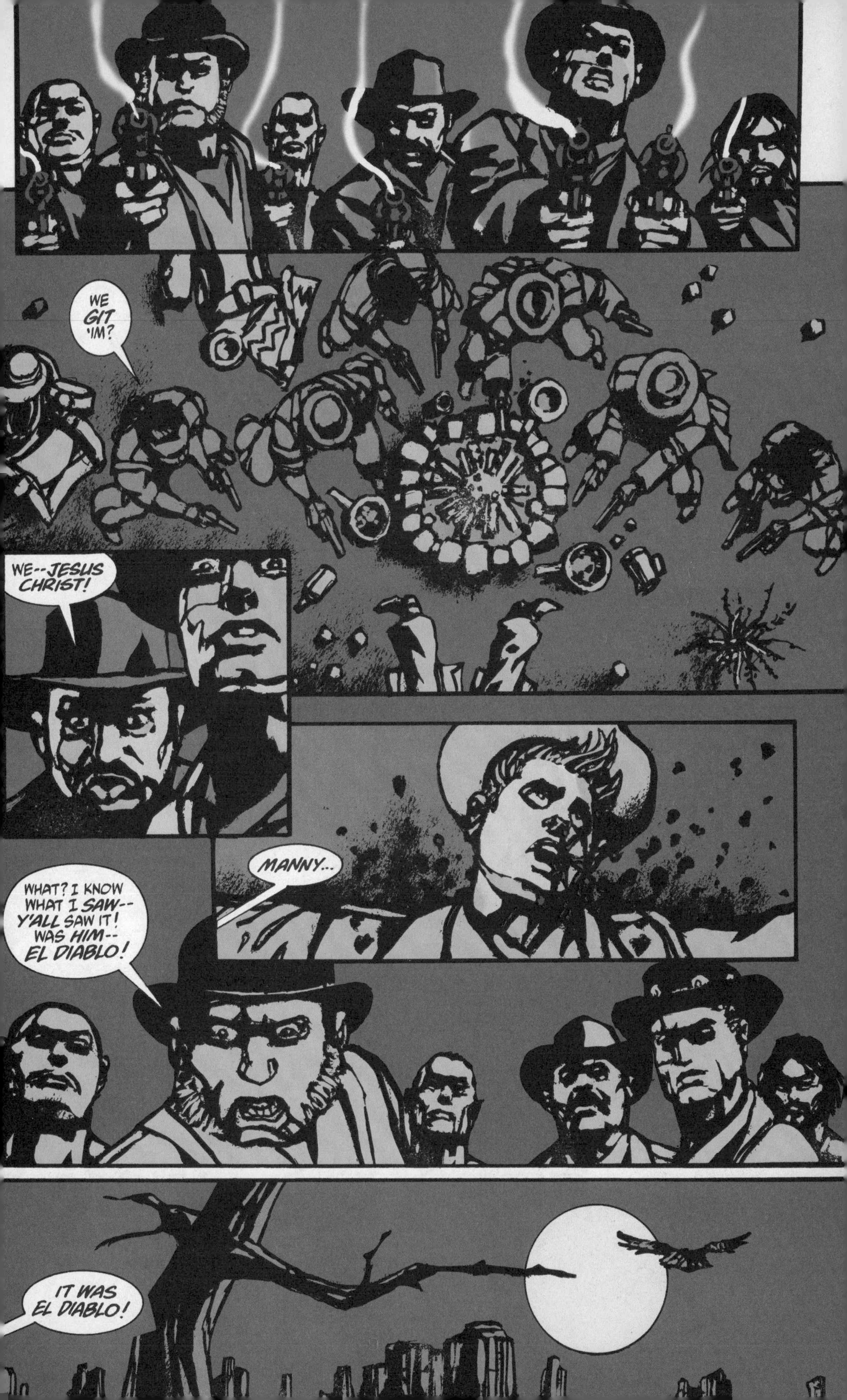
WE GIT 'IM?
WE--JESUS CHRIST!
MANNY...
WHAT? I KNOW WHAT I SAW-- Y'ALL SAW IT! WAS HIM-- EL DIABLO!
IT WAS EL DIABLO!

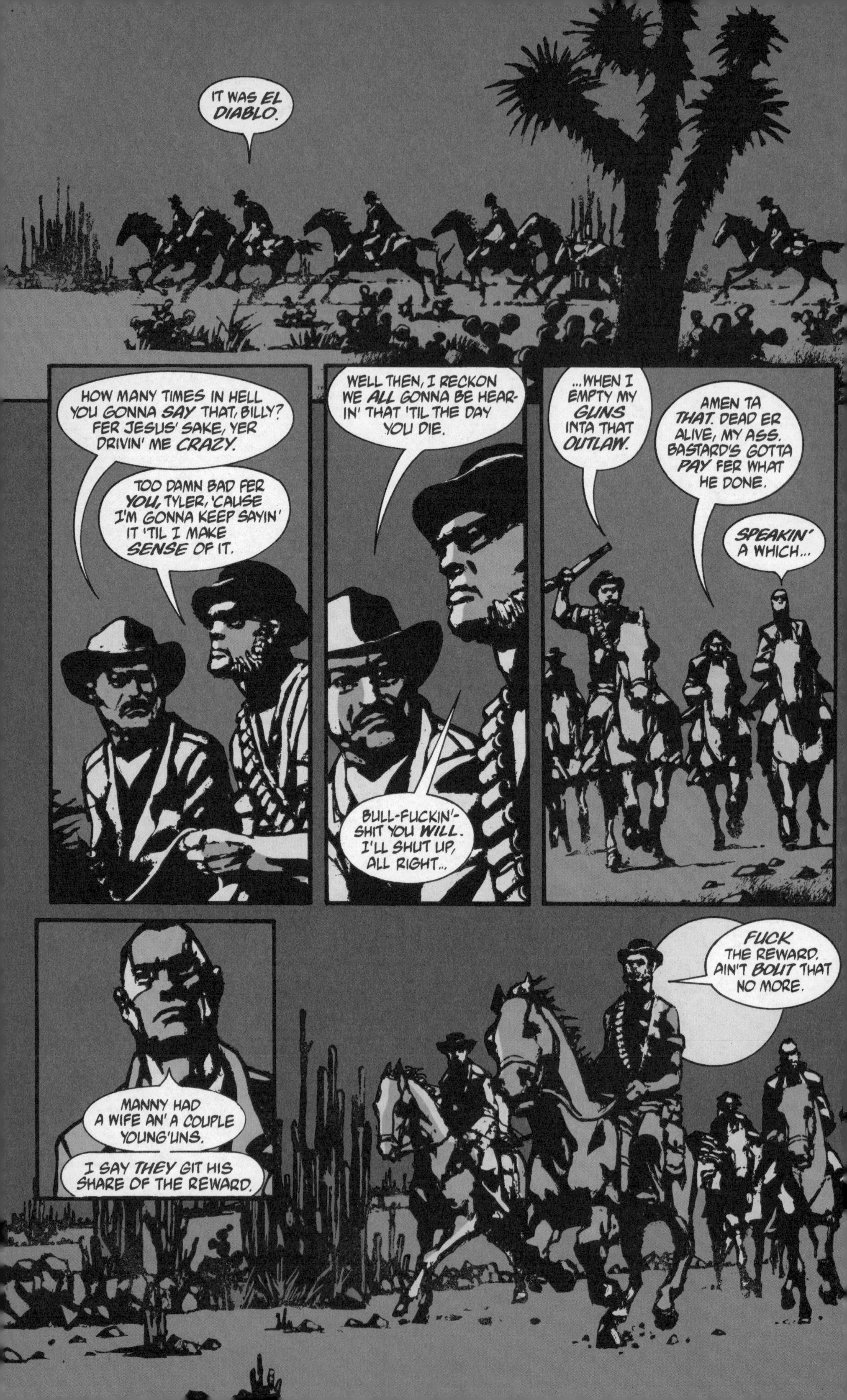

IT WAS *EL DIABLO*.
HOW MANY TIMES IN HELL YOU GONNA *SAY* THAT, BILLY? FER JESUS' SAKE, YER DRIVIN' ME *CRAZY*.
TOO DAMN BAD FER *YOU*, TYLER, 'CAUSE I'M GONNA KEEP SAYIN' IT 'TIL I MAKE *SENSE* OF IT.
WELL THEN, I RECKON WE *ALL* GONNA BE HEAR-IN' THAT 'TIL THE DAY YOU DIE.
BULL-FUCKIN'-SHIT YOU *WILL*. I'LL SHUT UP, ALL RIGHT...
...WHEN I EMPTY MY *GUNS* INTA THAT *OUTLAW*.
AMEN TA *THAT*. DEAD ER ALIVE, MY ASS. BASTARD'S GOTTA *PAY* FER WHAT HE DONE.
SPEAKIN' A WHICH...
MANNY HAD A WIFE AN' A COUPLE YOUNG'UNS.
I SAY *THEY* GIT HIS SHARE OF THE REWARD.
FUCK THE REWARD. AIN'T *BOUT* THAT NO MORE.

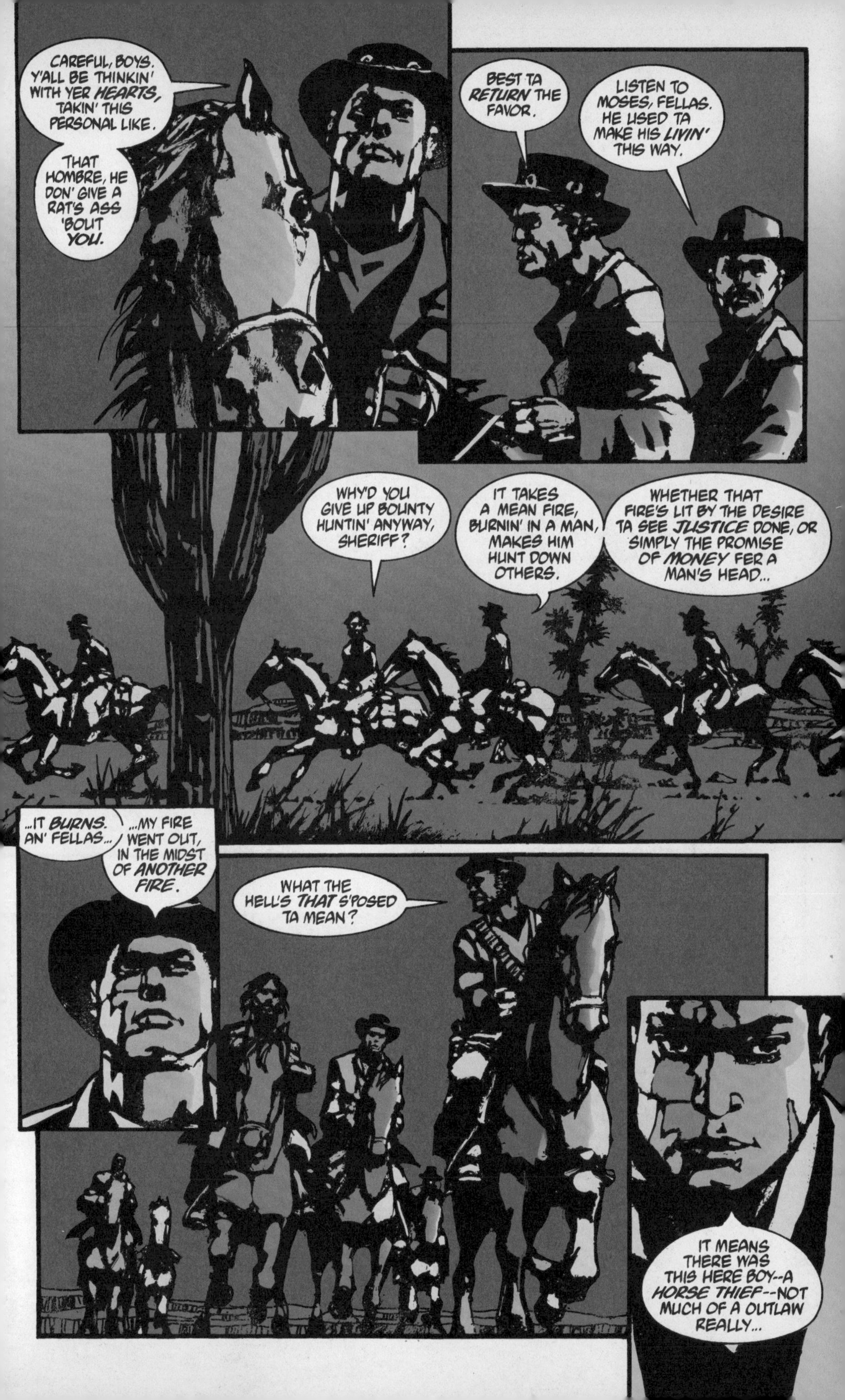
CAREFUL, BOYS. Y'ALL BE THINKIN' WITH YER HEARTS, TAKIN' THIS PERSONAL LIKE.
THAT HOMBRE, HE DON' GIVE A RAT'S ASS 'BOUT YOU.
BEST TA RETURN THE FAVOR.
LISTEN TO MOSES, FELLAS. HE USED TA MAKE HIS LIVIN' THIS WAY.
WHY'D YOU GIVE UP BOUNTY HUNTIN' ANYWAY, SHERIFF?
IT TAKES A MEAN FIRE, BURNIN' IN A MAN, MAKES HIM HUNT DOWN OTHERS.
WHETHER THAT FIRE'S LIT BY THE DESIRE TA SEE JUSTICE DONE, OR SIMPLY THE PROMISE OF MONEY FER A MAN'S HEAD...
...IT BURNS. AN' FELLAS...
...MY FIRE WENT OUT, IN THE MIDST OF ANOTHER FIRE.
WHAT THE HELL'S THAT S'POSED TA MEAN?
IT MEANS THERE WAS THIS HERE BOY--A HORSE THIEF--NOT MUCH OF A OUTLAW REALLY...

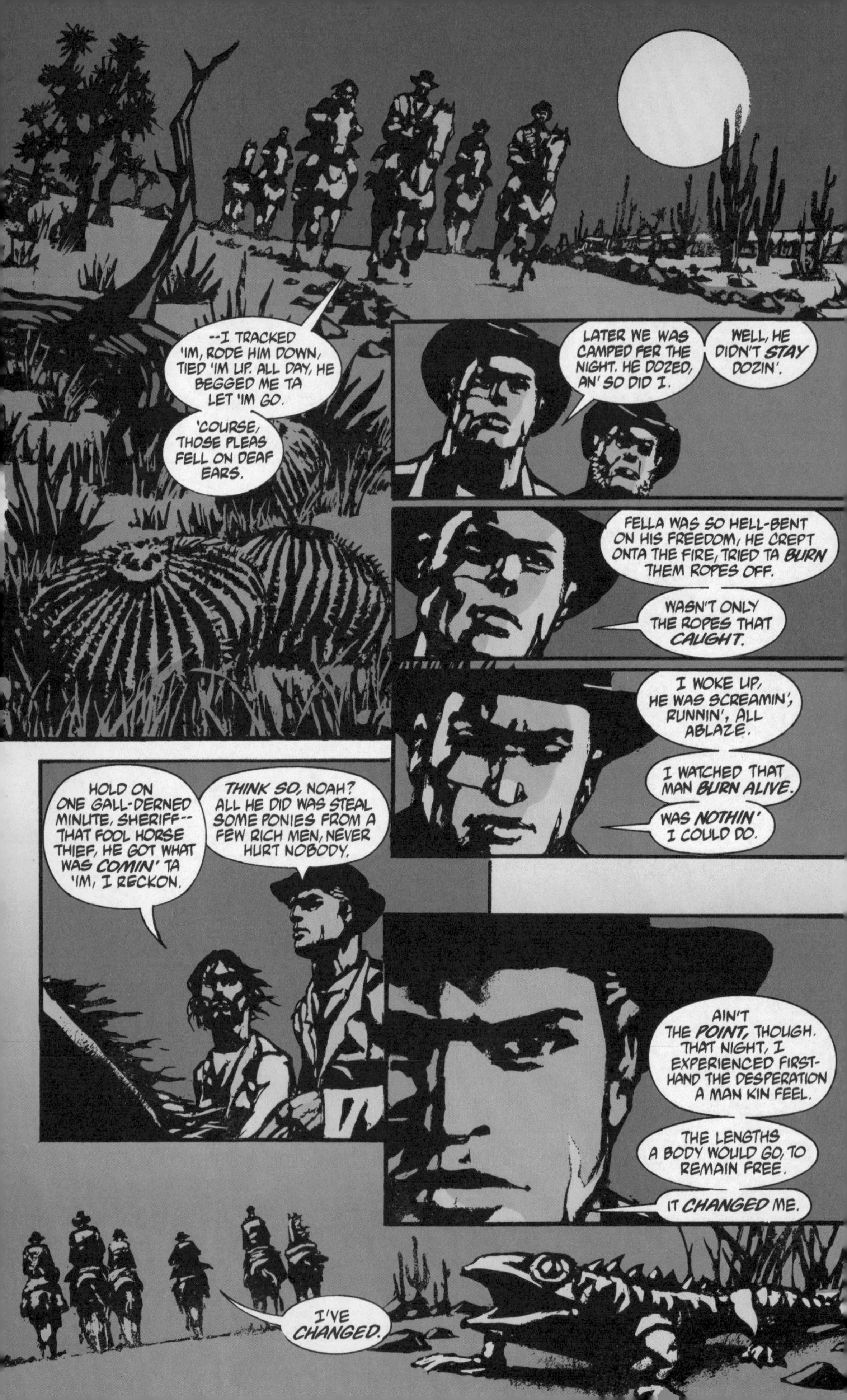
--I TRACKED 'IM, RODE HIM DOWN, TIED 'IM UP. ALL DAY, HE BEGGED ME TA LET 'IM GO.
'COURSE, THOSE PLEAS FELL ON DEAF EARS.
LATER WE WAS CAMPED FER THE NIGHT. HE DOZED, AN' SO DID I.
WELL, HE DIDN'T STAY DOZIN'.
FELLA WAS SO HELL-BENT ON HIS FREEDOM, HE CREPT ONTA THE FIRE, TRIED TA BURN THEM ROPES OFF.
WASN'T ONLY THE ROPES THAT CAUGHT.
I WOKE UP, HE WAS SCREAMIN', RUNNIN', ALL ABLAZE.
I WATCHED THAT MAN BURN ALIVE.
WAS NOTHIN' I COULD DO.
HOLD ON ONE GALL-DERNED MINUTE, SHERIFF--THAT FOOL HORSE THIEF, HE GOT WHAT WAS COMIN' TA 'IM, I RECKON.
THINK SO, NOAH? ALL HE DID WAS STEAL SOME PONIES FROM A FEW RICH MEN, NEVER HURT NOBODY.
AIN'T THE POINT, THOUGH. THAT NIGHT, I EXPERIENCED FIRST-HAND THE DESPERATION A MAN KIN FEEL.
THE LENGTHS A BODY WOULD GO, TO REMAIN FREE.
IT CHANGED ME.
I'VE CHANGED.

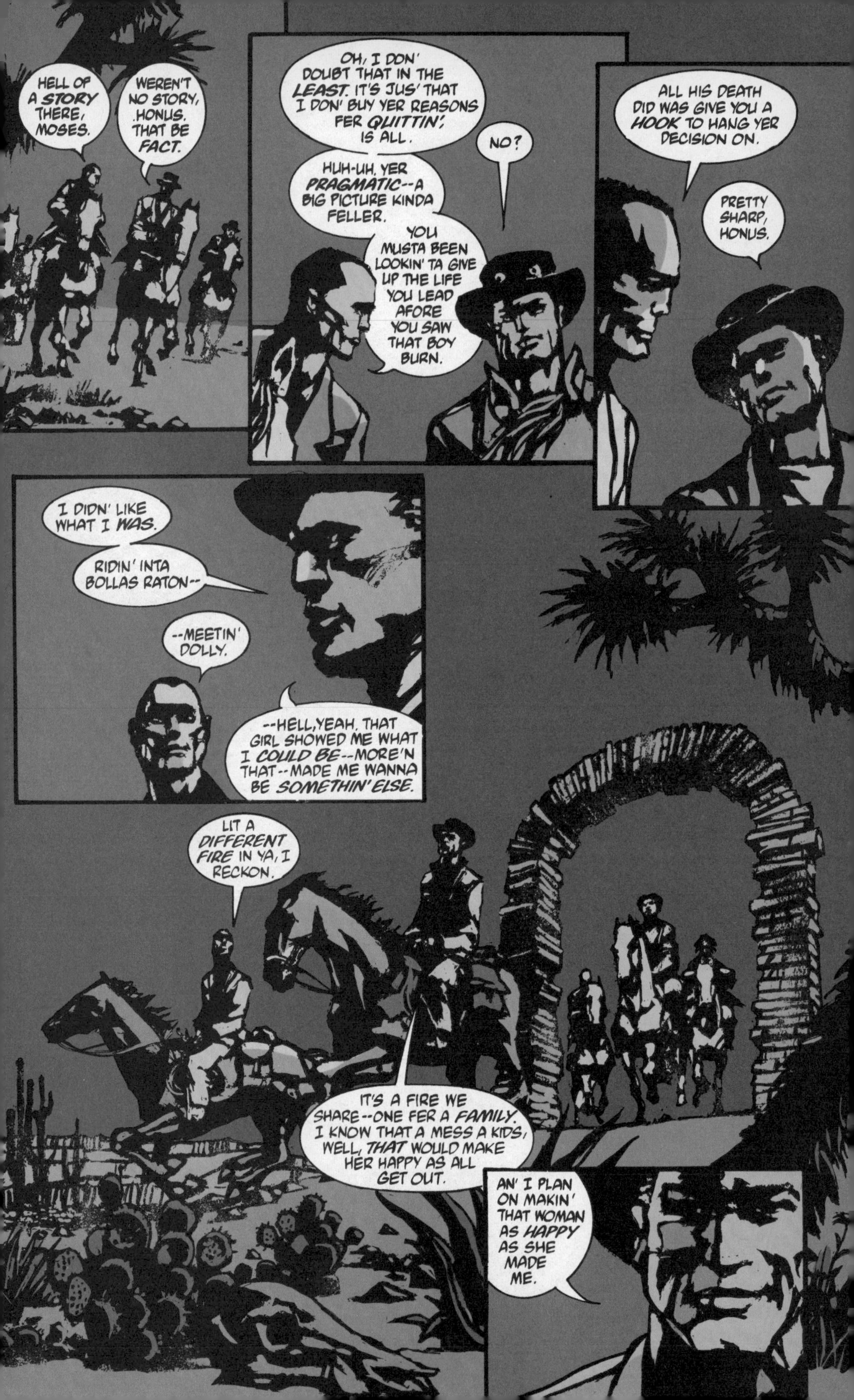
HELL OF A STORY THERE, MOSES.
WEREN'T NO STORY, HONUS. THAT BE FACT.
OH, I DON' DOUBT THAT IN THE LEAST. IT'S JUS' THAT I DON' BUY YER REASONS FER QUITTIN'; IS ALL.
NO?
HUH-UH. YER PRAGMATIC--A BIG PICTURE KINDA FELLER.
YOU MUSTA BEEN LOOKIN' TA GIVE UP THE LIFE YOU LEAD AFORE YOU SAW THAT BOY BURN.
ALL HIS DEATH DID WAS GIVE YOU A HOOK TO HANG YER DECISION ON.
PRETTY SHARP, HONUS.
I DIDN' LIKE WHAT I WAS.
RIDIN' INTA BOLLAS RATON--
--MEETIN' DOLLY.
--HELL, YEAH. THAT GIRL SHOWED ME WHAT I COULD BE--MORE'N THAT--MADE ME WANNA BE SOMETHIN' ELSE.
LIT A DIFFERENT FIRE IN YA, I RECKON.
IT'S A FIRE WE SHARE--ONE FER A FAMILY. I KNOW THAT A MESS A KIDS, WELL, THAT WOULD MAKE HER HAPPY AS ALL GET OUT.
AN' I PLAN ON MAKIN' THAT WOMAN AS HAPPY AS SHE MADE ME.

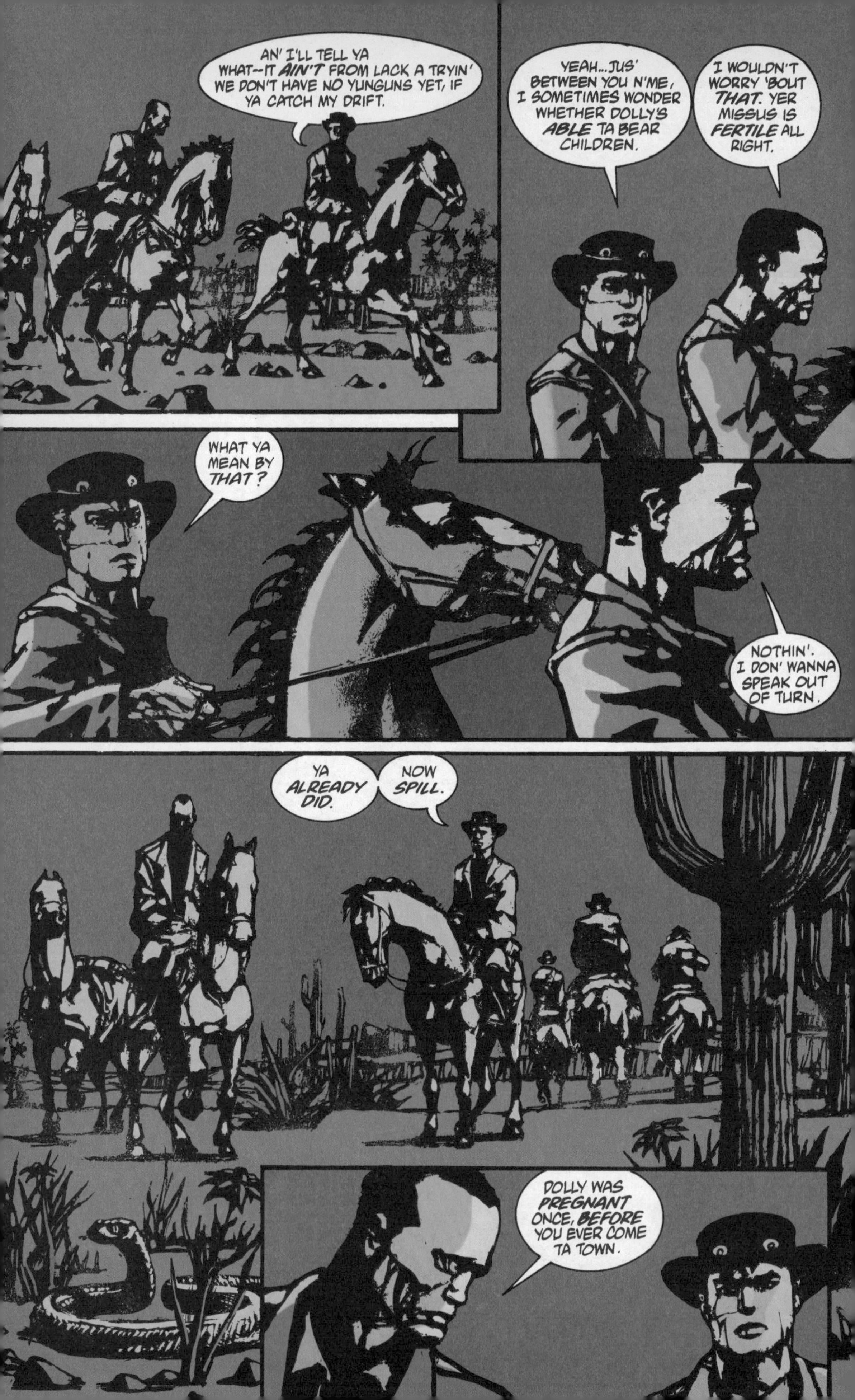
AN' I'LL TELL YA WHAT--IT AIN'T FROM LACK A TRYIN' WE DON'T HAVE NO YUNGUNS YET, IF YA CATCH MY DRIFT.
YEAH...JUS' BETWEEN YOU N'ME, I SOMETIMES WONDER WHETHER DOLLY'S ABLE TA BEAR CHILDREN.
I WOULDN'T WORRY 'BOUT THAT. YER MISSUS IS FERTILE ALL RIGHT.
WHAT YA MEAN BY THAT?
NOTHIN'. I DON' WANNA SPEAK OUT OF TURN.
YA ALREADY DID.
NOW SPILL.
DOLLY WAS PREGNANT ONCE, BEFORE YOU EVER COME TA TOWN.

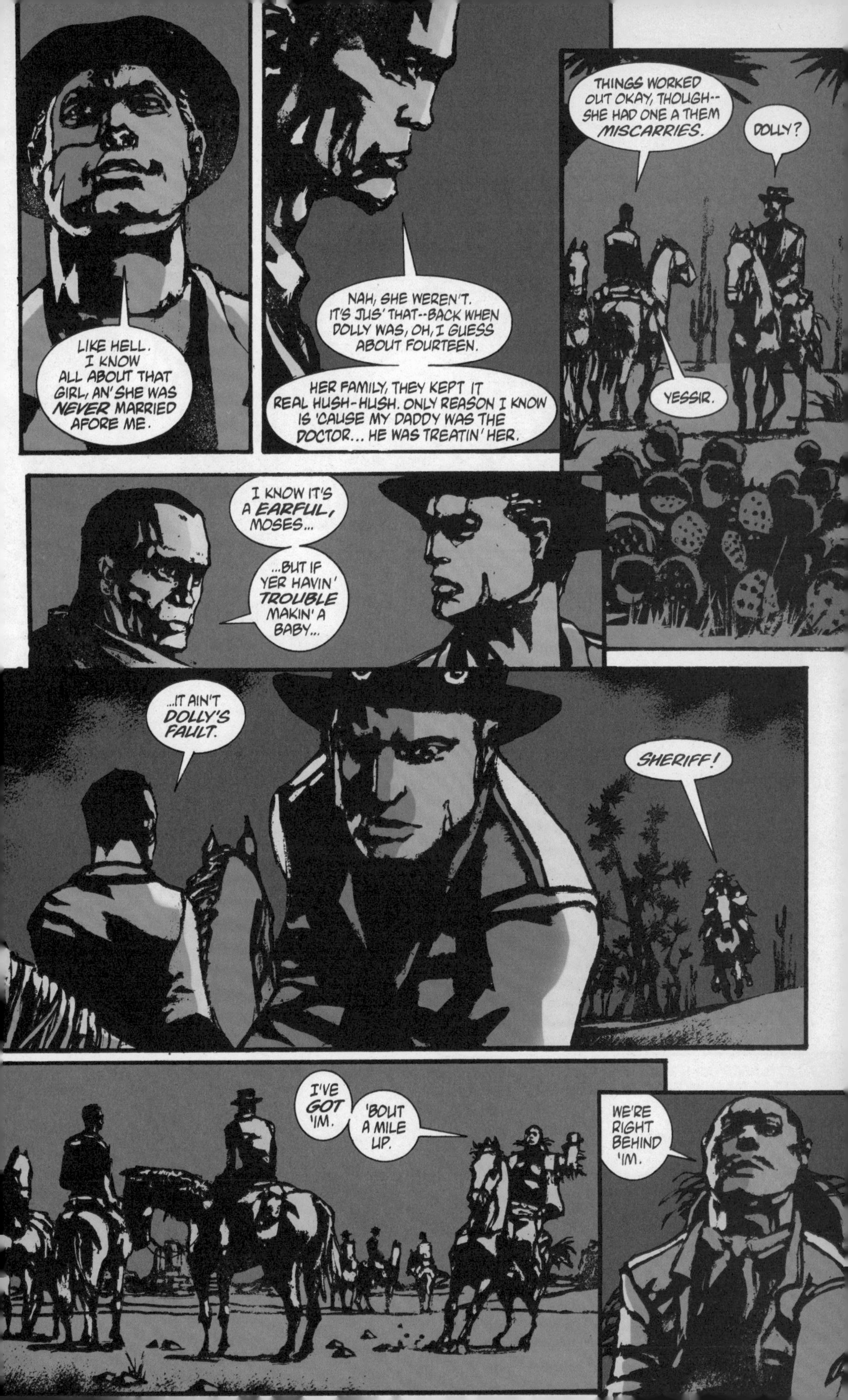
LIKE HELL. I KNOW ALL ABOUT THAT GIRL, AN' SHE WAS NEVER MARRIED AFORE ME.
NAH, SHE WEREN'T. IT'S JUS' THAT--BACK WHEN DOLLY WAS, OH, I GUESS ABOUT FOURTEEN.
HER FAMILY, THEY KEPT IT REAL HUSH-HUSH. ONLY REASON I KNOW IS 'CAUSE MY DADDY WAS THE DOCTOR... HE WAS TREATIN' HER.
THINGS WORKED OUT OKAY, THOUGH--SHE HAD ONE A THEM MISCARRIES.
DOLLY?
YESSIR.
I KNOW IT'S A EARFUL, MOSES...
...BUT IF YER HAVIN' TROUBLE MAKIN' A BABY...
...IT AIN'T DOLLY'S FAULT.
SHERIFF!
I'VE GOT 'IM.
'BOUT A MILE UP.
WE'RE RIGHT BEHIND 'IM.

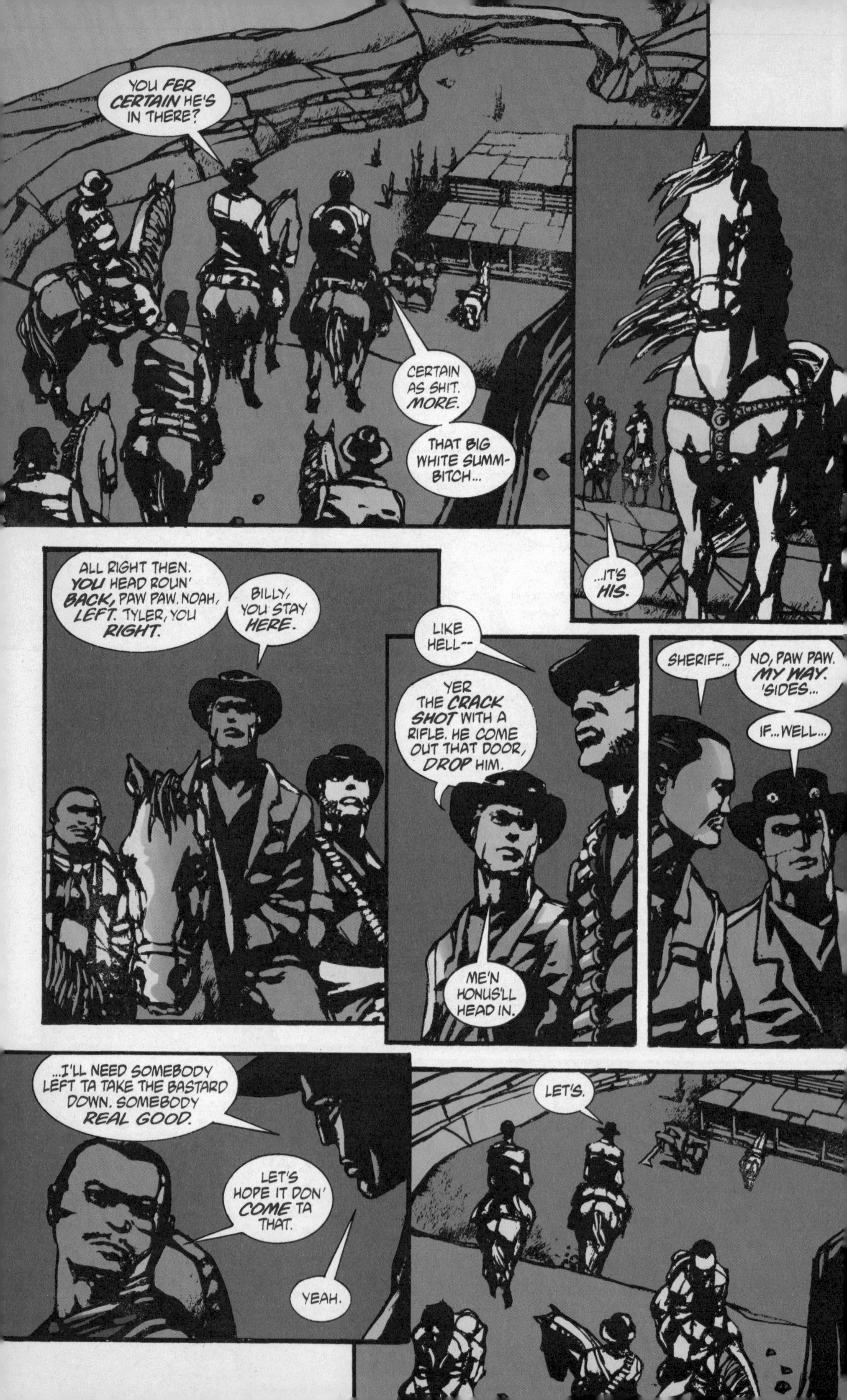
YOU FER CERTAIN HE'S IN THERE?
CERTAIN AS SHIT. MORE.
THAT BIG WHITE SUMM-BITCH...
...IT'S HIS.
ALL RIGHT THEN. YOU HEAD ROUN' BACK, PAW PAW. NOAH, LEFT. TYLER, YOU RIGHT.
BILLY, YOU STAY HERE.
LIKE HELL--
YER THE CRACK SHOT WITH A RIFLE. HE COME OUT THAT DOOR, DROP HIM.
ME'N HONUS'LL HEAD IN.
SHERIFF...
NO, PAW PAW. MY WAY. 'SIDES...
IF...WELL...
...I'LL NEED SOMEBODY LEFT TA TAKE THE BASTARD DOWN. SOMEBODY REAL GOOD.
LET'S HOPE IT DON' COME TA THAT.
YEAH.
LET'S.

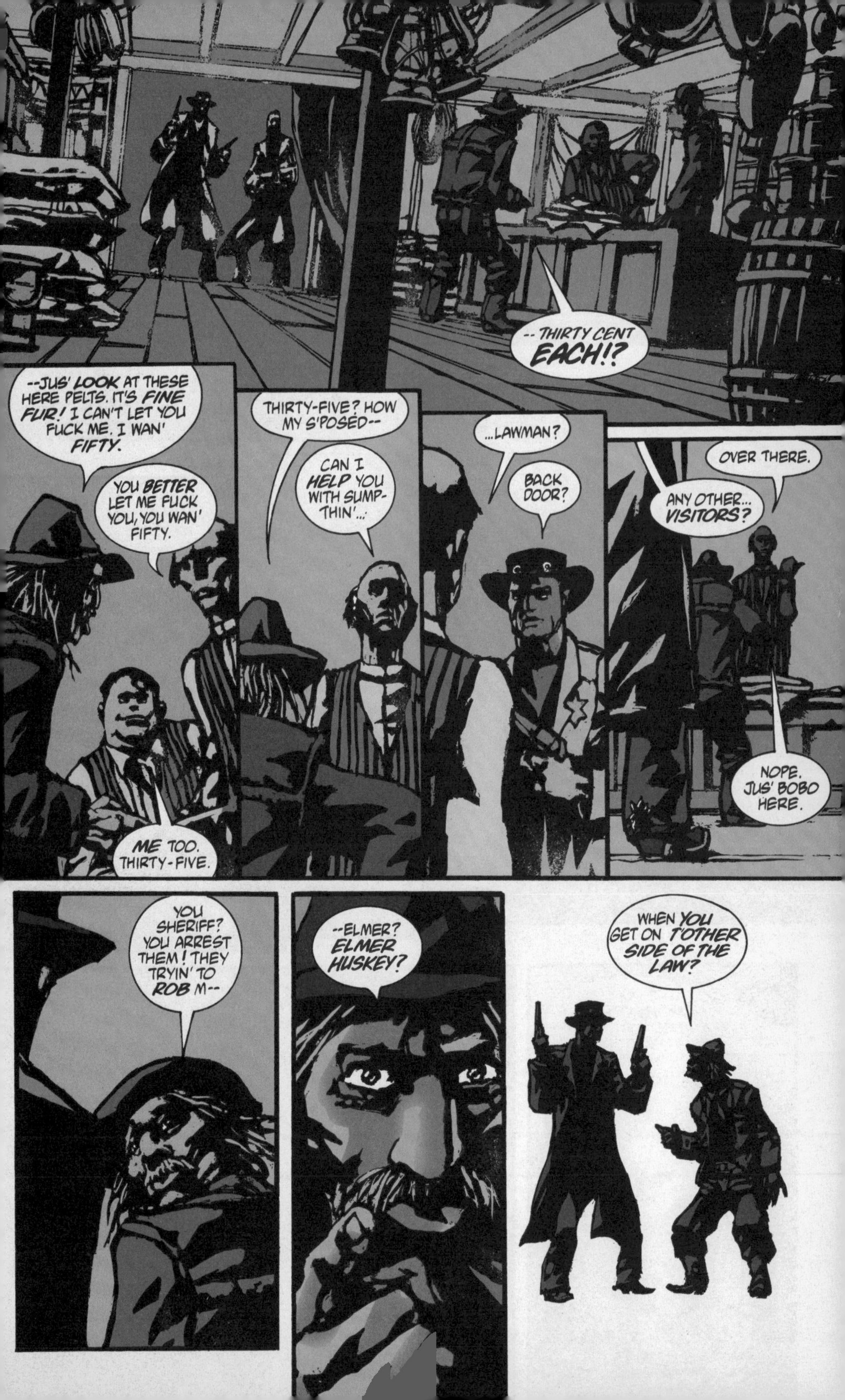
-- THIRTY CENT EACH!?
--JUS' LOOK AT THESE HERE PELTS. IT'S FINE FUR! I CAN'T LET YOU FUCK ME. I WAN' FIFTY.
YOU BETTER LET ME FUCK YOU, YOU WAN' FIFTY.
ME TOO. THIRTY-FIVE.
THIRTY-FIVE? HOW MY S'POSED--
CAN I HELP YOU WITH SUMP-THIN'...'
...LAWMAN?
BACK DOOR?
OVER THERE.
ANY OTHER... VISITORS?
NOPE. JUS' BOBO HERE.
YOU SHERIFF? YOU ARREST THEM! THEY TRYIN' TO ROB M--
--ELMER? ELMER HUSKEY?
WHEN YOU GET ON T'OTHER SIDE OF THE LAW?

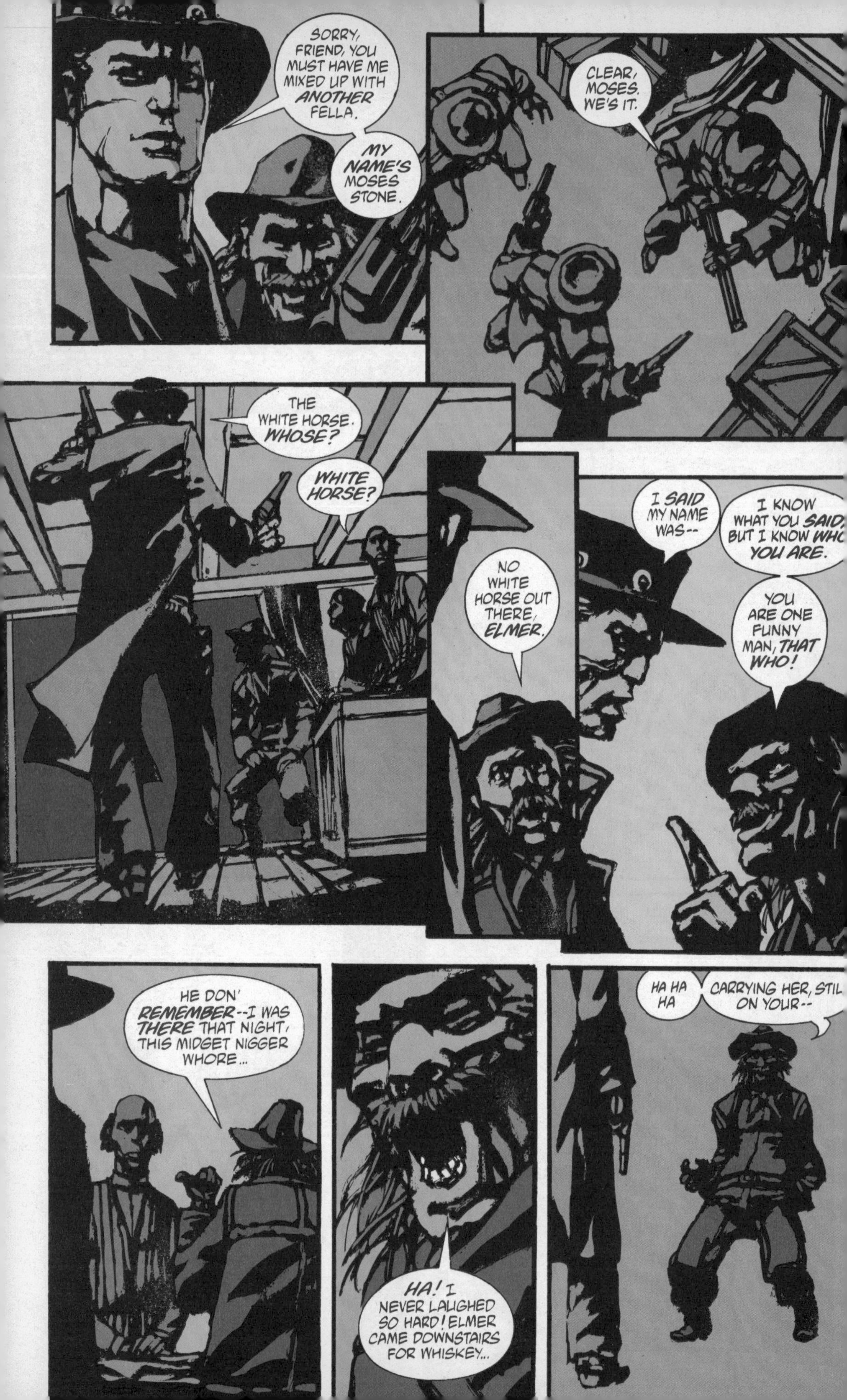
SORRY, FRIEND, YOU MUST HAVE ME MIXED UP WITH ANOTHER FELLA.
MY NAME'S MOSES STONE.
CLEAR, MOSES. WE'S IT.
THE WHITE HORSE. WHOSE?
WHITE HORSE?
NO WHITE HORSE OUT THERE, ELMER.
I SAID MY NAME WAS--
I KNOW WHAT YOU SAID, BUT I KNOW WHO YOU ARE.
YOU ARE ONE FUNNY MAN, THAT WHO!
HE DON' REMEMBER--I WAS THERE THAT NIGHT, THIS MIDGET NIGGER WHORE...
HA! I NEVER LAUGHED SO HARD! ELMER CAME DOWNSTAIRS FOR WHISKEY...
HA HA HA
CARRYING HER, STIL ON YOUR--

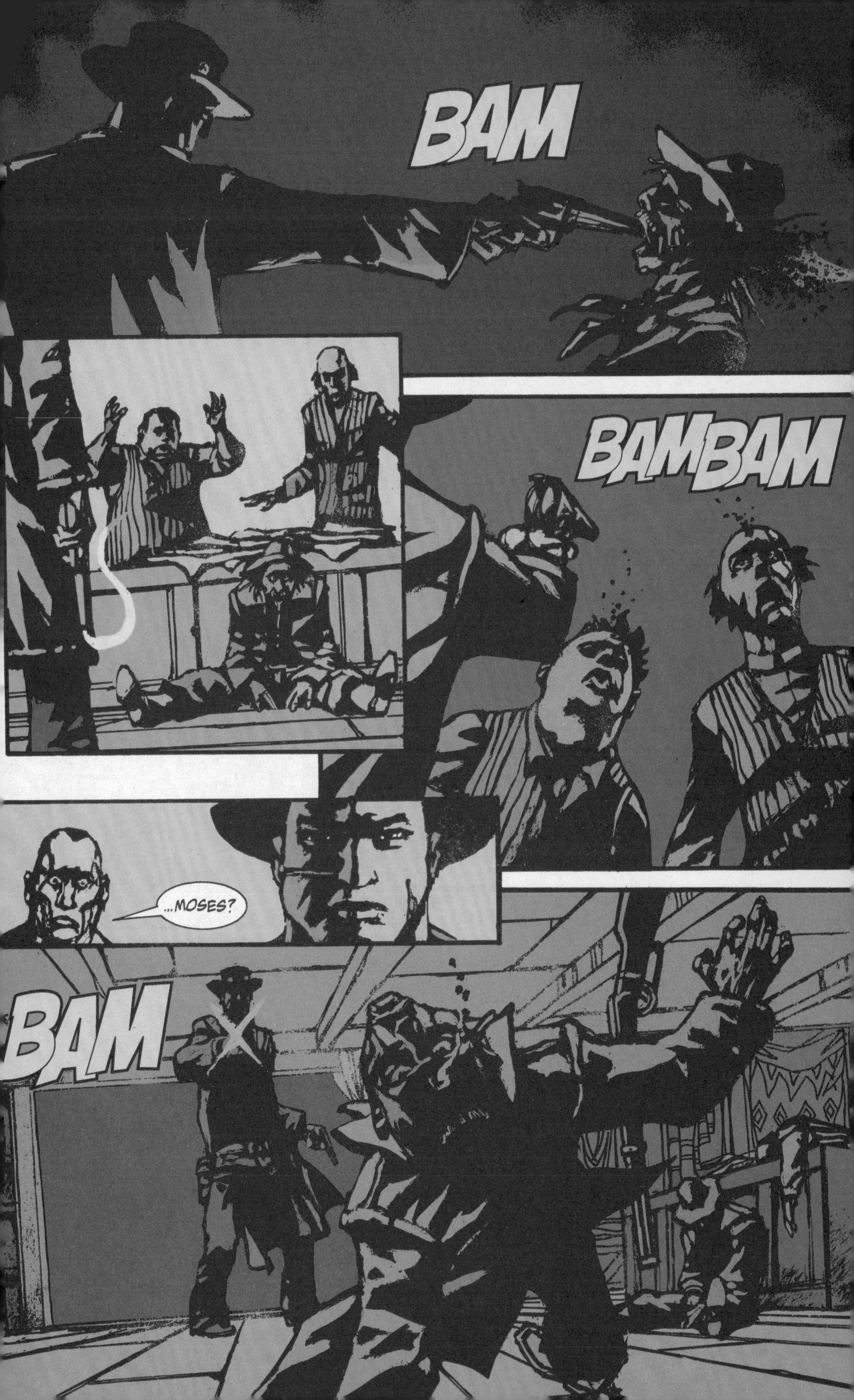
BAM
BAMBAM
...MOSES?
BAM

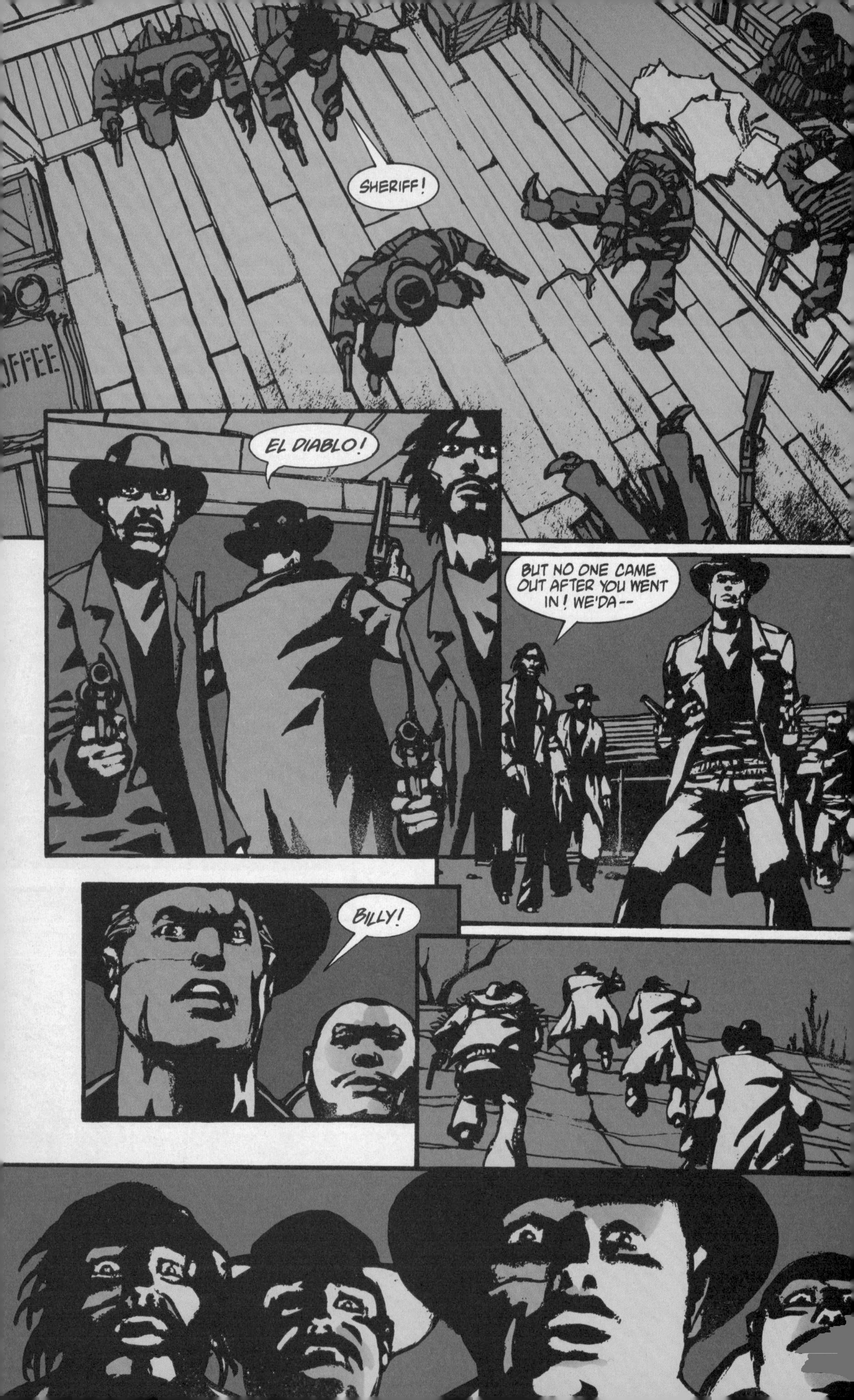
SHERIFF!
COFFEE
EL DIABLO!
BUT NO ONE CAME OUT AFTER YOU WENT IN! WE'DA--
BILLY!

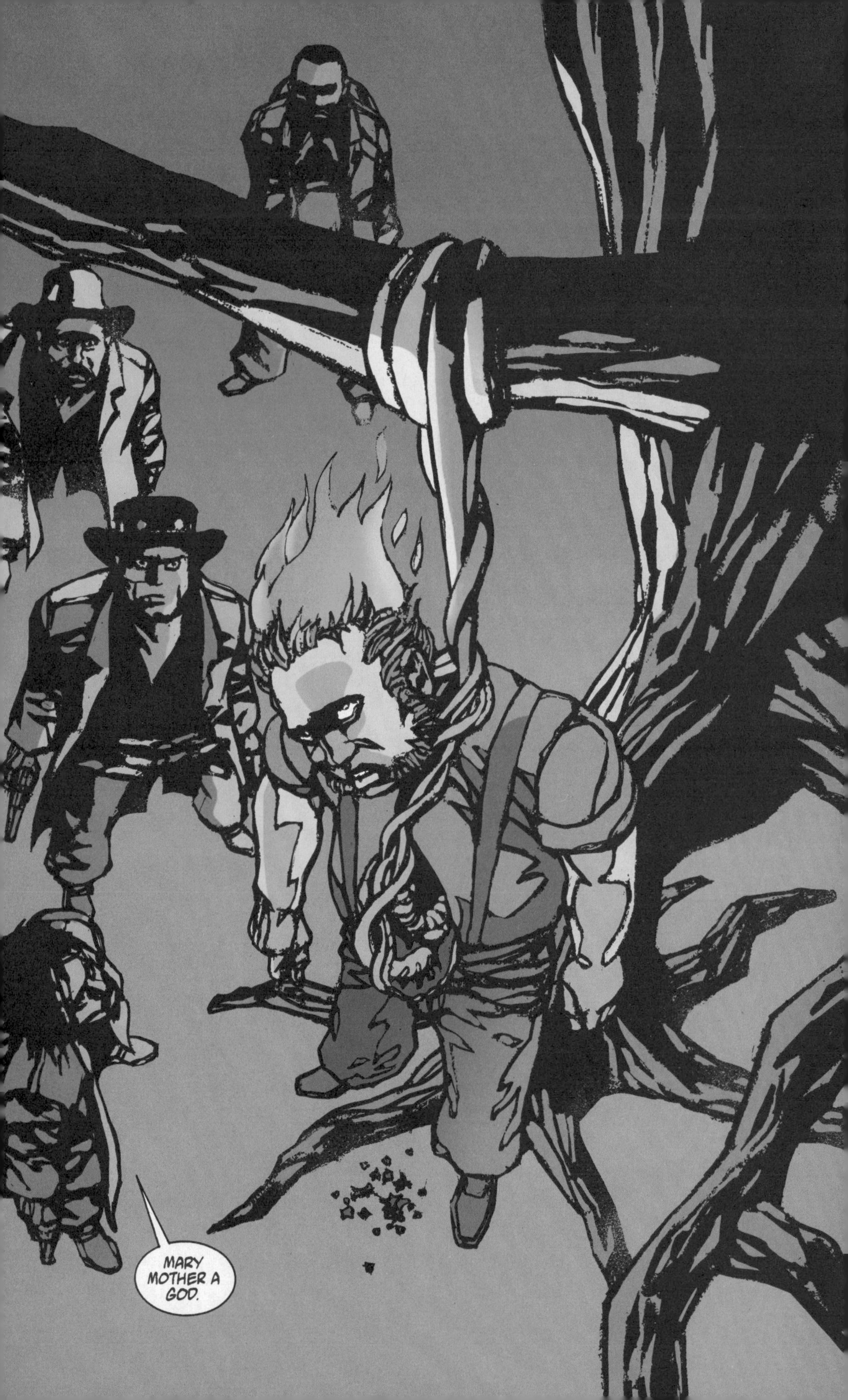
MARY MOTHER A GOD.

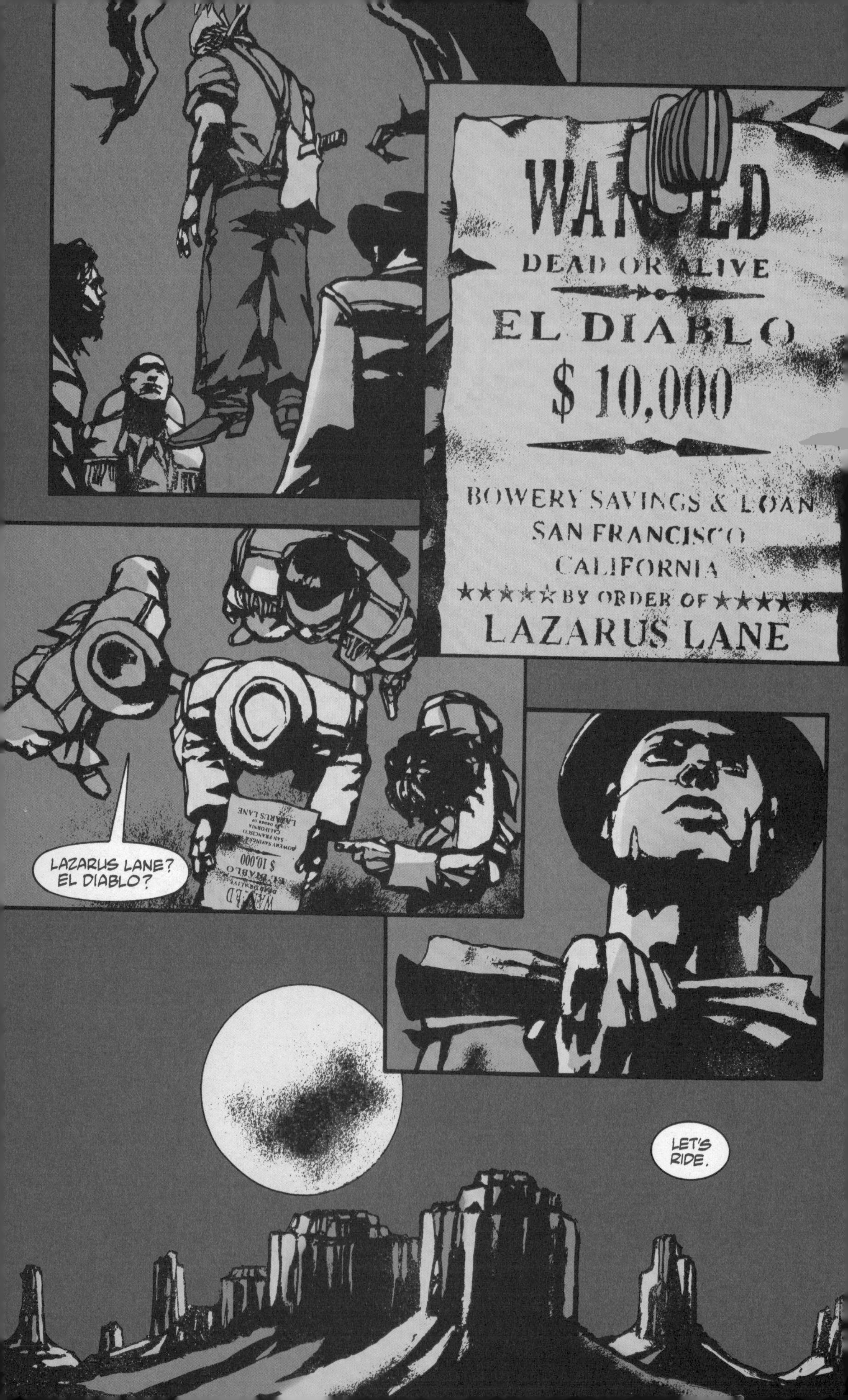

WAN ED
DEAD OR ALIVE
EL DIABLO
$ 10,000
BOWERY SAVINGS & LOAN
SAN FRANCISCO
CALIFORNIA
★★★★★ BY ORDER OF ★★★★★
LAZARUS LANE
LAZARUS LANE? EL DIABLO?
LET'S RIDE.

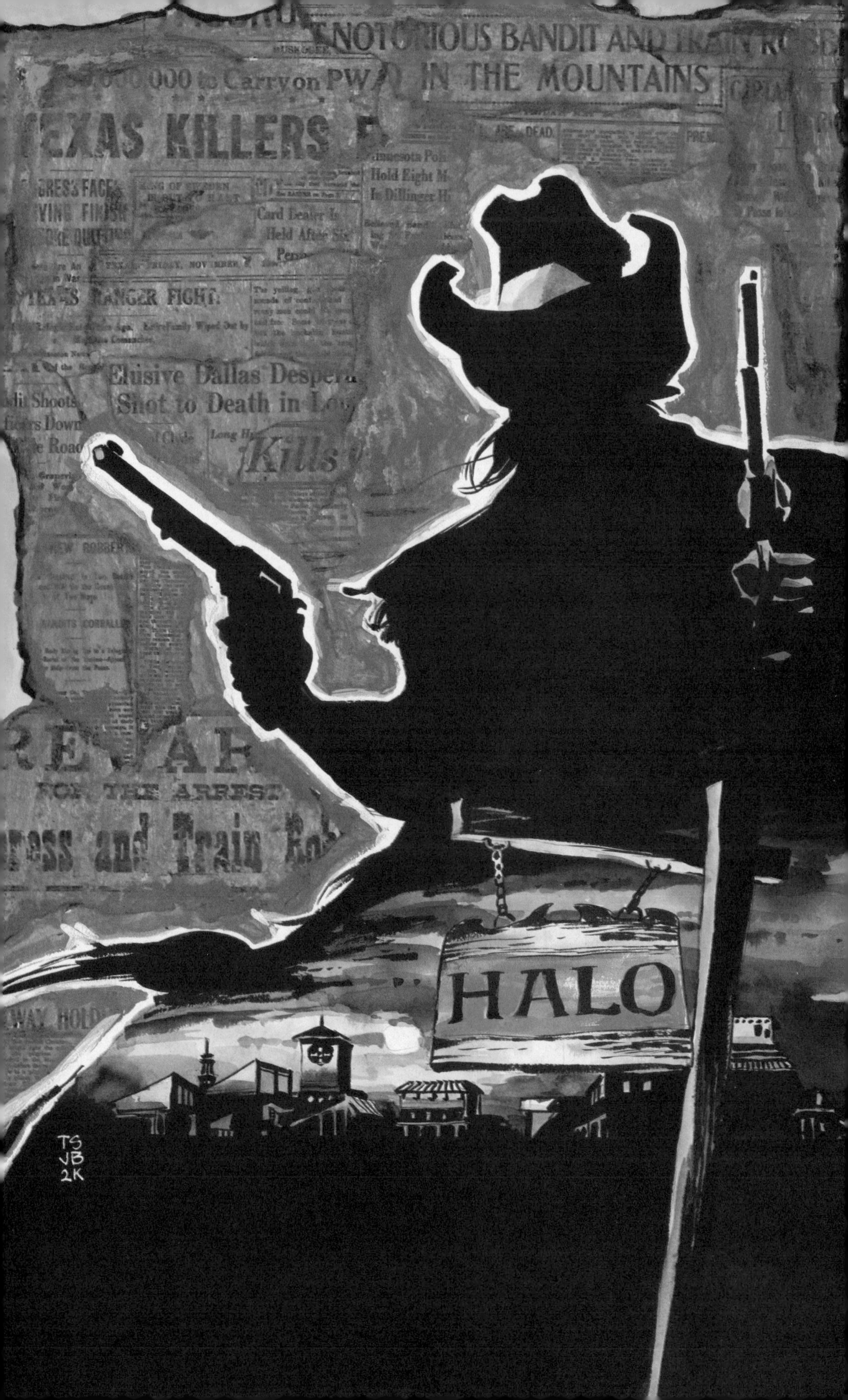
NOTORIOUS BANDIT AND
IN THE MOUNTAINS
EXAS KILLERS
Hold Eight
Card Dealer Is
Held After Six
TEXAS RANGER FIGHT
Elusive Dallas
Shot to Death in
Kills
FOR THE ARREST
and Train
HALO
TS
JB
2K

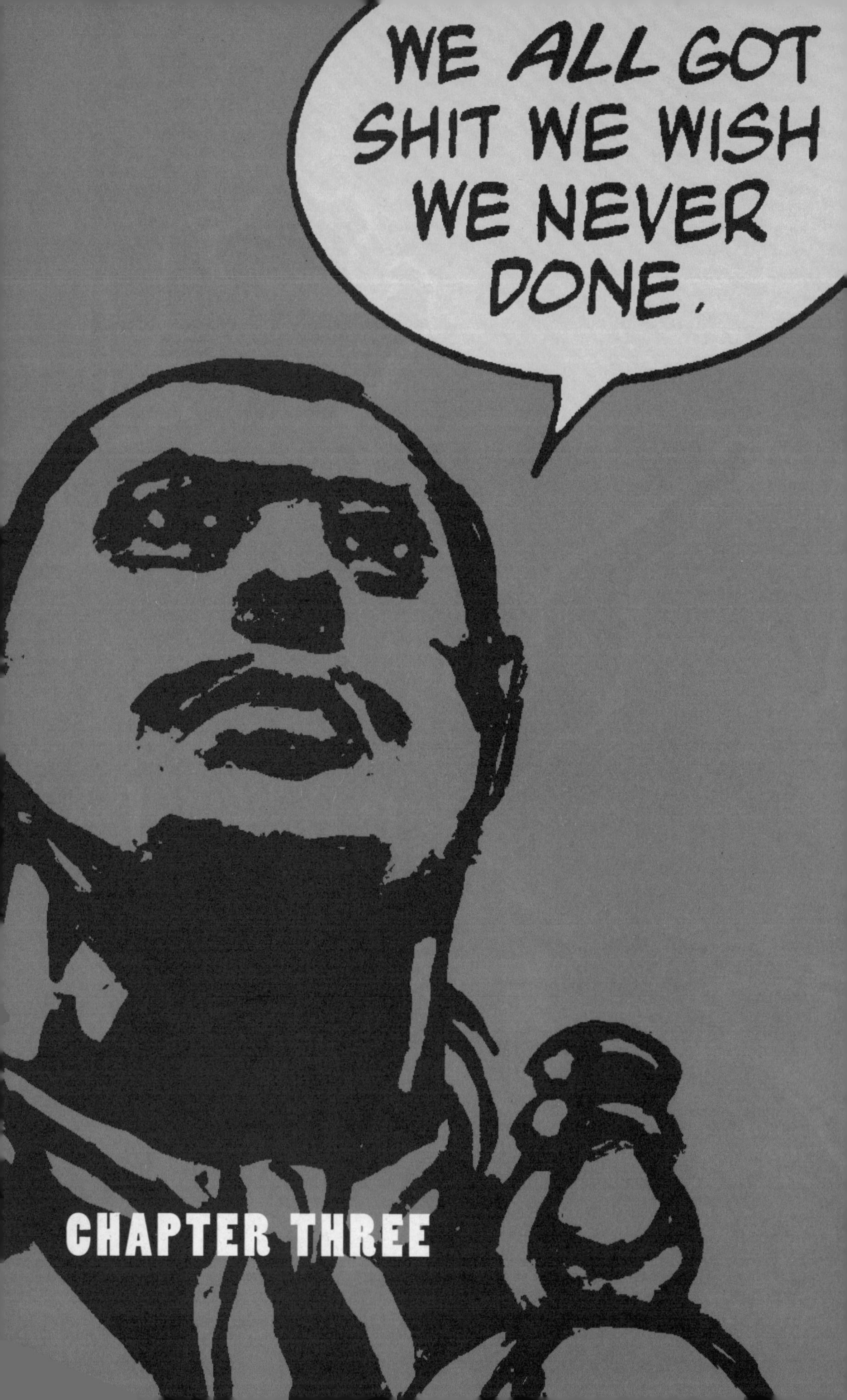

CHAPTER THREE

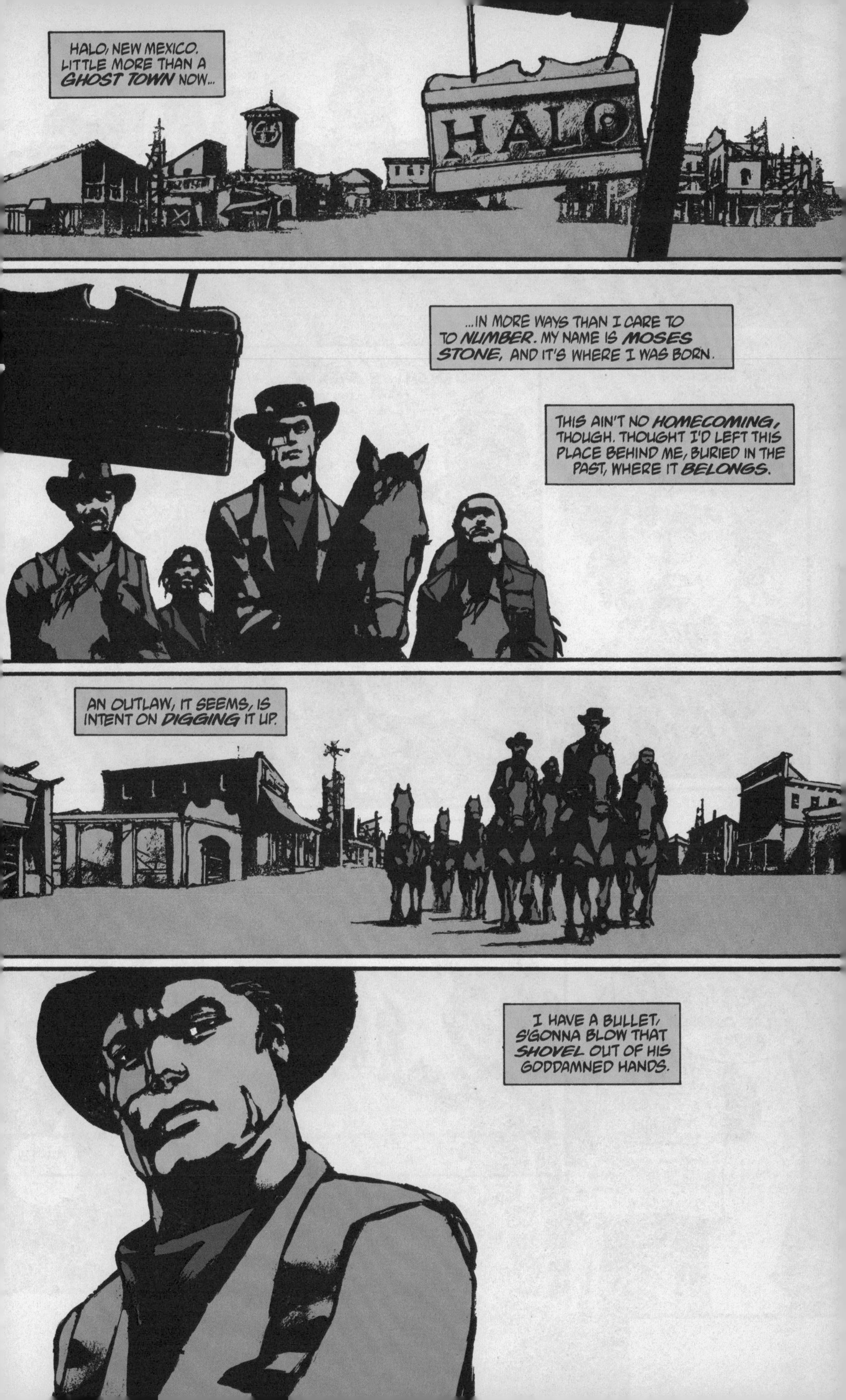
HALO, NEW MEXICO. LITTLE MORE THAN A GHOST TOWN NOW...
HALO
...IN MORE WAYS THAN I CARE TO TO NUMBER. MY NAME IS MOSES STONE, AND IT'S WHERE I WAS BORN.
THIS AIN'T NO HOMECOMING, THOUGH. THOUGHT I'D LEFT THIS PLACE BEHIND ME, BURIED IN THE PAST, WHERE IT BELONGS.
AN OUTLAW, IT SEEMS, IS INTENT ON DIGGING IT UP.
I HAVE A BULLET, S'GONNA BLOW THAT SHOVEL OUT OF HIS GODDAMNED HANDS.

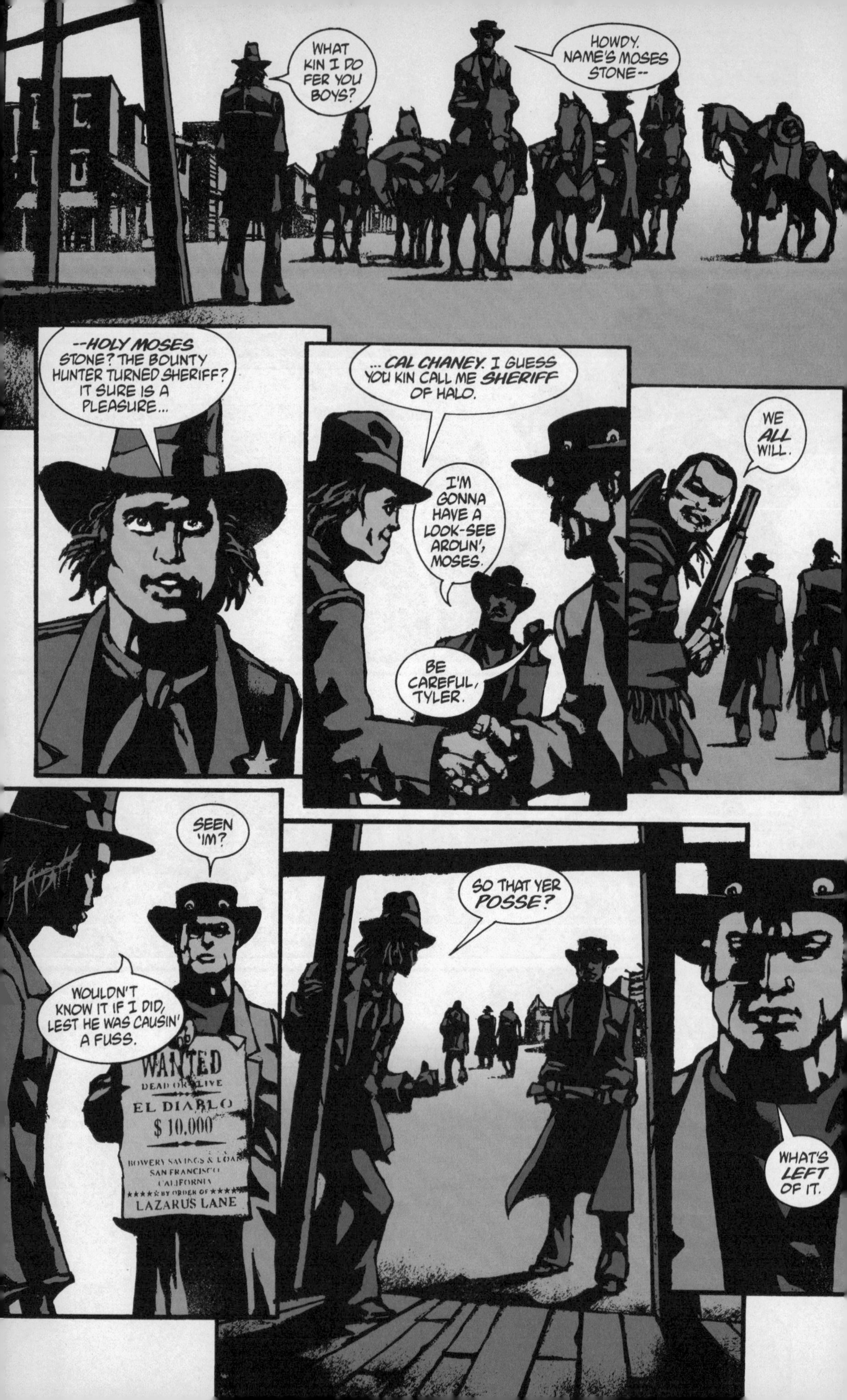
WHAT KIN I DO FER YOU BOYS?
HOWDY. NAME'S MOSES STONE--
--HOLY MOSES STONE? THE BOUNTY HUNTER TURNED SHERIFF? IT SURE IS A PLEASURE...
...CAL CHANEY. I GUESS YOU KIN CALL ME SHERIFF OF HALO.
I'M GONNA HAVE A LOOK-SEE AROUN', MOSES.
BE CAREFUL, TYLER.
WE ALL WILL.
SEEN 'IM?
WOULDN'T KNOW IT IF I DID, LEST HE WAS CAUSIN' A FUSS.
WANTED
DEAD OR ALIVE
EL DIABLO
$ 10.000
BOWERY SAVINGS & LOAN
SAN FRANCISCO
CALIFORNIA
BY ORDER OF
LAZARUS LANE
SO THAT YER POSSE?
WHAT'S LEFT OF IT.

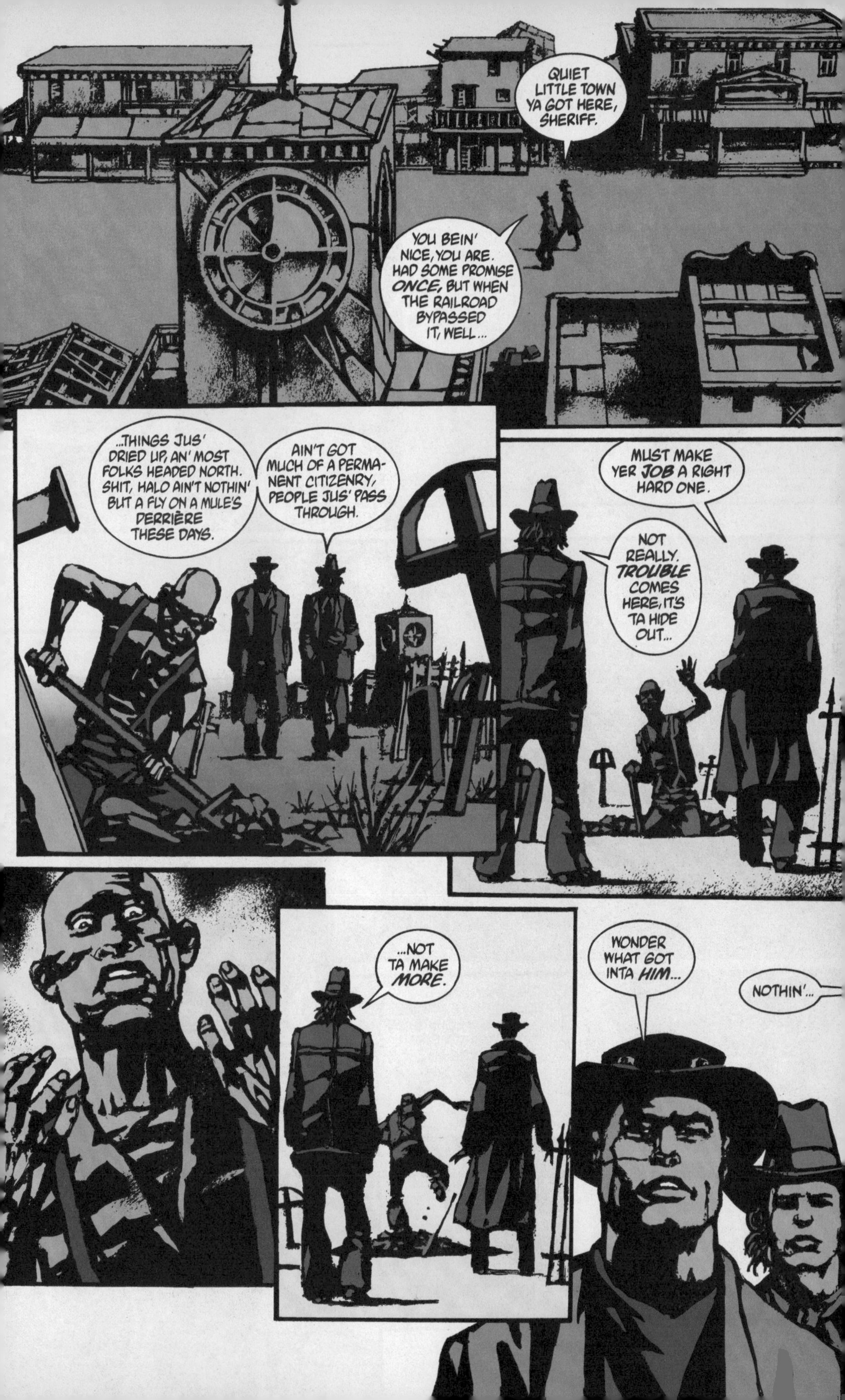
QUIET LITTLE TOWN YA GOT HERE, SHERIFF.
YOU BEIN' NICE, YOU ARE. HAD SOME PROMISE ONCE, BUT WHEN THE RAILROAD BYPASSED IT, WELL...
...THINGS JUS' DRIED UP, AN' MOST FOLKS HEADED NORTH. SHIT, HALO AIN'T NOTHIN' BUT A FLY ON A MULE'S DERRIÈRE THESE DAYS.
AIN'T GOT MUCH OF A PERMANENT CITIZENRY, PEOPLE JUS' PASS THROUGH.
MUST MAKE YER JOB A RIGHT HARD ONE.
NOT REALLY. TROUBLE COMES HERE, IT'S TA HIDE OUT...
...NOT TA MAKE MORE.
WONDER WHAT GOT INTA HIM...
NOTHIN'...

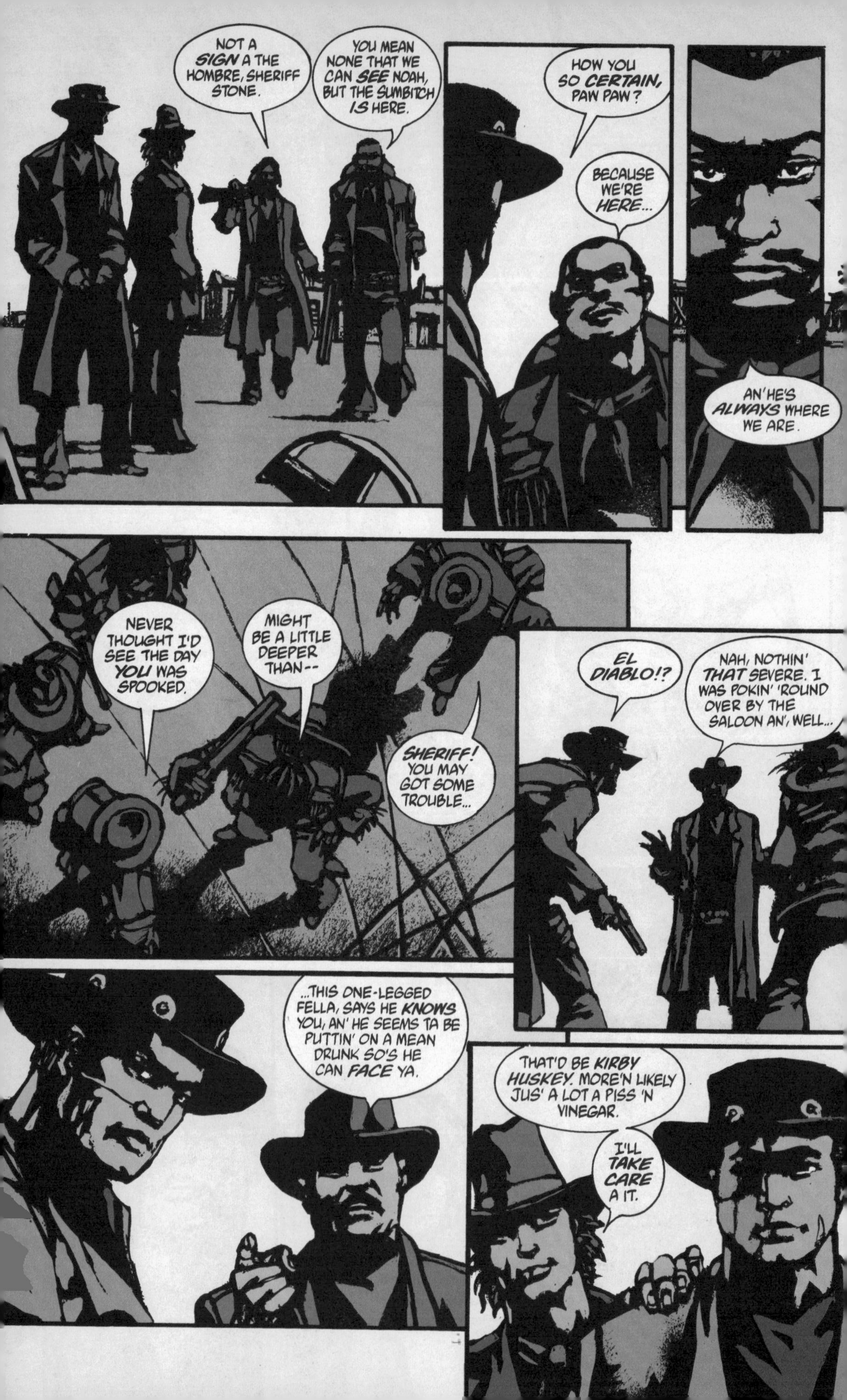
NOT A SIGN A THE HOMBRE, SHERIFF STONE.
YOU MEAN NONE THAT WE CAN SEE NOAH, BUT THE SUMBITCH IS HERE.
HOW YOU SO CERTAIN, PAW PAW?
BECAUSE WE'RE HERE...
AN' HE'S ALWAYS WHERE WE ARE.
NEVER THOUGHT I'D SEE THE DAY YOU WAS SPOOKED.
MIGHT BE A LITTLE DEEPER THAN--
SHERIFF! YOU MAY GOT SOME TROUBLE...
EL DIABLO!?
NAH, NOTHIN' THAT SEVERE. I WAS POKIN' 'ROUND OVER BY THE SALOON AN', WELL...
...THIS ONE-LEGGED FELLA, SAYS HE KNOWS YOU, AN' HE SEEMS TA BE PUTTIN' ON A MEAN DRUNK SO'S HE CAN FACE YA.
THAT'D BE KIRBY HUSKEY. MORE'N LIKELY JUS' A LOT A PISS 'N VINEGAR.
I'LL TAKE CARE A IT.

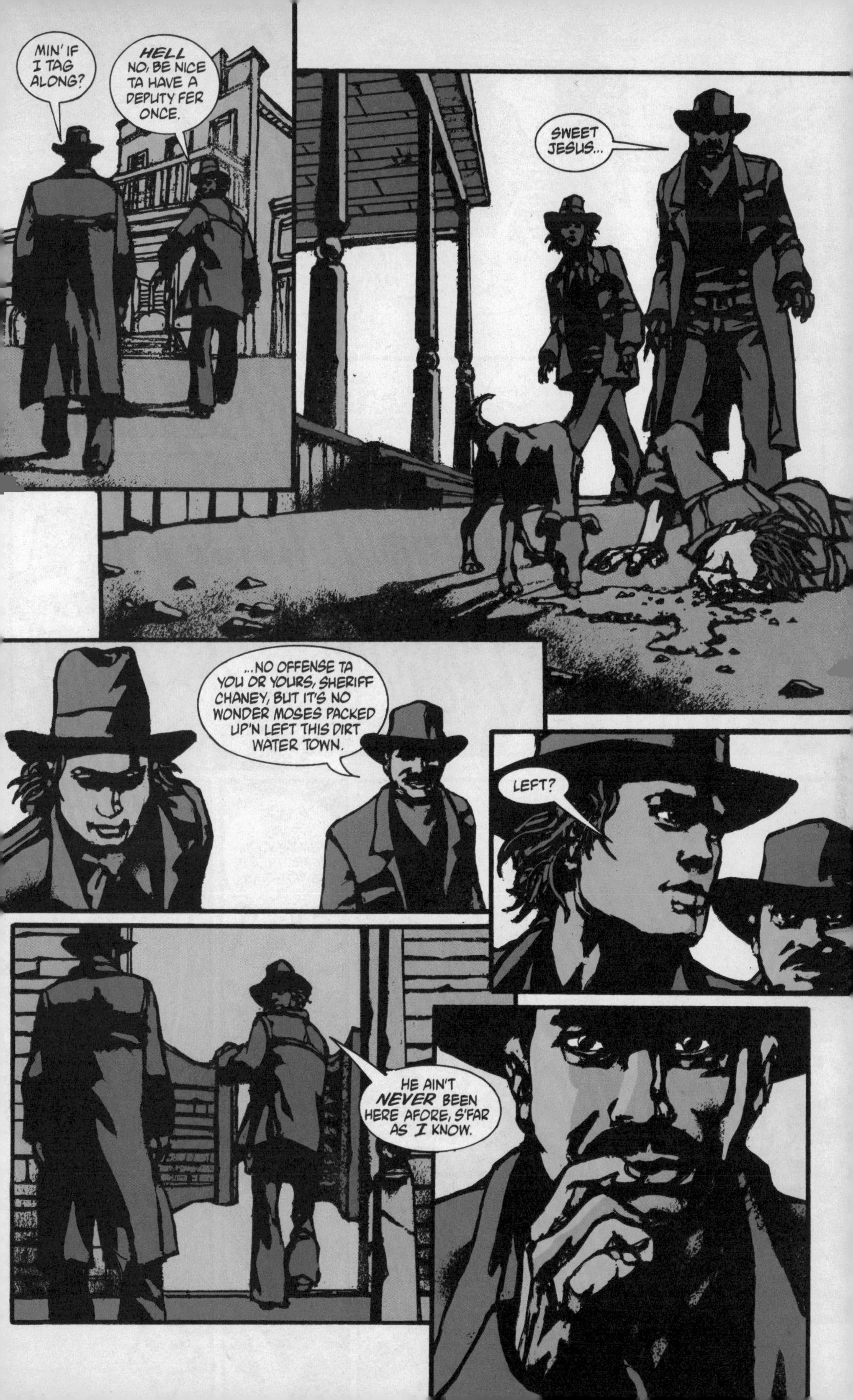
MIN' IF I TAG ALONG?
HELL NO, BE NICE TA HAVE A DEPUTY FER ONCE.
SWEET JESUS...
...NO OFFENSE TA YOU OR YOURS, SHERIFF CHANEY, BUT IT'S NO WONDER MOSES PACKED UP'N LEFT THIS DIRT WATER TOWN.
LEFT?
HE AIN'T NEVER BEEN HERE AFORE, S'FAR AS I KNOW.

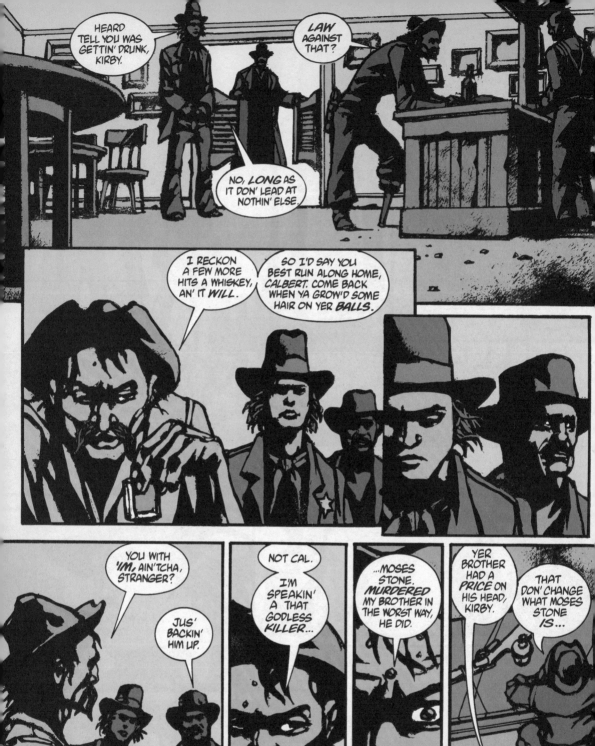

HEARD TELL YOU WAS GETTIN' DRUNK, KIRBY.

LAW AGAINST THAT?

NO, *LONG* AS IT DON' LEAD AT NOTHIN' ELSE.

I RECKON A FEW MORE HITS A WHISKEY, AN' IT *WILL*.

SO I'D SAY YOU BEST RUN ALONG HOME, *CALBERT*. COME BACK WHEN YA GROW'D SOME HAIR ON YER *BALLS*.

YOU WITH *'IM*, AIN'TCHA, STRANGER?

JUS' *BACKIN'* HIM UP.

NOT CAL. I'M SPEAKIN' A THAT GODLESS *KILLER*...

...MOSES STONE. *MURDERED* MY BROTHER IN THE WORST WAY, HE DID.

YER BROTHER HAD A *PRICE* ON HIS HEAD, KIRBY.

THAT DON' CHANGE WHAT MOSES STONE *IS*...

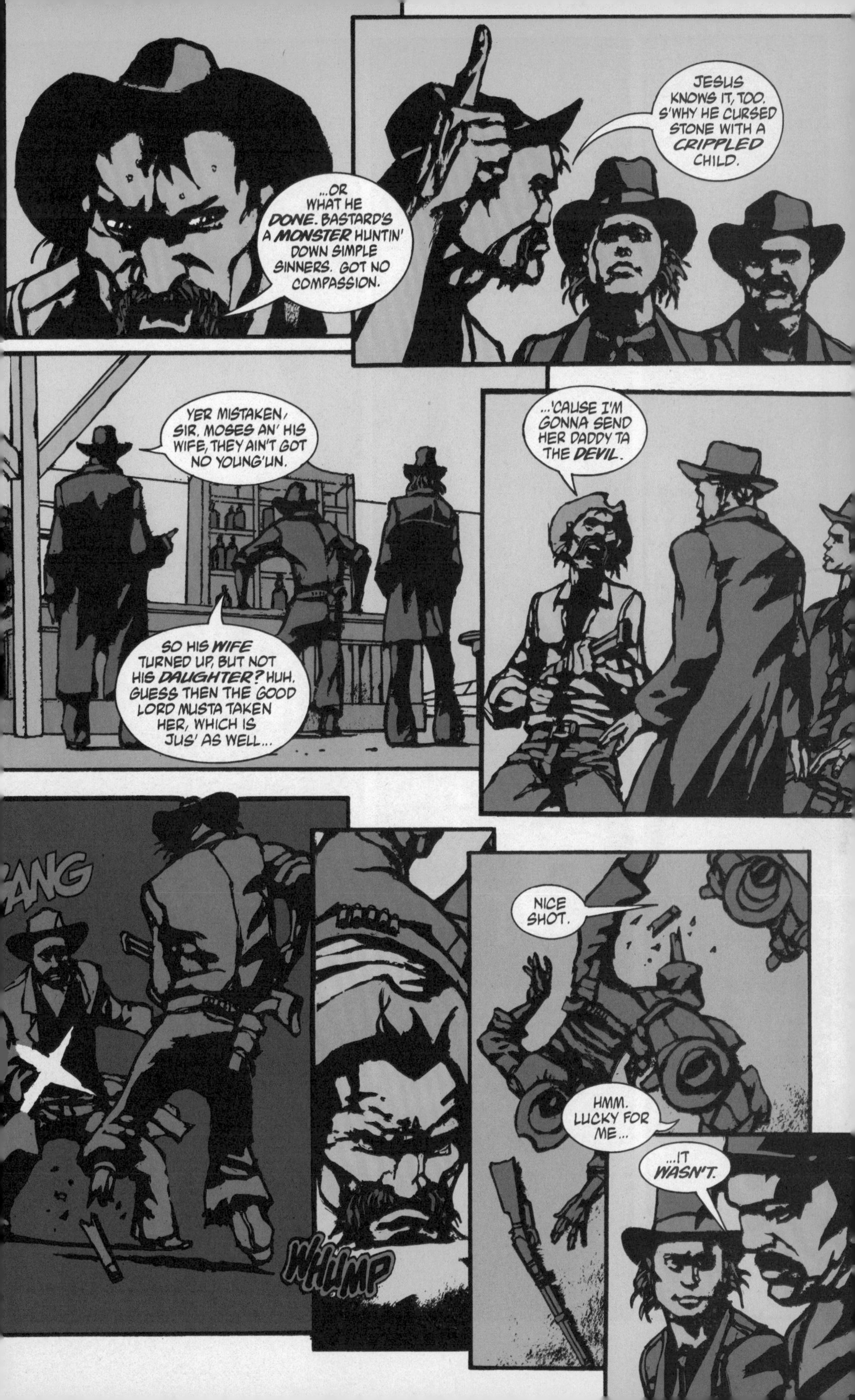
...OR WHAT HE DONE. BASTARD'S A MONSTER HUNTIN' DOWN SIMPLE SINNERS. GOT NO COMPASSION.
JESUS KNOWS IT, TOO. S'WHY HE CURSED STONE WITH A CRIPPLED CHILD.
YER MISTAKEN, SIR. MOSES AN' HIS WIFE, THEY AIN'T GOT NO YOUNG'UN.
SO HIS WIFE TURNED UP, BUT NOT HIS DAUGHTER? HUH. GUESS THEN THE GOOD LORD MUSTA TAKEN HER, WHICH IS JUS' AS WELL...
...'CAUSE I'M GONNA SEND HER DADDY TA THE DEVIL.
ANG
WHUMP
NICE SHOT.
HMM. LUCKY FOR ME...
...IT WASN'T.

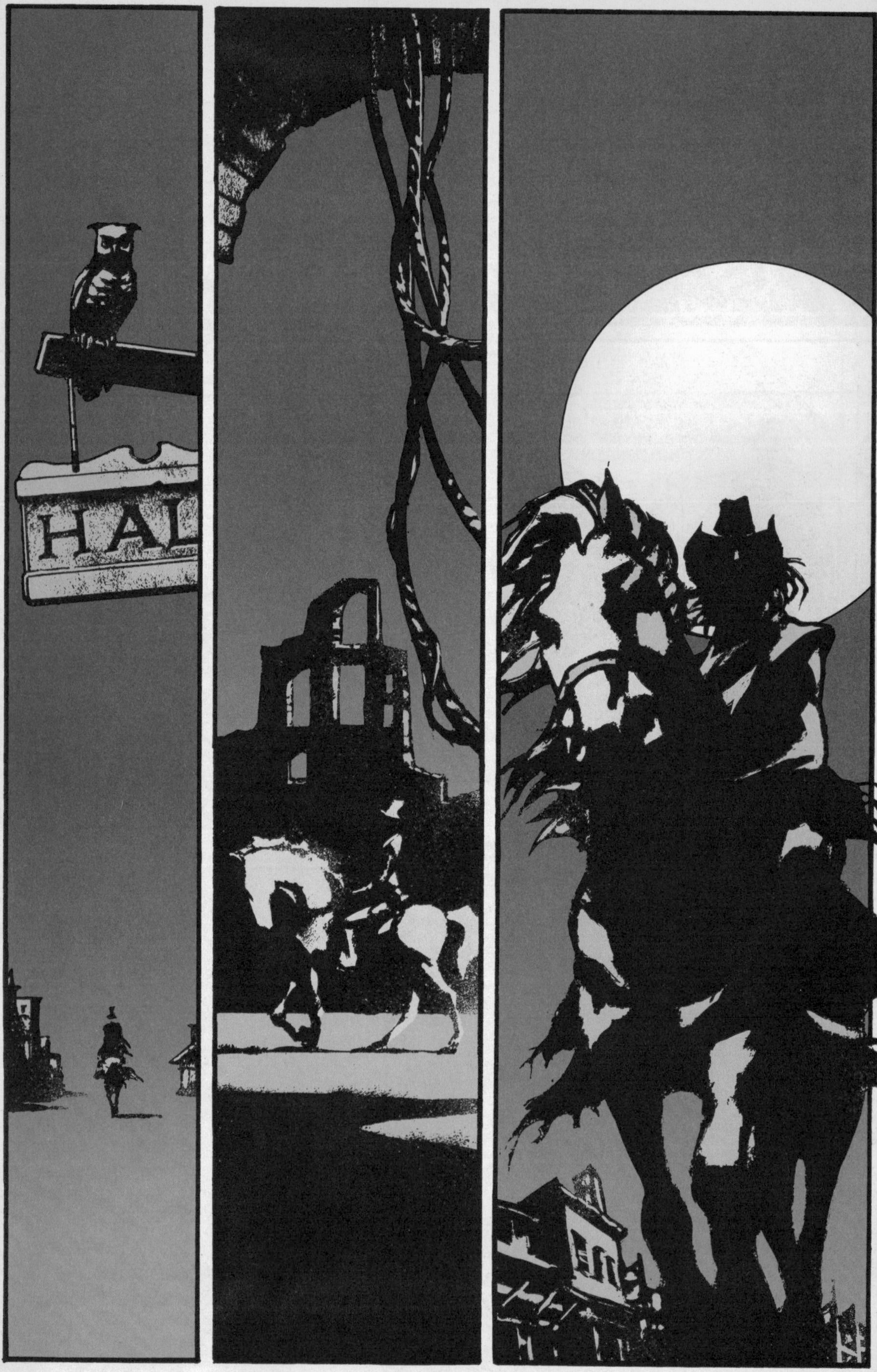
HAL

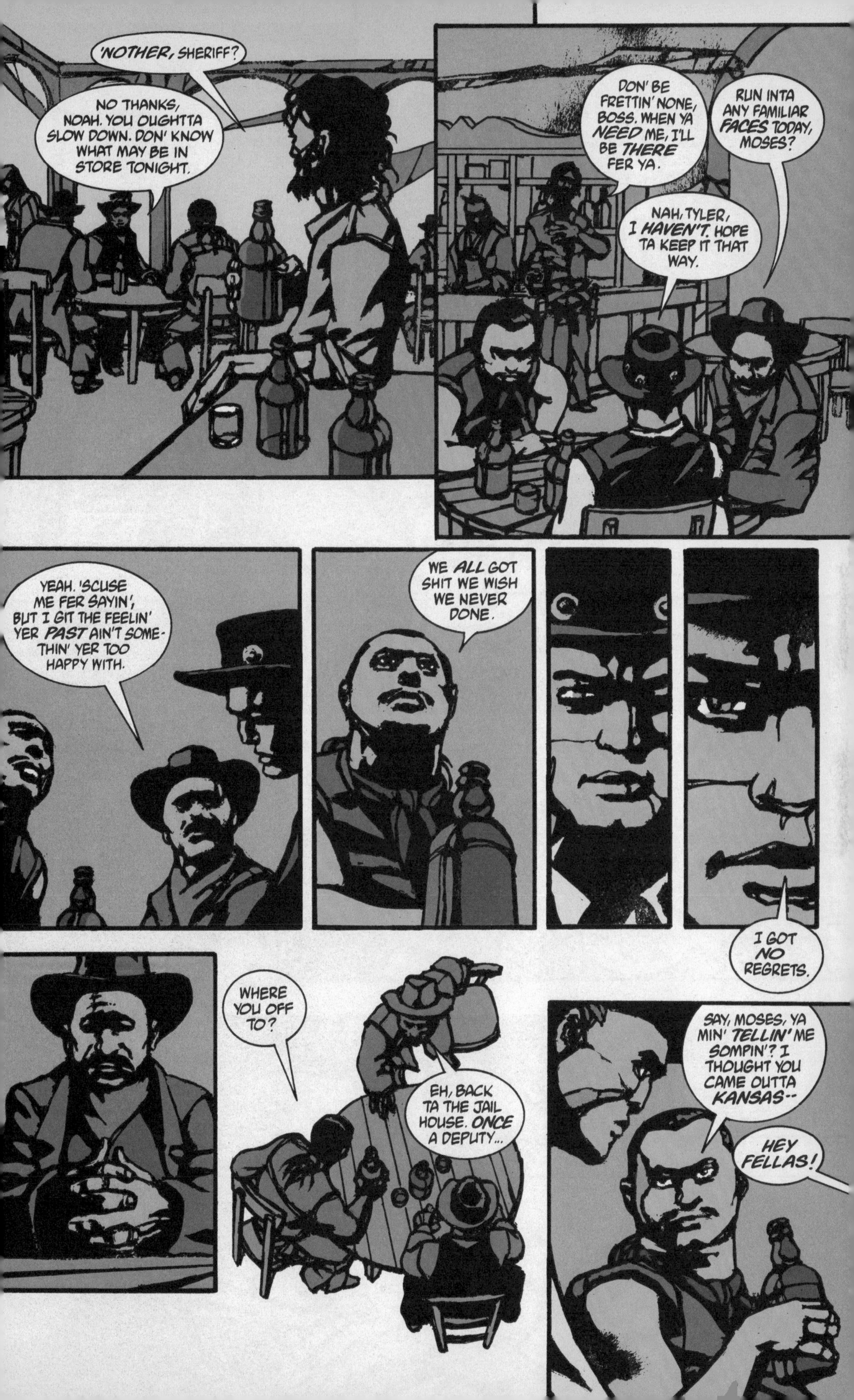
'NOTHER, SHERIFF?
NO THANKS, NOAH. YOU OUGHTTA SLOW DOWN. DON' KNOW WHAT MAY BE IN STORE TONIGHT.
DON' BE FRETTIN' NONE, BOSS. WHEN YA NEED ME, I'LL BE THERE FER YA.
RUN INTA ANY FAMILIAR FACES TODAY, MOSES?
NAH, TYLER, I HAVEN'T. HOPE TA KEEP IT THAT WAY.
YEAH. 'SCUSE ME FER SAYIN', BUT I GIT THE FEELIN' YER PAST AIN'T SOMETHIN' YER TOO HAPPY WITH.
WE ALL GOT SHIT WE WISH WE NEVER DONE.
I GOT NO REGRETS.
WHERE YOU OFF TO?
EH, BACK TA THE JAIL HOUSE. ONCE A DEPUTY...
SAY, MOSES, YA MIN' TELLIN' ME SOMPIN'? I THOUGHT YOU CAME OUTTA KANSAS--
HEY FELLAS!

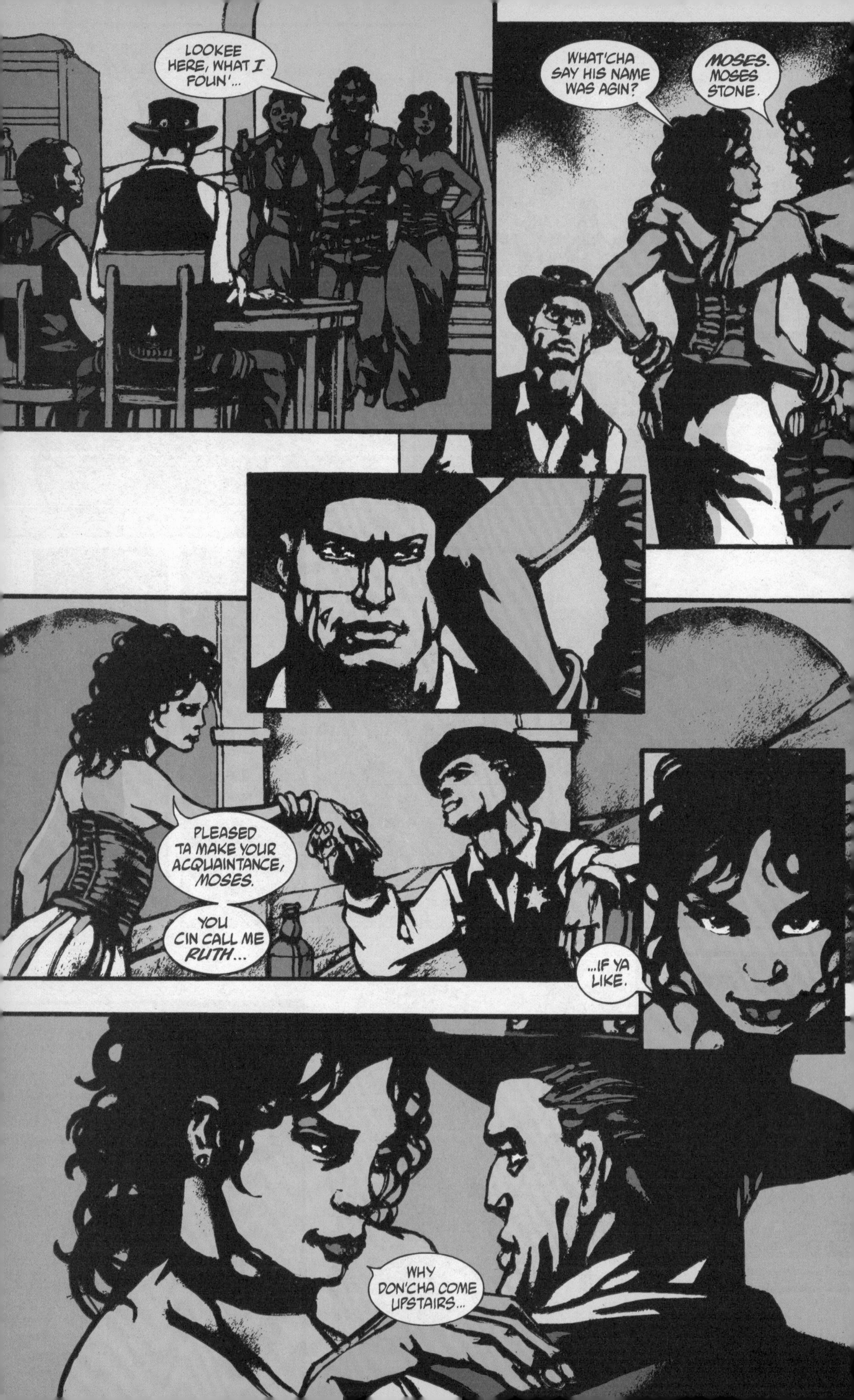
LOOKEE HERE, WHAT I FOUN'...
WHAT'CHA SAY HIS NAME WAS AGIN?
MOSES. MOSES STONE.
PLEASED TA MAKE YOUR ACQUAINTANCE, MOSES.
YOU CIN CALL ME RUTH...
...IF YA LIKE.
WHY DON'CHA COME UPSTAIRS...

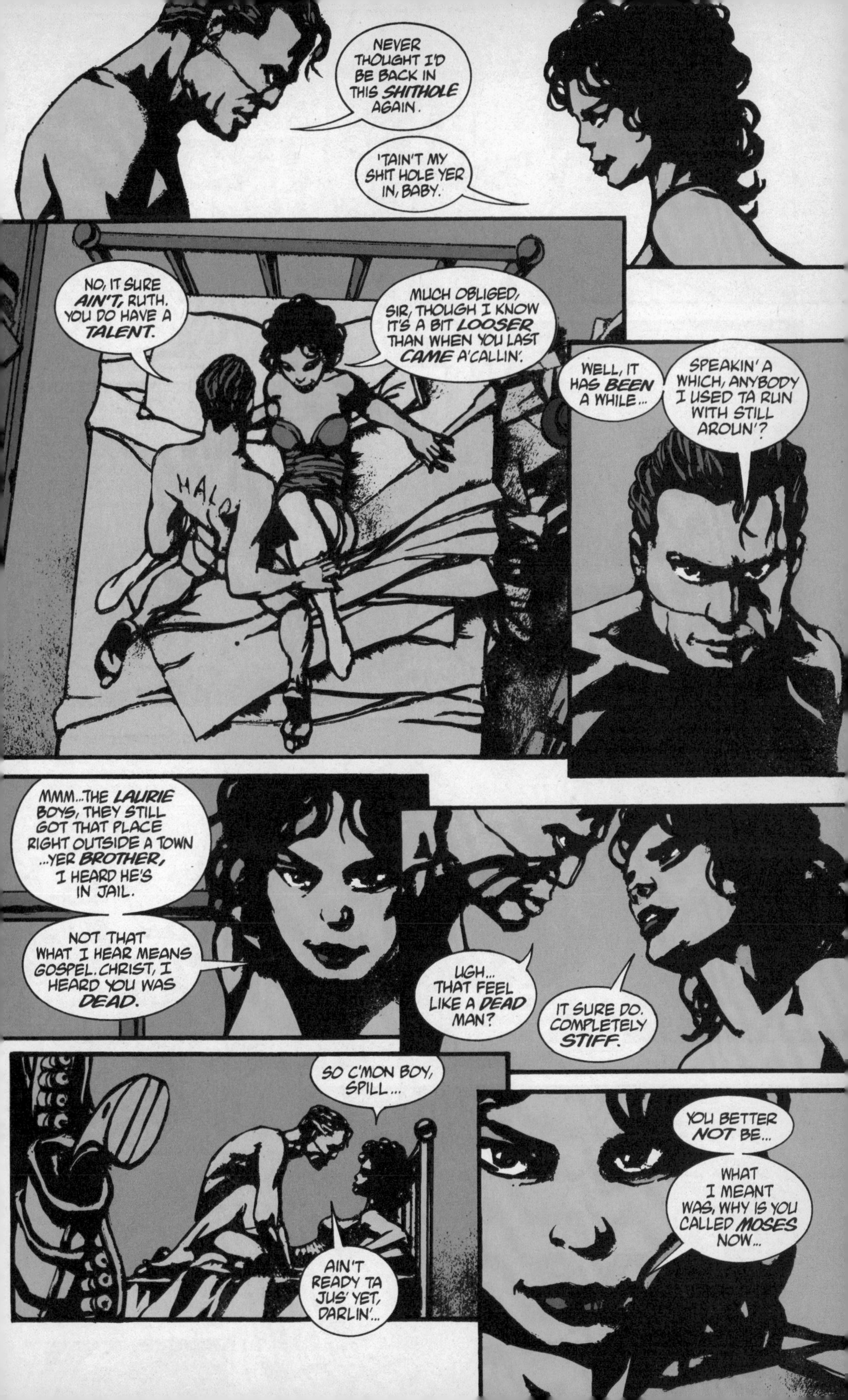
NEVER THOUGHT I'D BE BACK IN THIS SHITHOLE AGAIN.
'TAIN'T MY SHIT HOLE YER IN, BABY.
NO, IT SURE AIN'T, RUTH. YOU DO HAVE A TALENT.
MUCH OBLIGED, SIR, THOUGH I KNOW IT'S A BIT LOOSER THAN WHEN YOU LAST CAME A'CALLIN'.
WELL, IT HAS BEEN A WHILE...
SPEAKIN' A WHICH, ANYBODY I USED TA RUN WITH STILL AROUN'?
MMM...THE LAURIE BOYS, THEY STILL GOT THAT PLACE RIGHT OUTSIDE A TOWN ...YER BROTHER, I HEARD HE'S IN JAIL.
NOT THAT WHAT I HEAR MEANS GOSPEL. CHRIST, I HEARD YOU WAS DEAD.
UGH... THAT FEEL LIKE A DEAD MAN?
IT SURE DO. COMPLETELY STIFF.
SO C'MON BOY, SPILL...
AIN'T READY TA JUS' YET, DARLIN'...
YOU BETTER NOT BE...
WHAT I MEANT WAS, WHY IS YOU CALLED MOSES NOW...

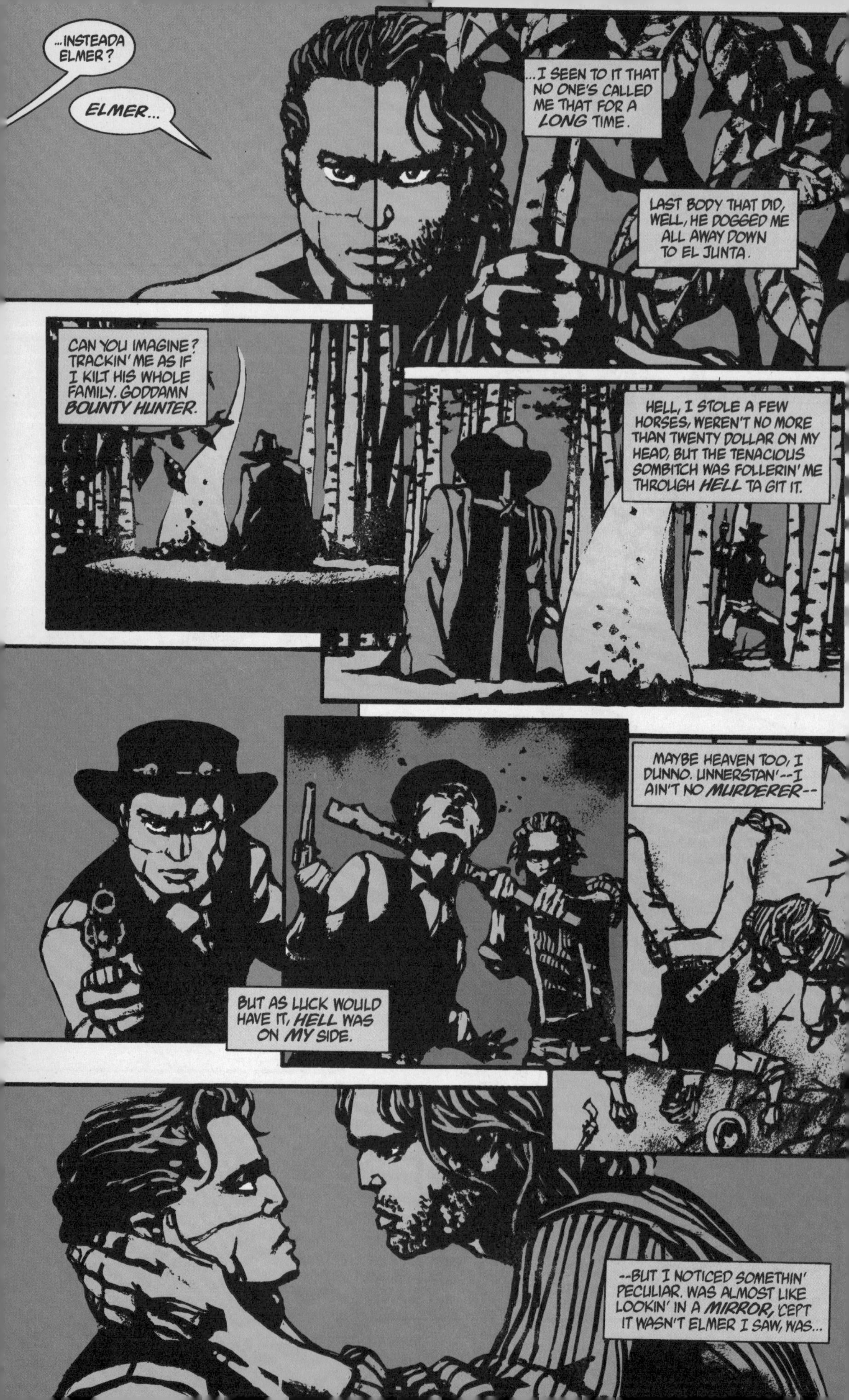
...INSTEADA ELMER?
ELMER...
...I SEEN TO IT THAT NO ONE'S CALLED ME THAT FOR A LONG TIME.
LAST BODY THAT DID, WELL, HE DOGGED ME ALL AWAY DOWN TO EL JUNTA.
CAN YOU IMAGINE? TRACKIN' ME AS IF I KILT HIS WHOLE FAMILY. GODDAMN BOUNTY HUNTER.
HELL, I STOLE A FEW HORSES, WEREN'T NO MORE THAN TWENTY DOLLAR ON MY HEAD, BUT THE TENACIOUS SOMBITCH WAS FOLLERIN' ME THROUGH HELL TA GIT IT.
BUT AS LUCK WOULD HAVE IT, HELL WAS ON MY SIDE.
MAYBE HEAVEN TOO, I DUNNO. UNNERSTAN'--I AIN'T NO MURDERER--
--BUT I NOTICED SOMETHIN' PECULIAR. WAS ALMOST LIKE LOOKIN' IN A MIRROR, 'CEPT IT WASN'T ELMER I SAW, WAS...

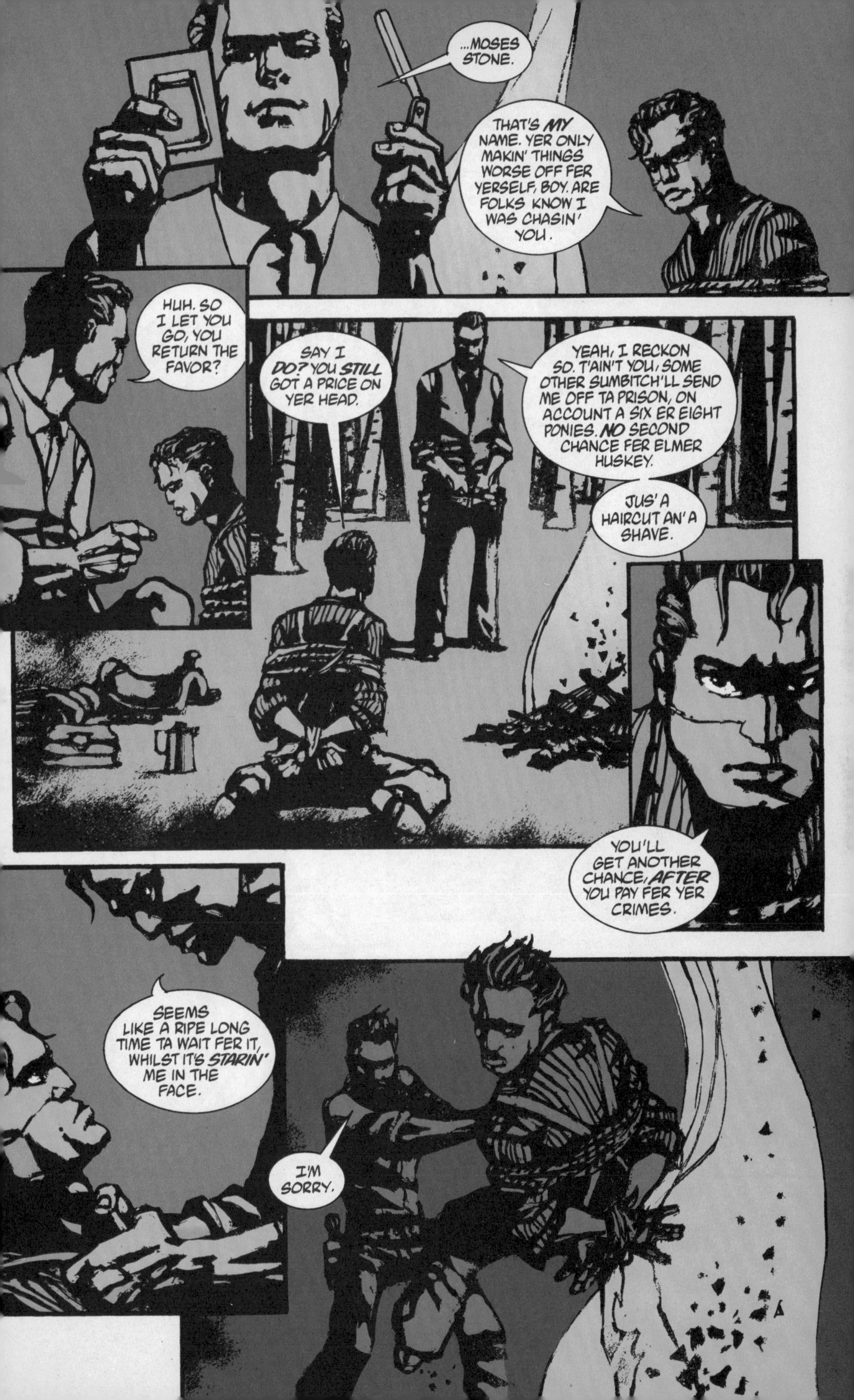
...MOSES STONE.
THAT'S MY NAME. YER ONLY MAKIN' THINGS WORSE OFF FER YERSELF, BOY. ARE FOLKS KNOW I WAS CHASIN' YOU.
HUH. SO I LET YOU GO, YOU RETURN THE FAVOR?
SAY I DO? YOU STILL GOT A PRICE ON YER HEAD.
YEAH, I RECKON SO. T'AIN'T YOU, SOME OTHER SUMBITCH'LL SEND ME OFF TA PRISON, ON ACCOUNT A SIX ER EIGHT PONIES. NO SECOND CHANCE FER ELMER HUSKEY.
JUS' A HAIRCUT AN' A SHAVE.
YOU'LL GET ANOTHER CHANCE, AFTER YOU PAY FER YER CRIMES.
SEEMS LIKE A RIPE LONG TIME TA WAIT FER IT, WHILST IT'S STARIN' ME IN THE FACE.
I'M SORRY.

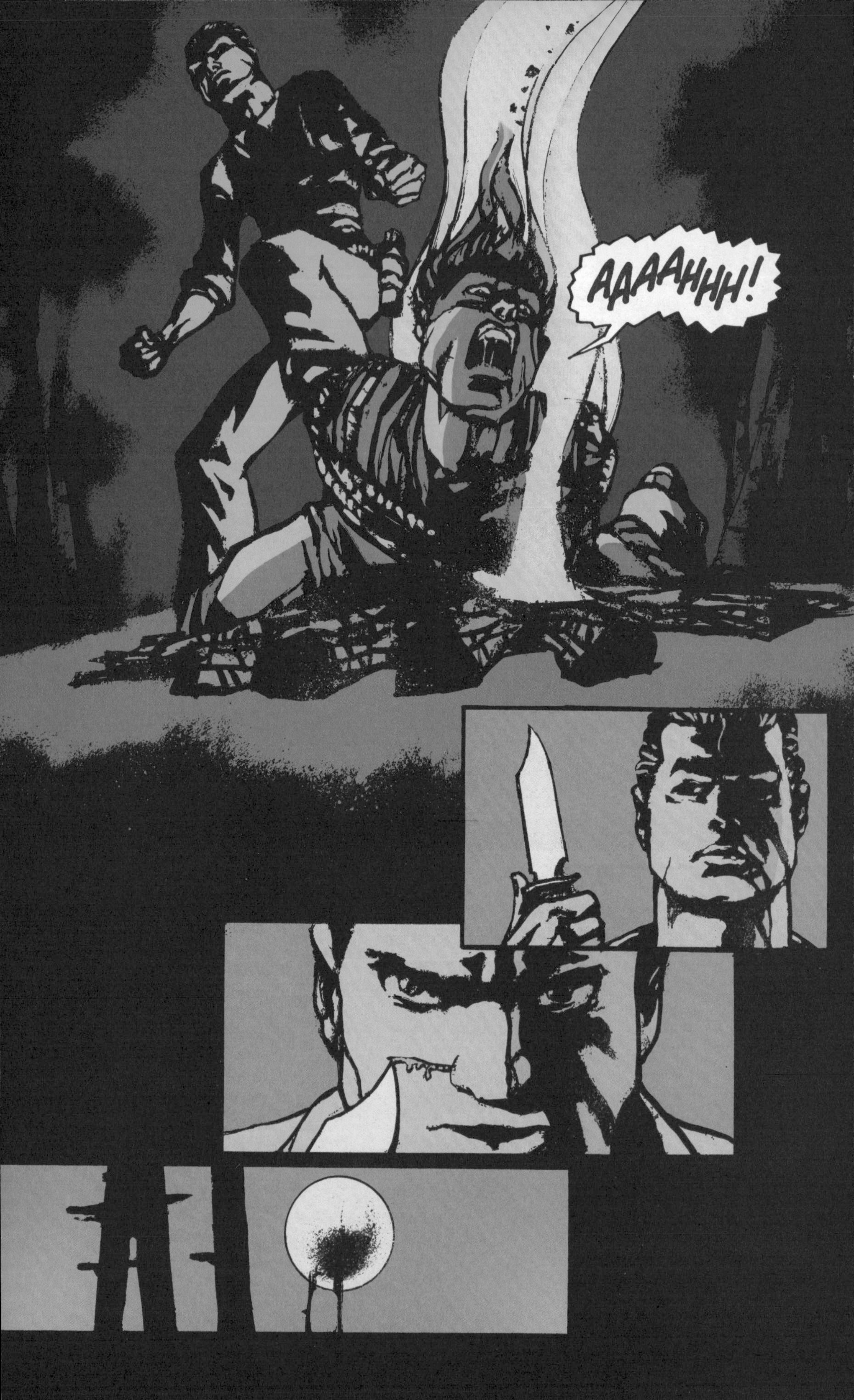
AAAAHHH!

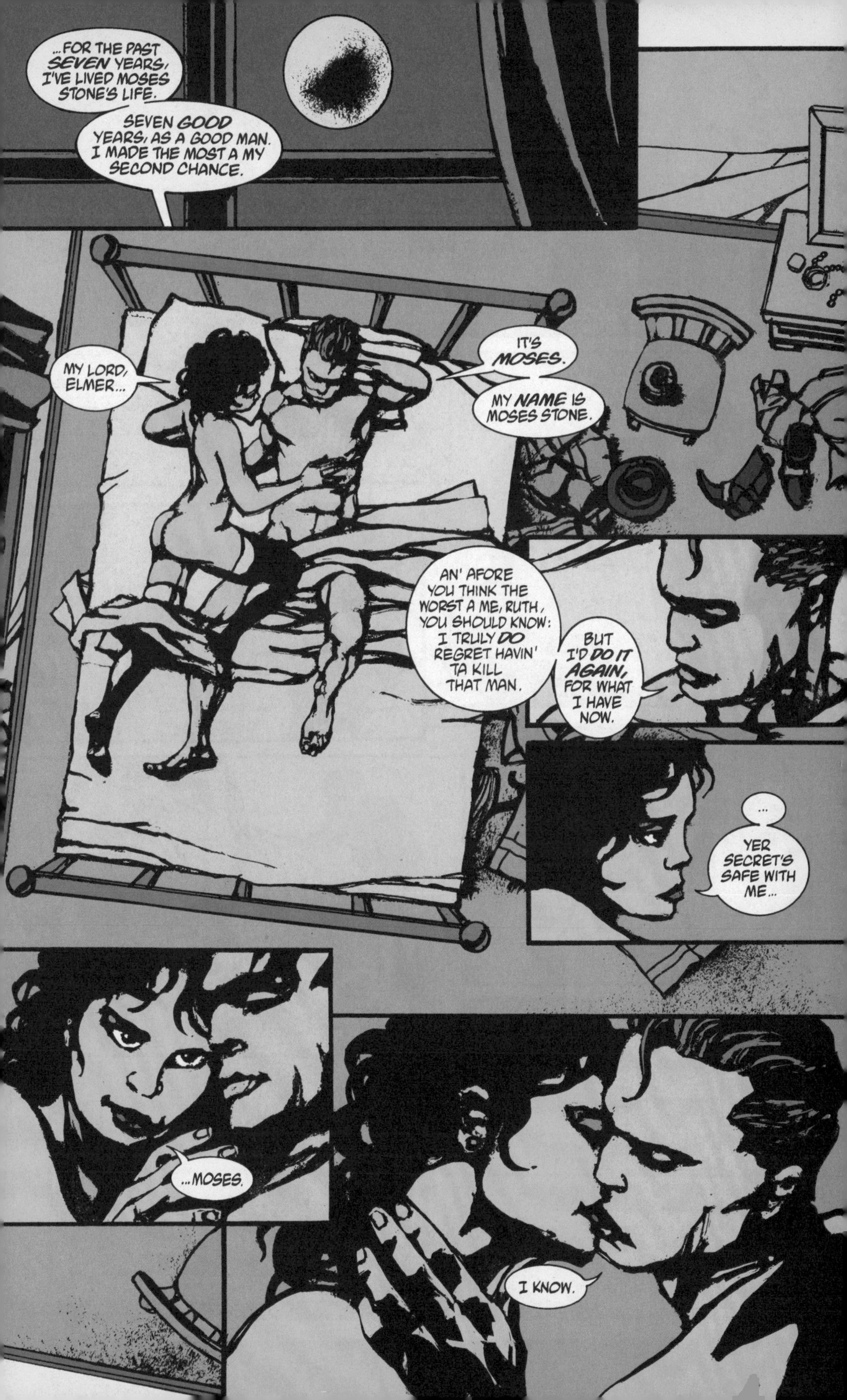

...FOR THE PAST SEVEN YEARS, I'VE LIVED MOSES STONE'S LIFE.
SEVEN GOOD YEARS, AS A GOOD MAN. I MADE THE MOST A MY SECOND CHANCE.
MY LORD, ELMER...
IT'S MOSES.
MY NAME IS MOSES STONE.
AN' AFORE YOU THINK THE WORST A ME, RUTH, YOU SHOULD KNOW: I TRULY DO REGRET HAVIN' TA KILL THAT MAN.
BUT I'D DO IT AGAIN, FOR WHAT I HAVE NOW.
...
YER SECRET'S SAFE WITH ME...
...MOSES.
I KNOW.

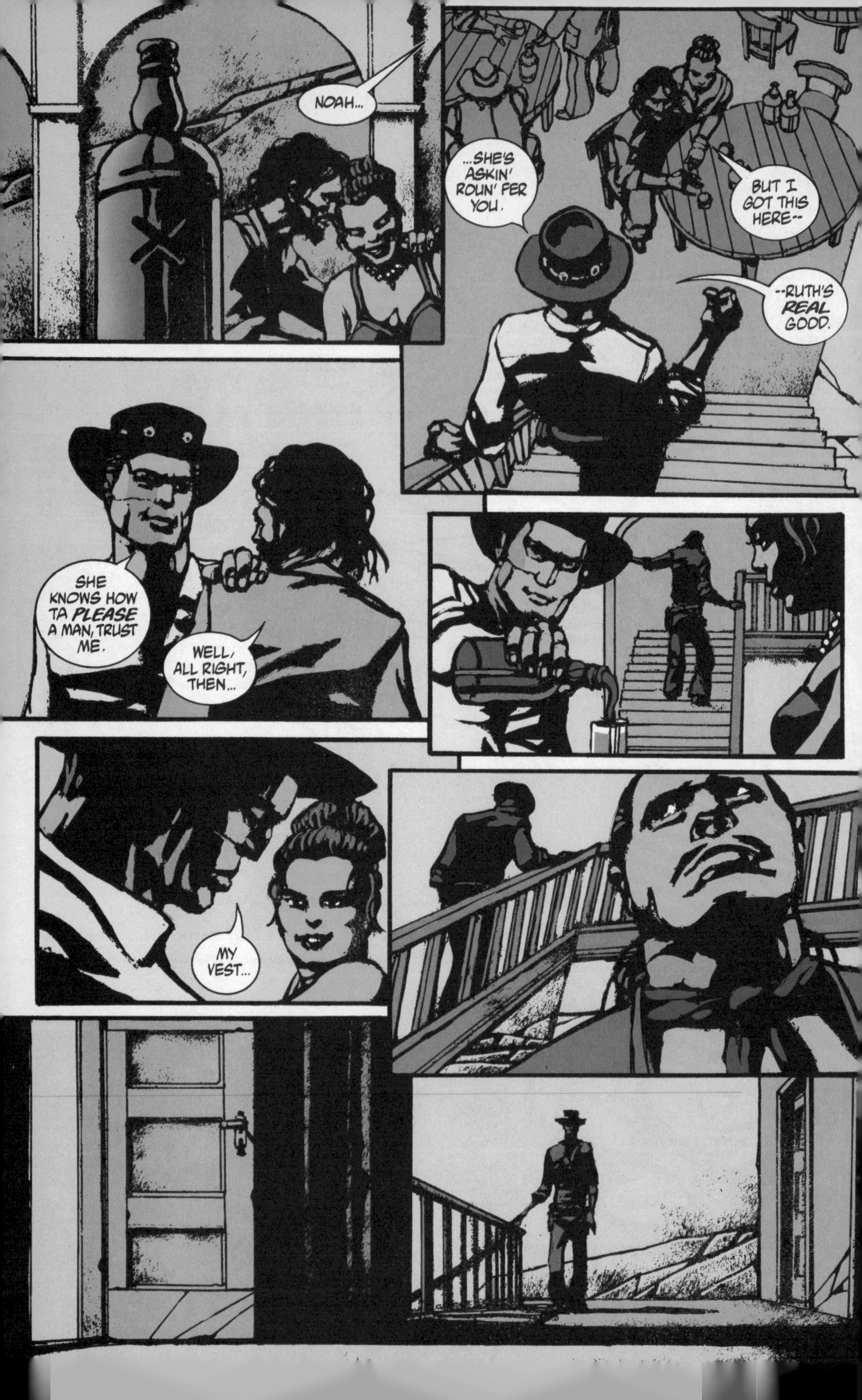
NOAH...
...SHE'S ASKIN' ROUN' FER YOU.
BUT I GOT THIS HERE--
--RUTH'S REAL GOOD.
SHE KNOWS HOW TA PLEASE A MAN, TRUST ME.
WELL, ALL RIGHT, THEN...
MY VEST...

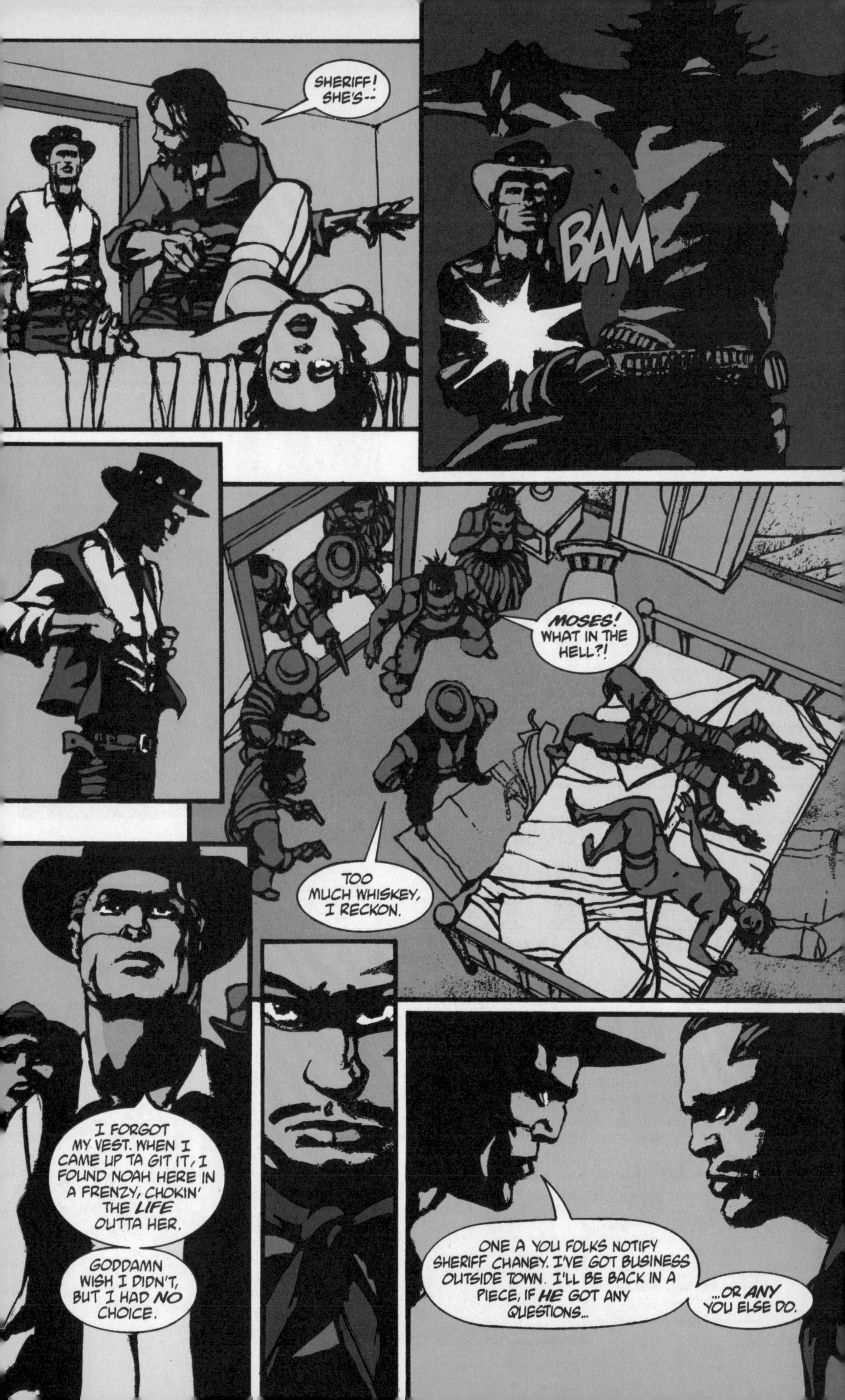
SHERIFF! SHE'S--
BAM
MOSES! WHAT IN THE HELL?!
TOO MUCH WHISKEY, I RECKON.
I FORGOT MY VEST. WHEN I CAME UP TA GIT IT, I FOUND NOAH HERE IN A FRENZY, CHOKIN' THE LIFE OUTTA HER.
GODDAMN WISH I DIDN'T, BUT I HAD NO CHOICE.
ONE A YOU FOLKS NOTIFY SHERIFF CHANEY. I'VE GOT BUSINESS OUTSIDE TOWN. I'LL BE BACK IN A PIECE, IF HE GOT ANY QUESTIONS...
...OR ANY YOU ELSE DO.

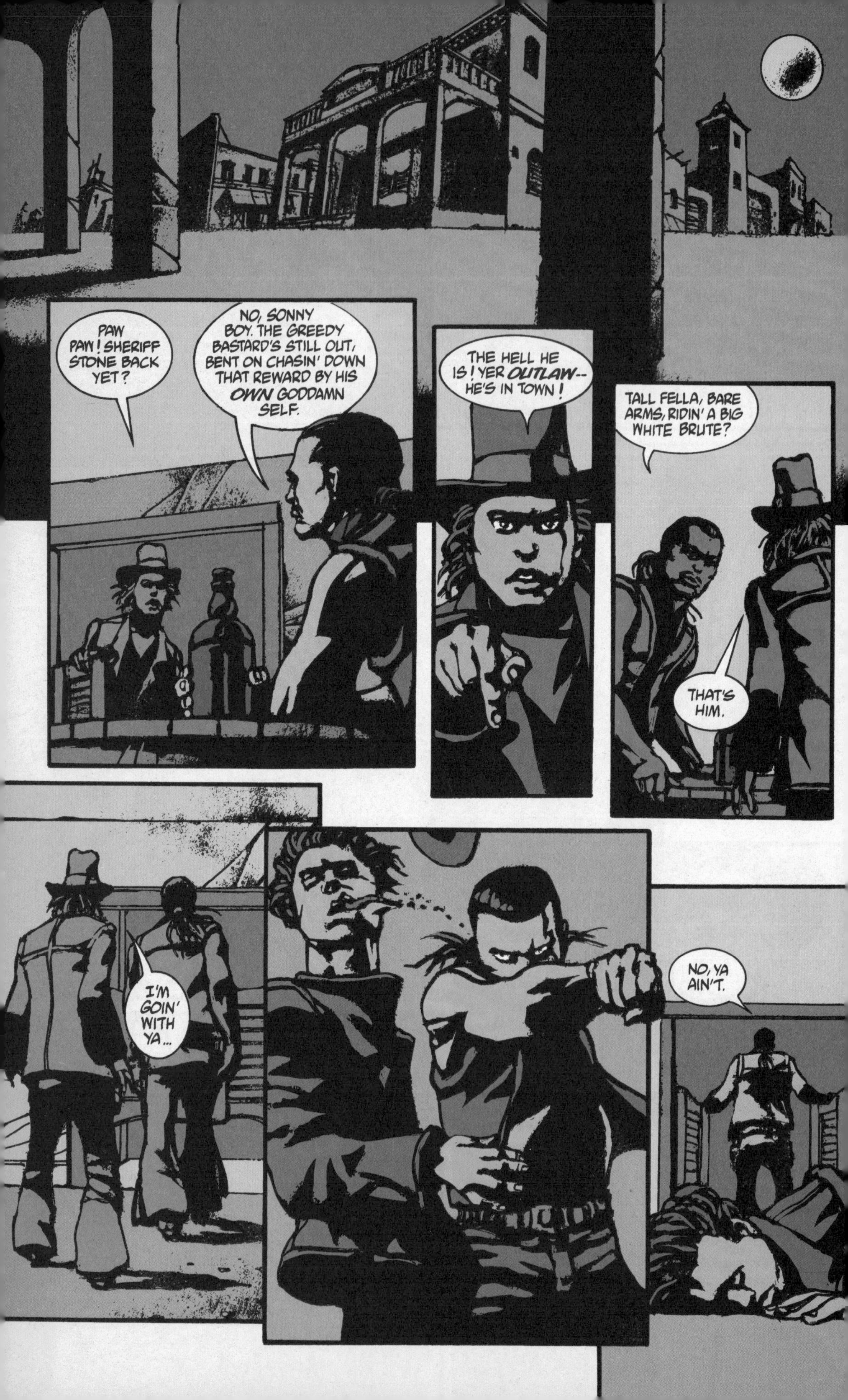
PAW PAW! SHERIFF STONE BACK YET?
NO, SONNY BOY. THE GREEDY BASTARD'S STILL OUT, BENT ON CHASIN' DOWN THAT REWARD BY HIS OWN GODDAMN SELF.
THE HELL HE IS! YER OUTLAW-- HE'S IN TOWN!
TALL FELLA, BARE ARMS, RIDIN' A BIG WHITE BRUTE?
THAT'S HIM.
I'M GOIN' WITH YA...
NO, YA AIN'T.

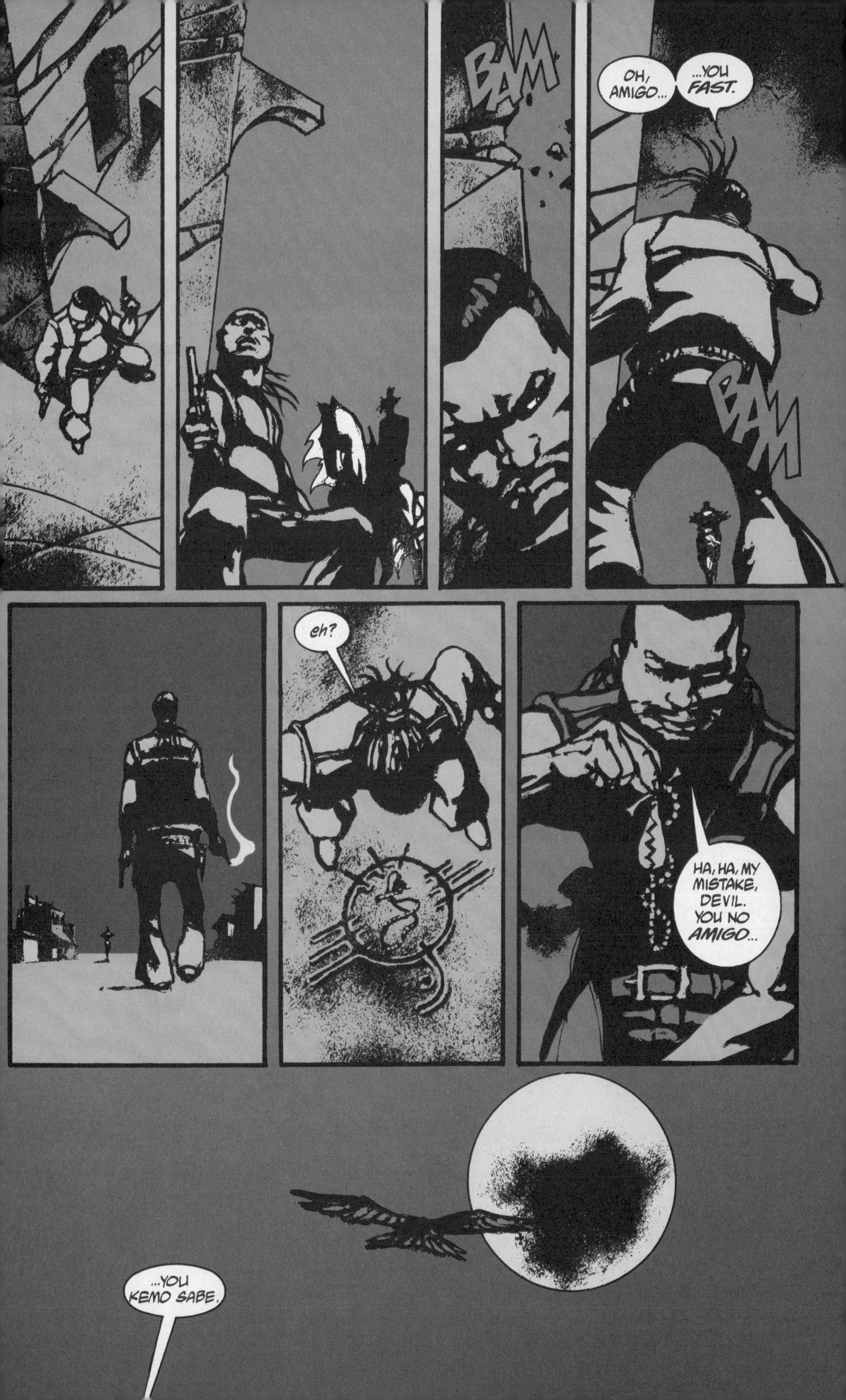
BAM
OH, AMIGO...
...YOU FAST.
BAM
eh?
HA, HA, MY MISTAKE, DEVIL. YOU NO AMIGO...
...YOU KEMO SABE.

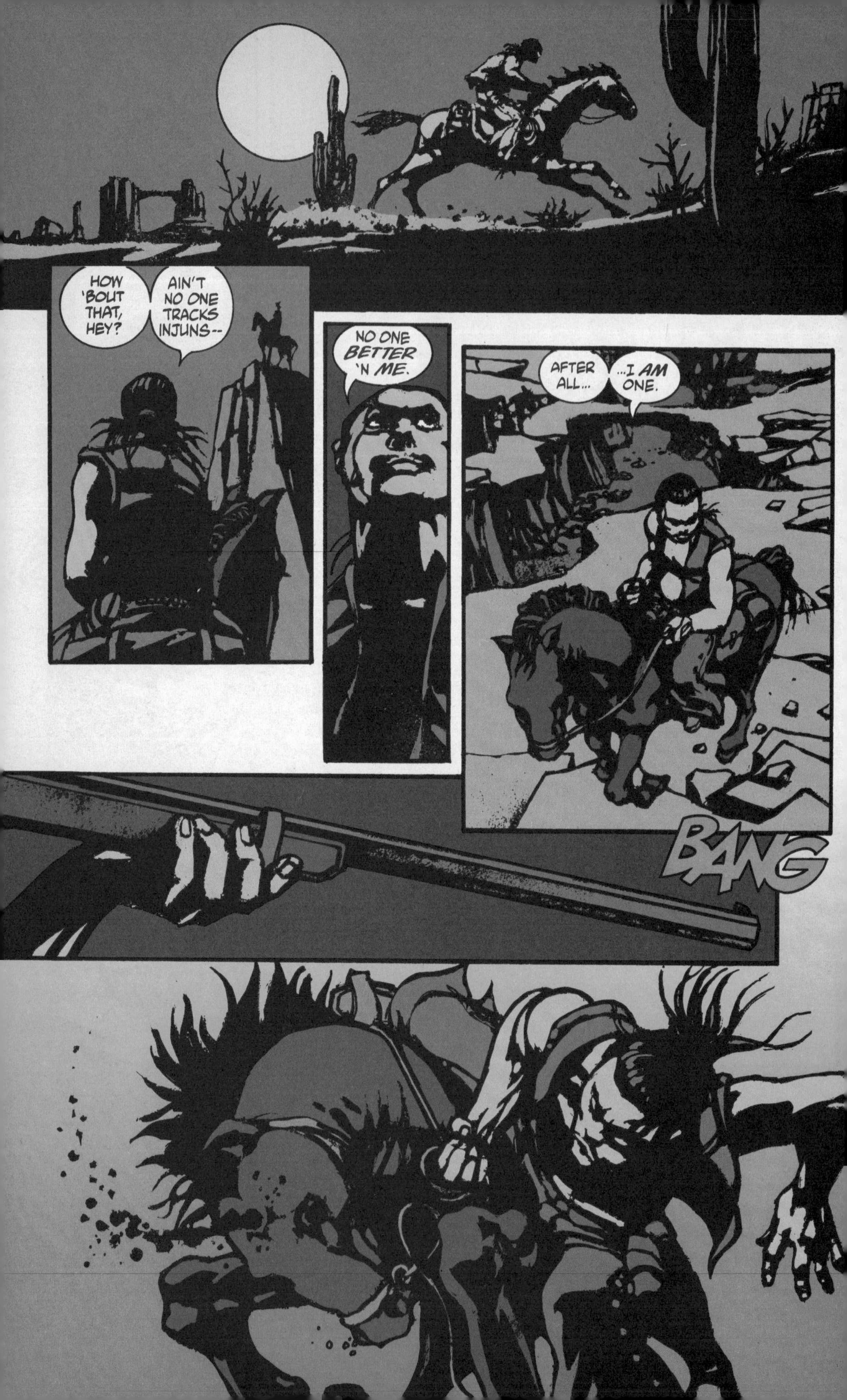
HOW 'BOUT THAT, HEY?
AIN'T NO ONE TRACKS INJUNS--
NO ONE BETTER 'N ME.
AFTER ALL...
...I AM ONE.
BANG

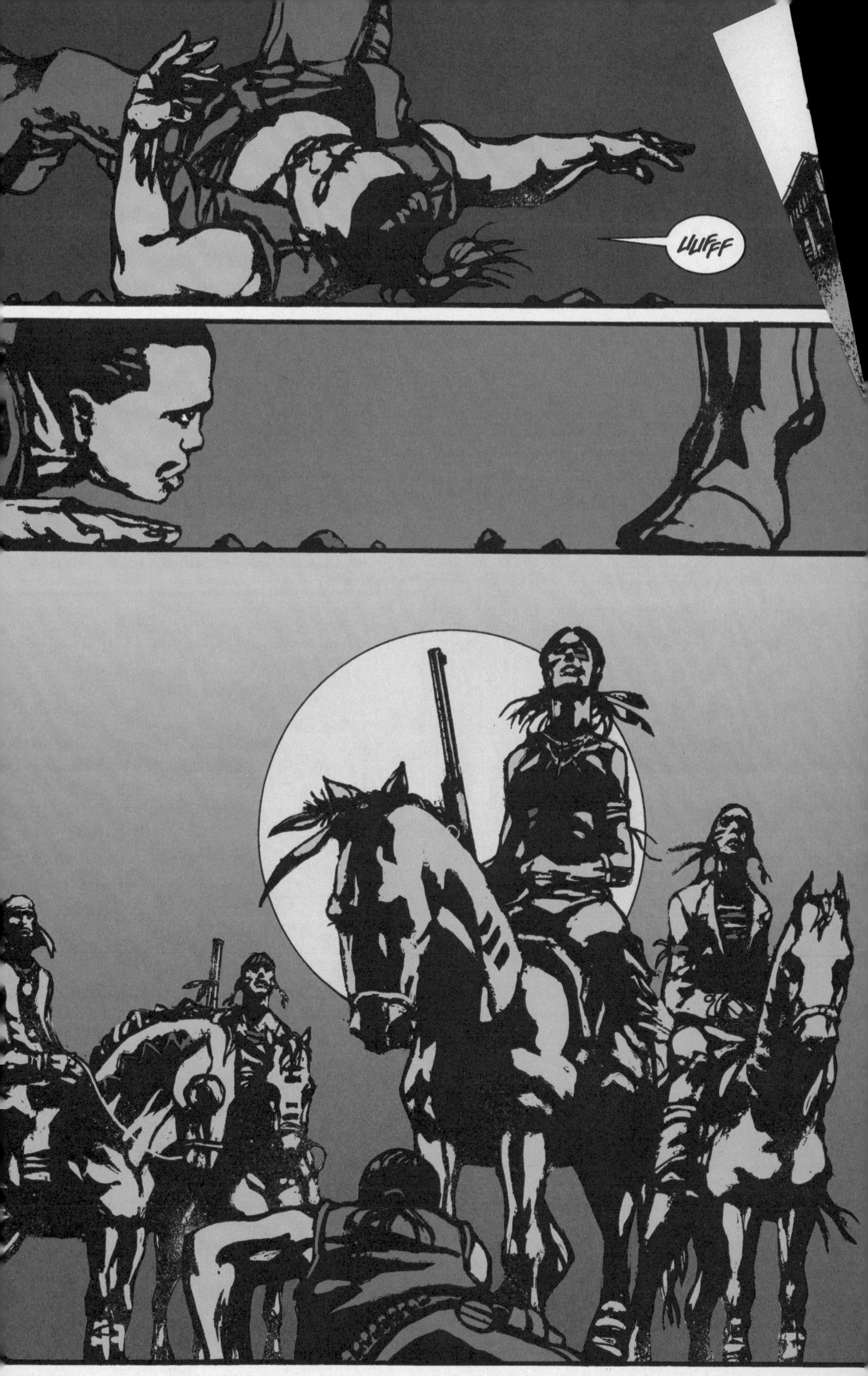
UUFFF

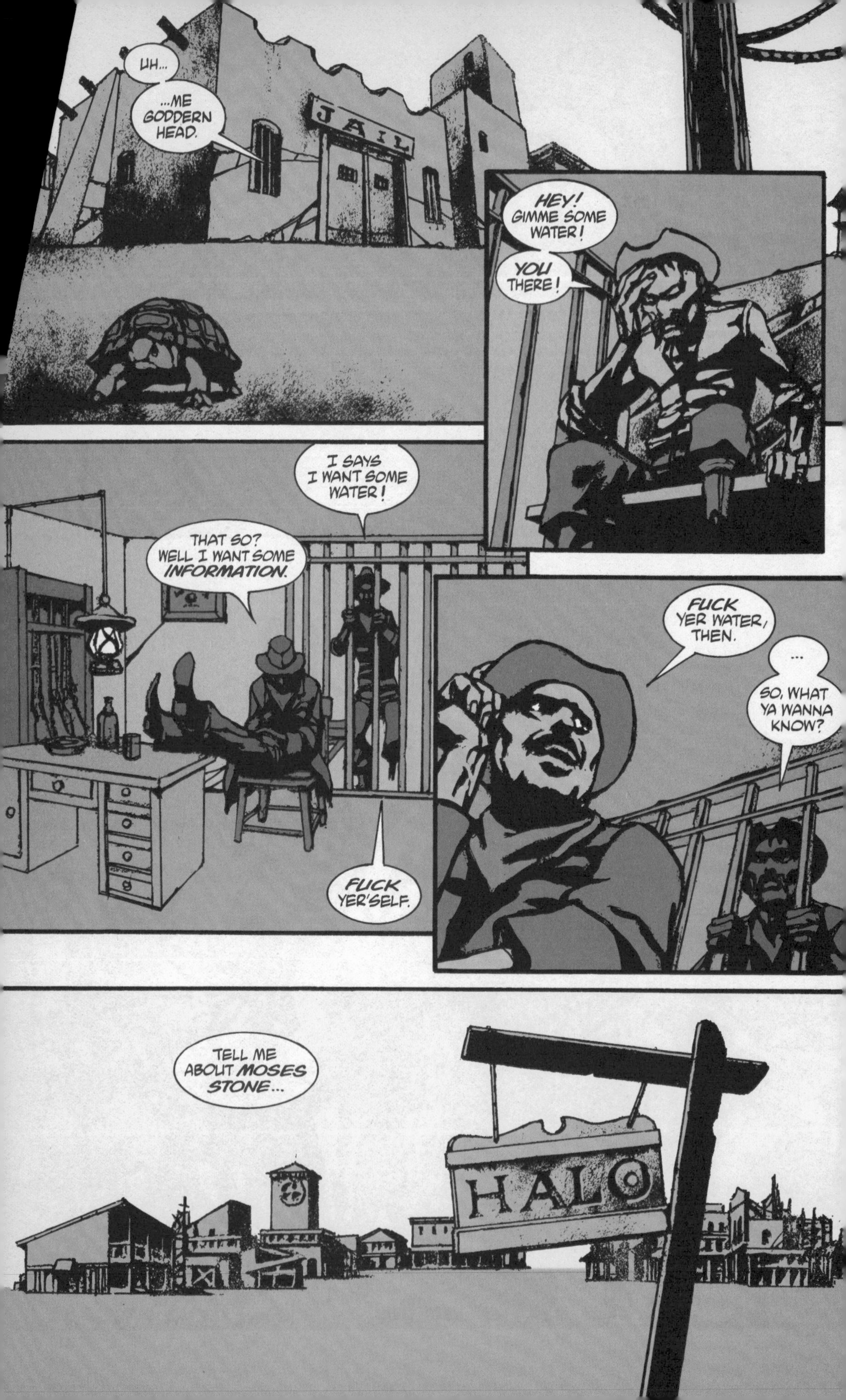
UH...
...ME GODDERN HEAD.
JAIL
HEY! GIMME SOME WATER!
YOU THERE!
I SAYS I WANT SOME WATER!
THAT SO? WELL I WANT SOME INFORMATION.
FUCK YER'SELF.
FUCK YER WATER, THEN.
...
SO, WHAT YA WANNA KNOW?
TELL ME ABOUT MOSES STONE...
HALO

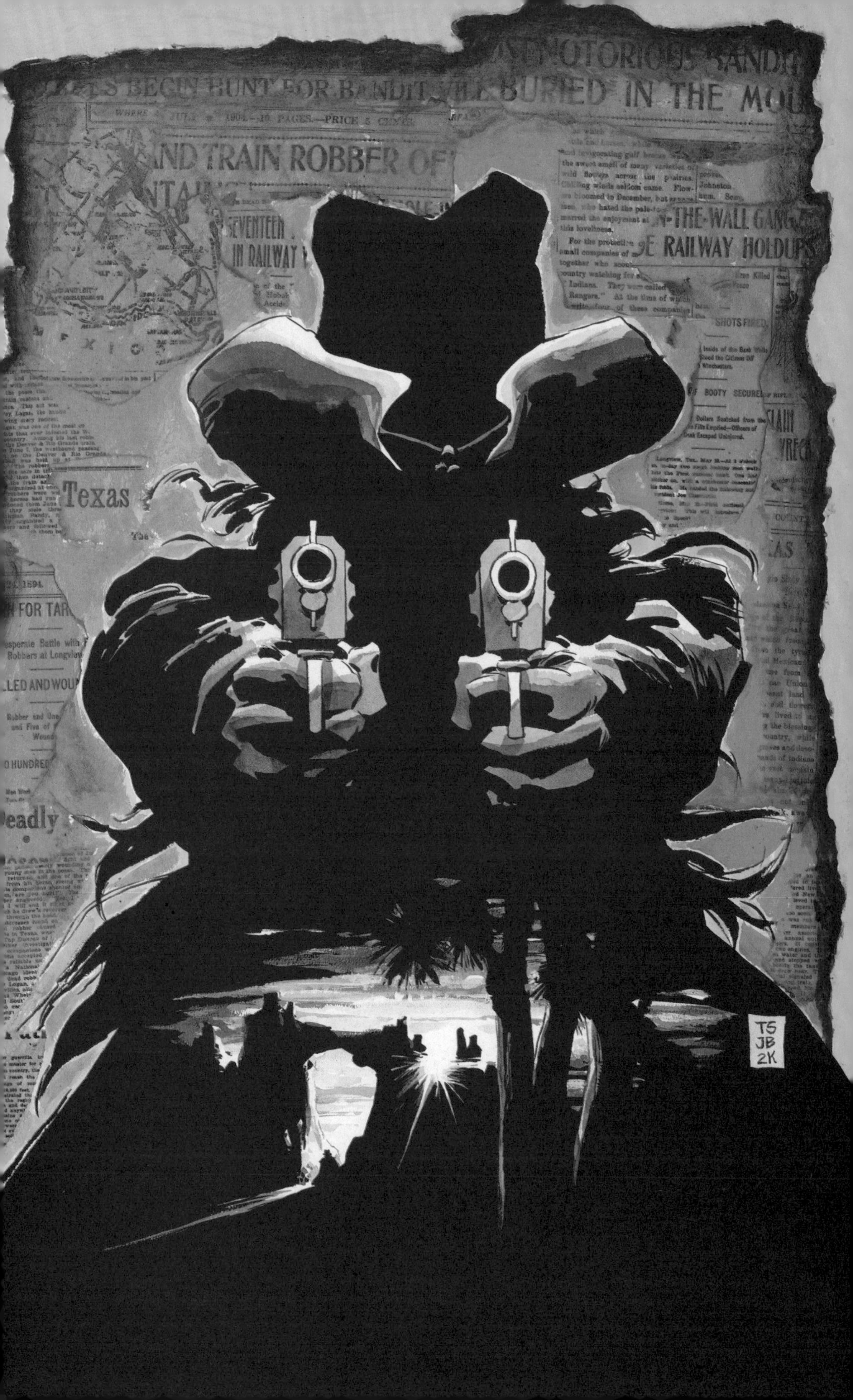

BURIED IN THE
TRAIN ROBBER OF
RAILWAY HOLDUPS
SHOTS FIRED
Texas
Desperate Battle with
Robbers at Longview
Deadly
TS JB 2K

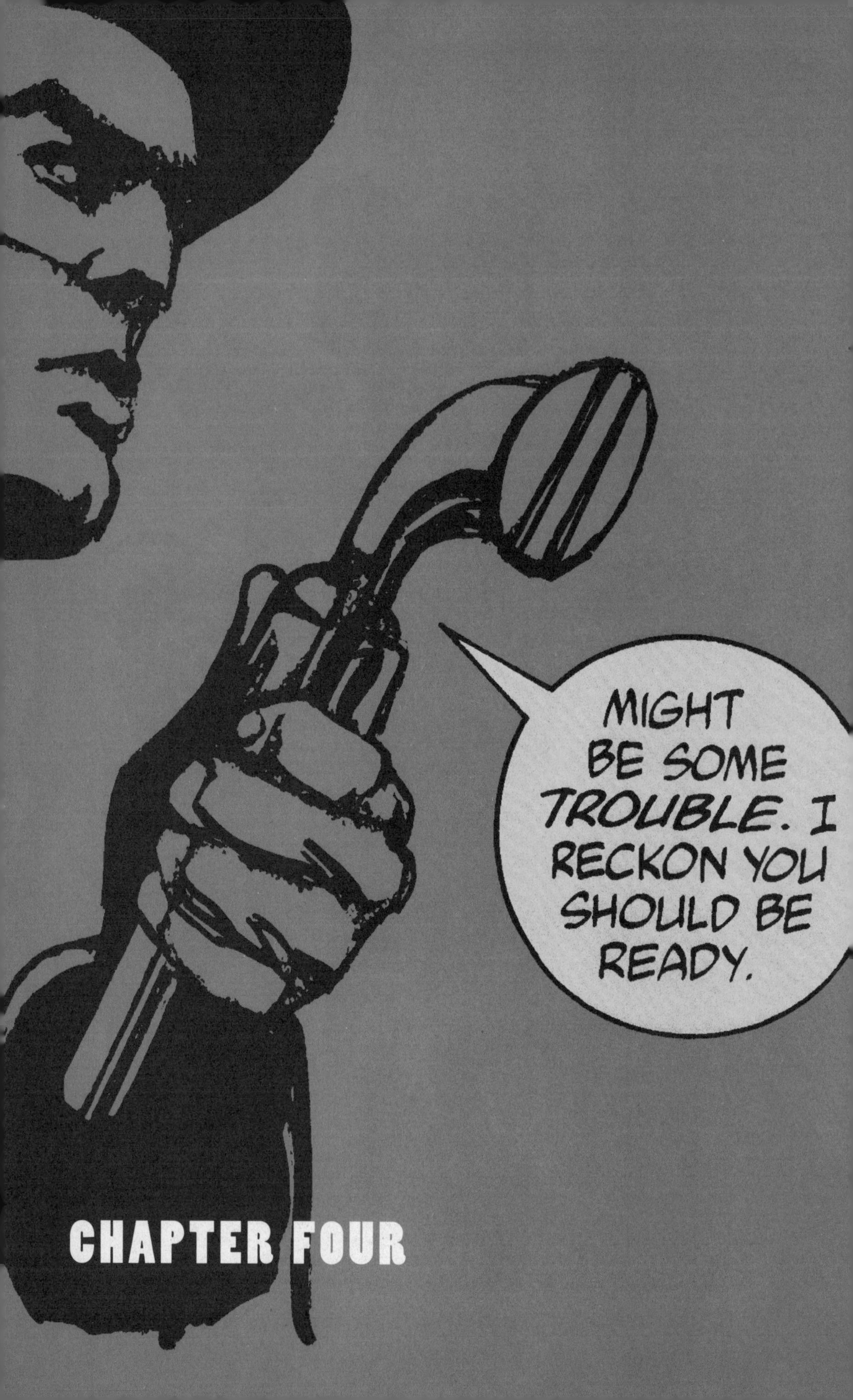
MIGHT BE SOME TROUBLE. I RECKON YOU SHOULD BE READY.

CHAPTER FOUR

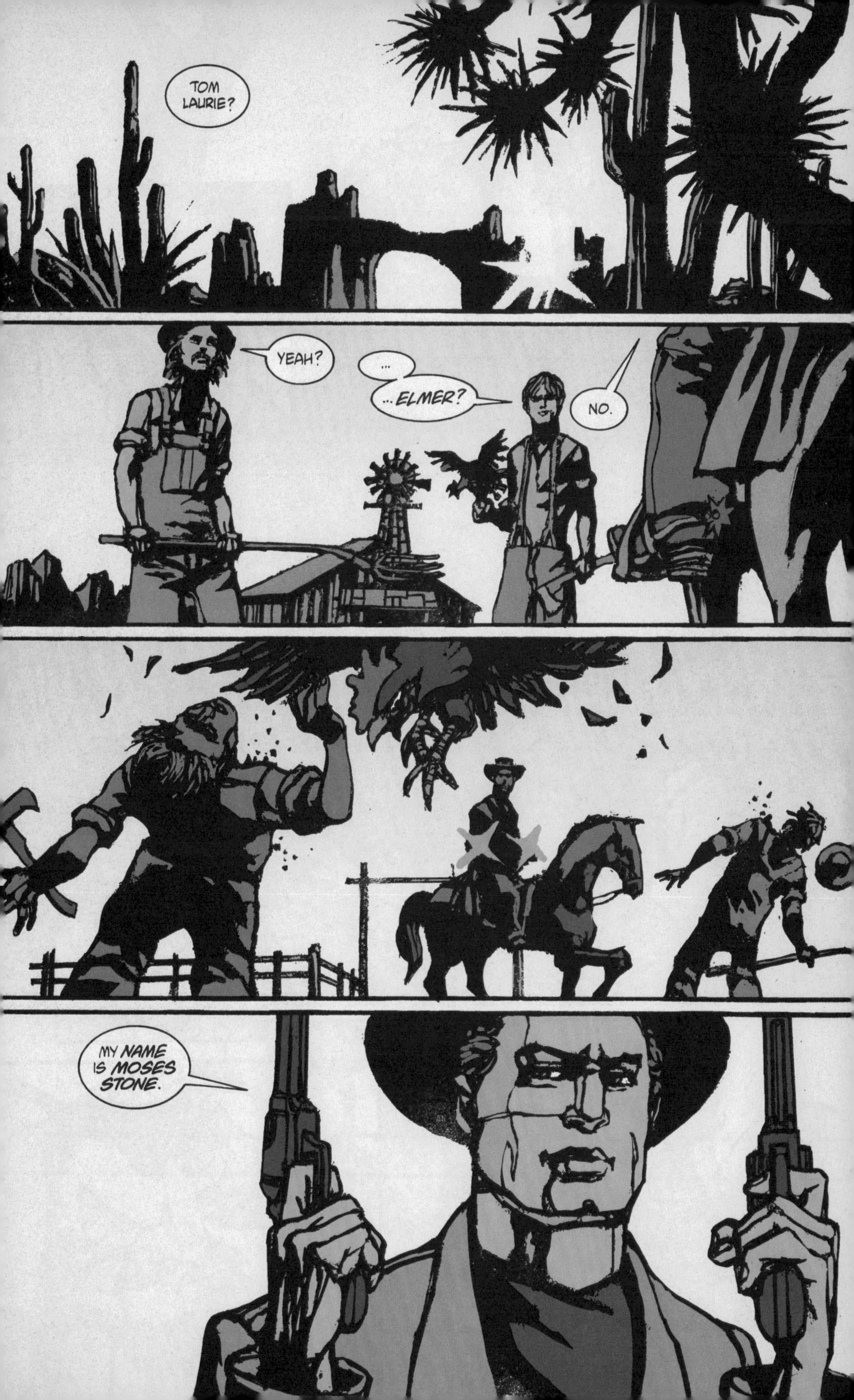
TOM LAURIE?
YEAH?
...
...ELMER?
NO.
MY NAME IS MOSES STONE.

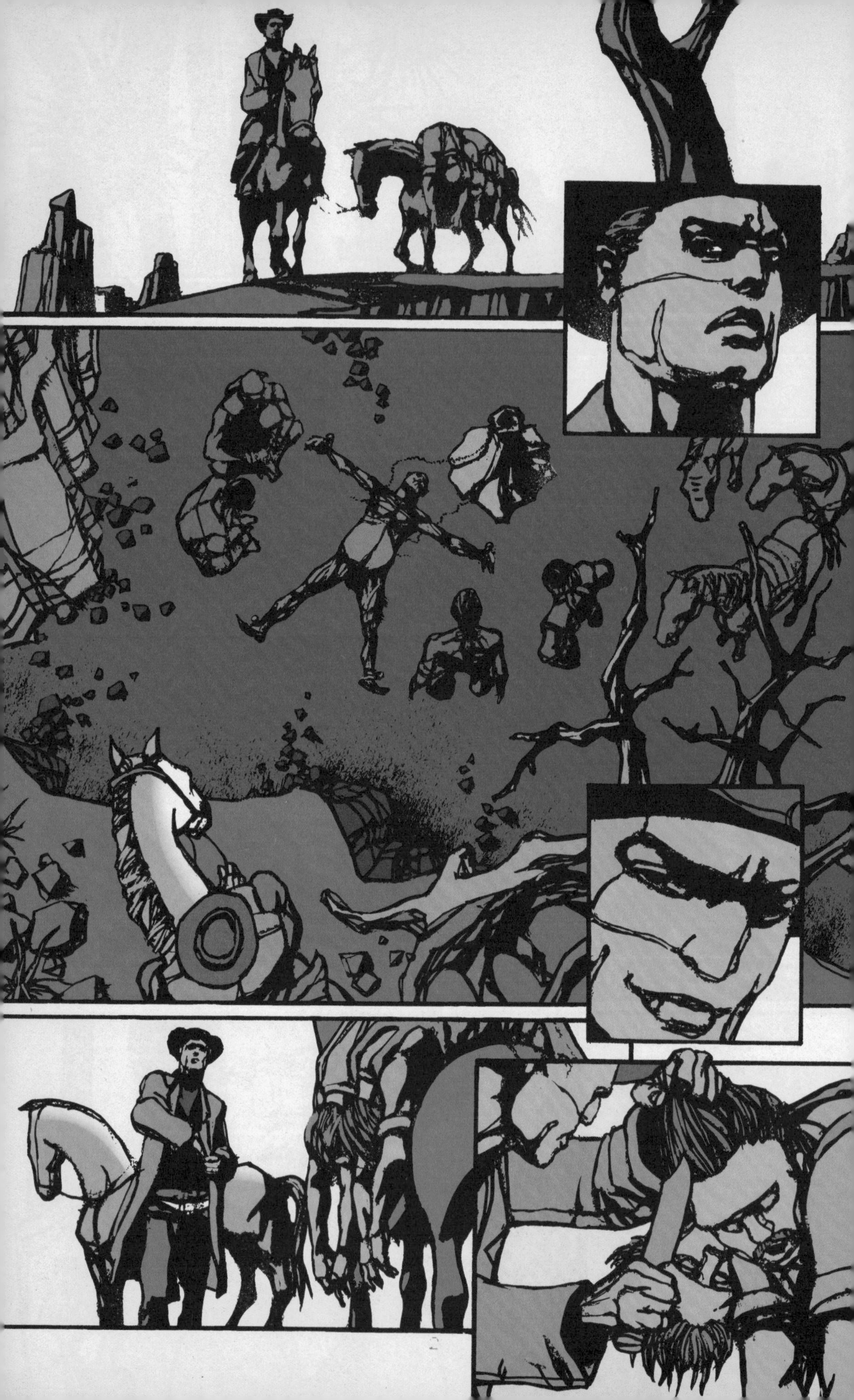

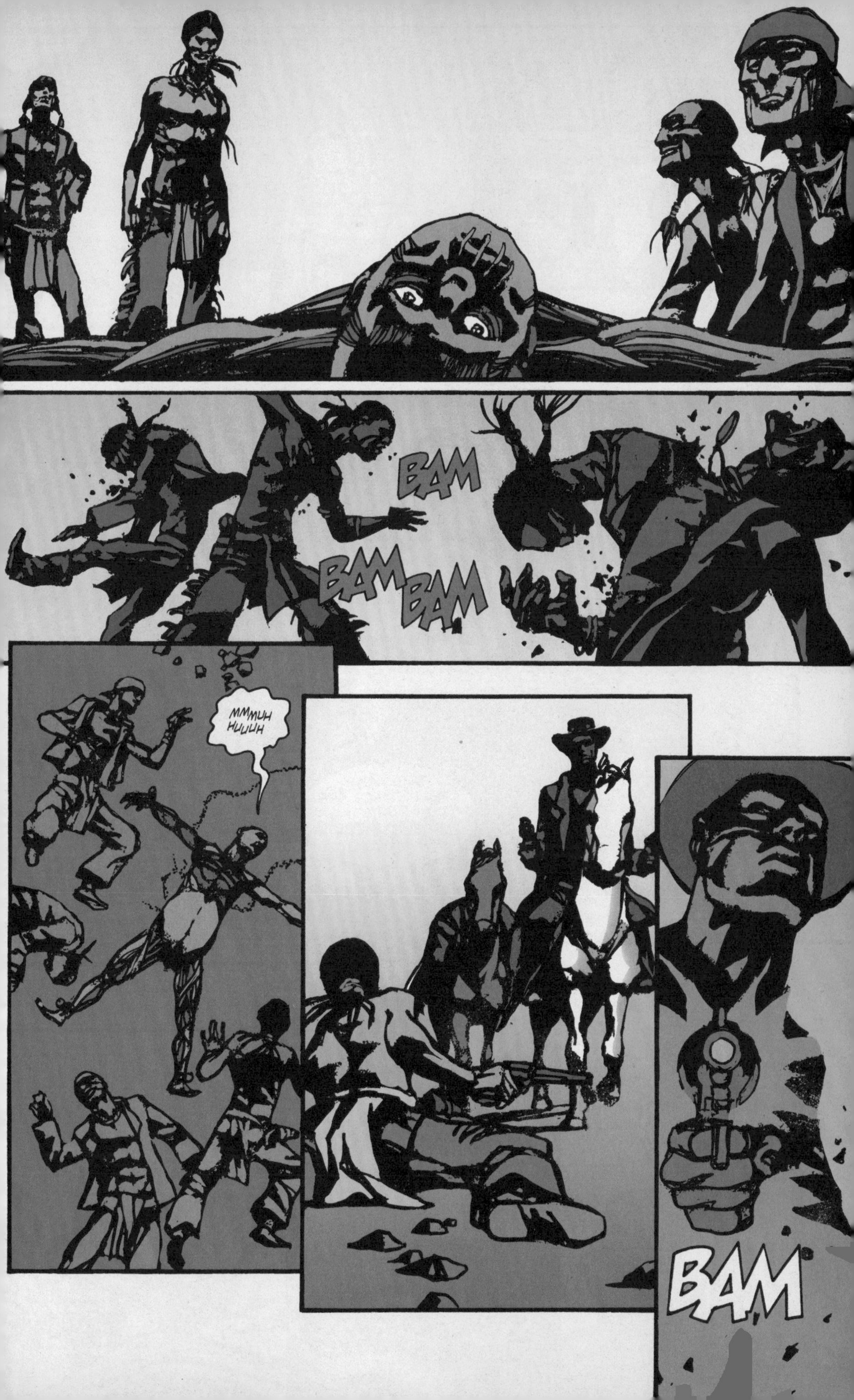
BAM
BAM BAM
MMMUH HUUUH
BAM

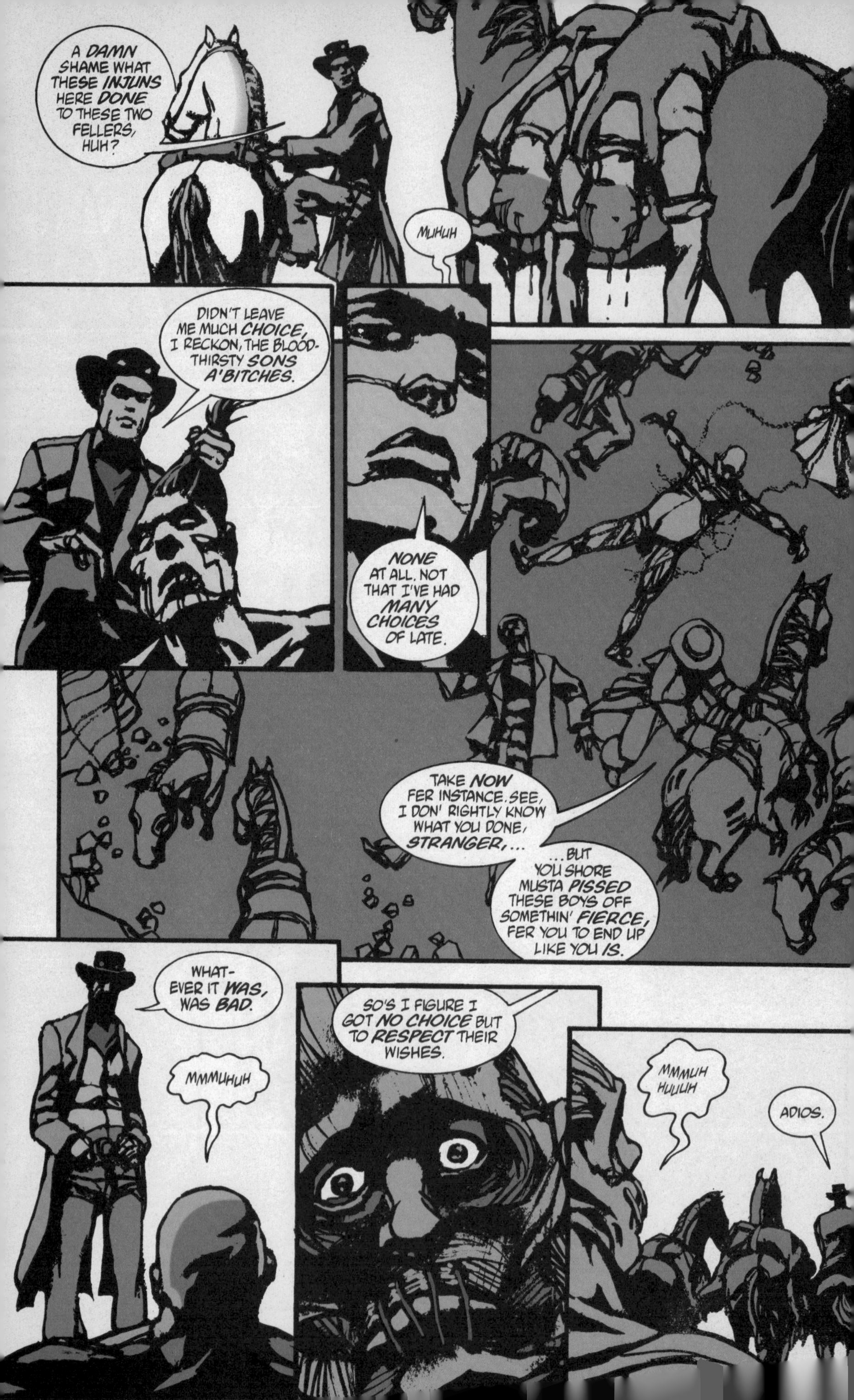
A DAMN SHAME WHAT THESE INJUNS HERE DONE TO THESE TWO FELLERS, HUH?
MUHUH
DIDN'T LEAVE ME MUCH CHOICE, I RECKON, THE BLOOD-THIRSTY SONS A'BITCHES.
NONE AT ALL. NOT THAT I'VE HAD MANY CHOICES OF LATE.
TAKE NOW FER INSTANCE. SEE, I DON' RIGHTLY KNOW WHAT YOU DONE, STRANGER, ...
...BUT YOU SHORE MUSTA PISSED THESE BOYS OFF SOMETHIN' FIERCE, FER YOU TO END UP LIKE YOU IS.
WHAT-EVER IT WAS, WAS BAD.
MMMUHUH
SO'S I FIGURE I GOT NO CHOICE BUT TO RESPECT THEIR WISHES.
MMMUH HUUUH
ADIOS.

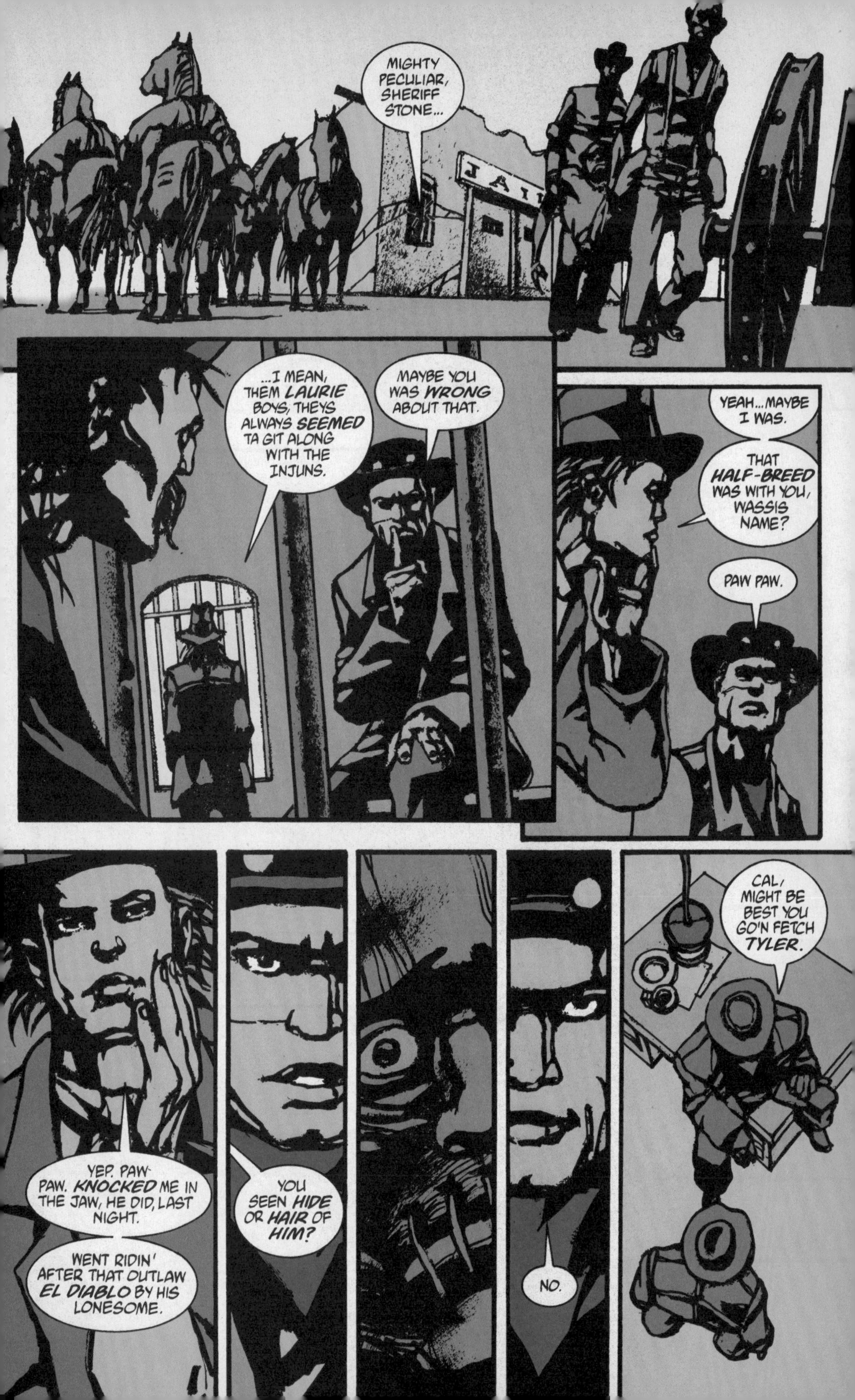
MIGHTY PECULIAR, SHERIFF STONE...
...I MEAN, THEM LAURIE BOYS, THEYS ALWAYS SEEMED TA GIT ALONG WITH THE INJUNS.
MAYBE YOU WAS WRONG ABOUT THAT.
YEAH...MAYBE I WAS.
THAT HALF-BREED WAS WITH YOU, WASSIS NAME?
PAW PAW.
YEP. PAW-PAW. KNOCKED ME IN THE JAW, HE DID, LAST NIGHT.
WENT RIDIN' AFTER THAT OUTLAW EL DIABLO BY HIS LONESOME.
YOU SEEN HIDE OR HAIR OF HIM?
NO.
CAL, MIGHT BE BEST YOU GO'N FETCH TYLER.

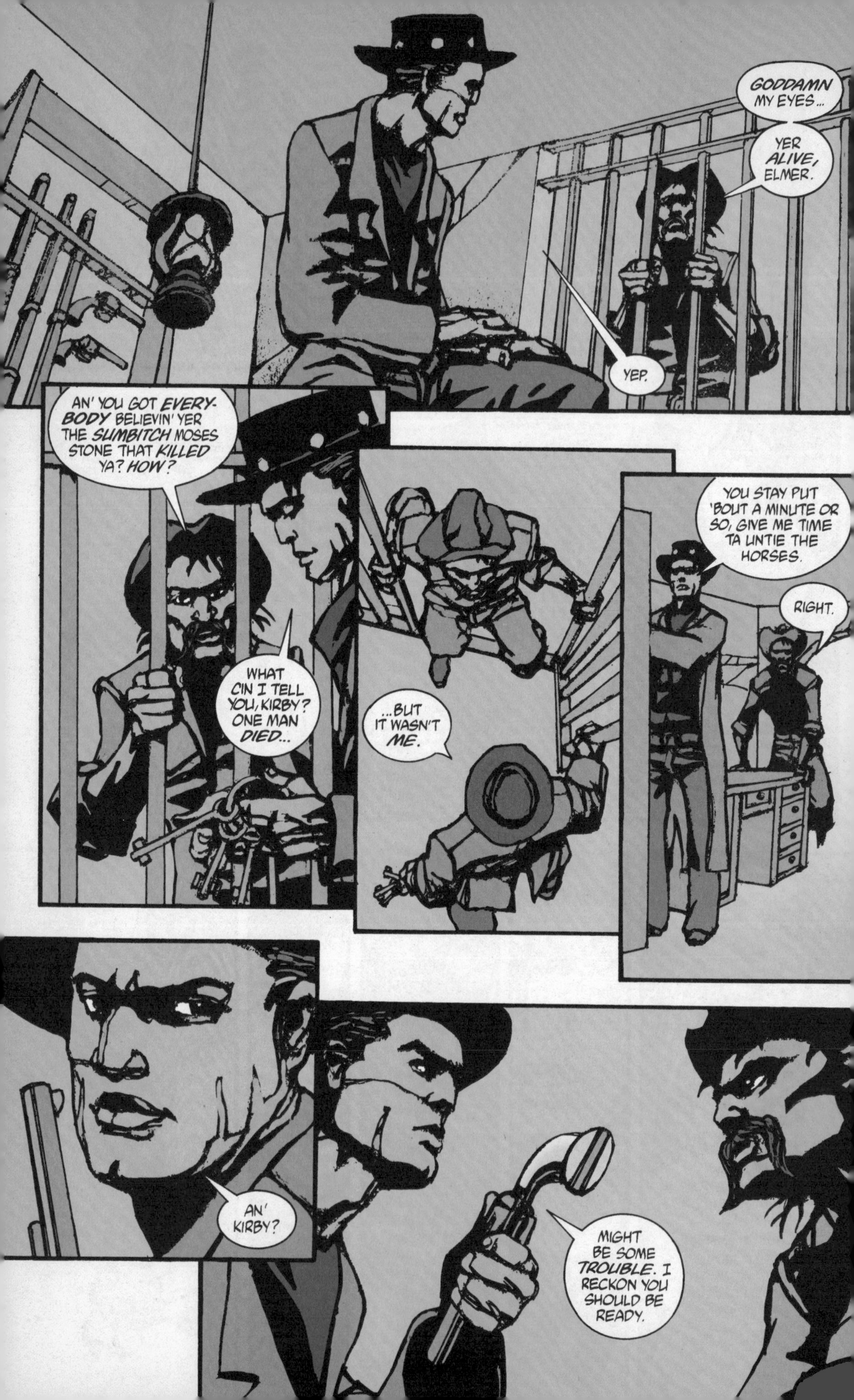
GODDAMN MY EYES...
YER ALIVE, ELMER.
YEP.
AN' YOU GOT EVERYBODY BELIEVIN' YER THE SUMBITCH MOSES STONE THAT KILLED YA? HOW?
WHAT CIN I TELL YOU, KIRBY? ONE MAN DIED...
...BUT IT WASN'T ME.
YOU STAY PUT 'BOUT A MINUTE OR SO, GIVE ME TIME TA UNTIE THE HORSES.
RIGHT.
AN' KIRBY?
MIGHT BE SOME TROUBLE. I RECKON YOU SHOULD BE READY.

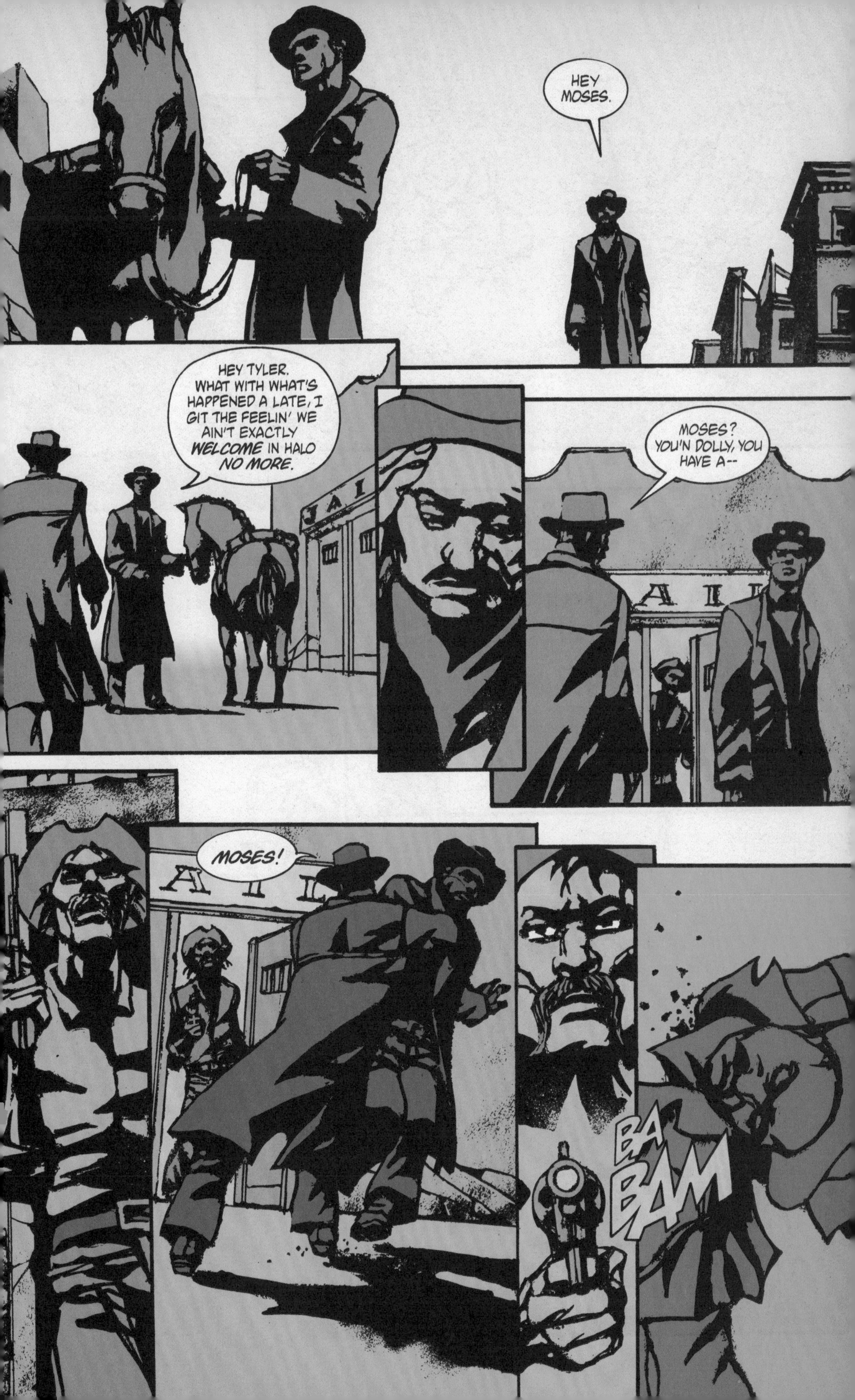
HEY
MOSES.
HEY TYLER.
WHAT WITH WHAT'S
HAPPENED A LATE, I
GIT THE FEELIN' WE
AIN'T EXACTLY
WELCOME IN HALO
NO MORE.
MOSES?
YOU'N DOLLY, YOU
HAVE A--
MOSES!
BA
BAM

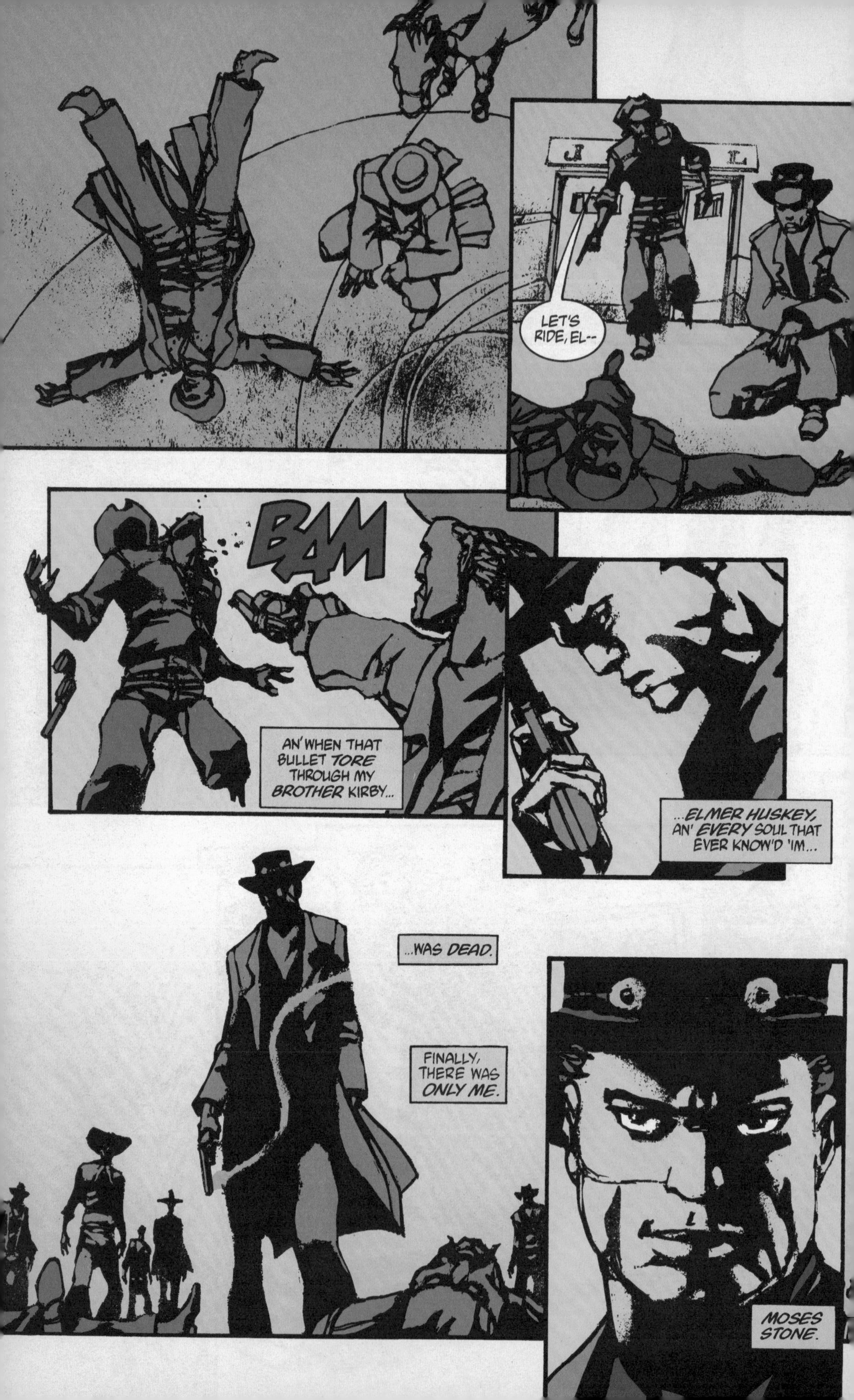
LET'S RIDE, EL--
BAM
AN' WHEN THAT BULLET TORE THROUGH MY BROTHER KIRBY...
...ELMER HUSKEY, AN' EVERY SOUL THAT EVER KNOW'D 'IM...
...WAS DEAD.
FINALLY, THERE WAS ONLY ME.
MOSES STONE.

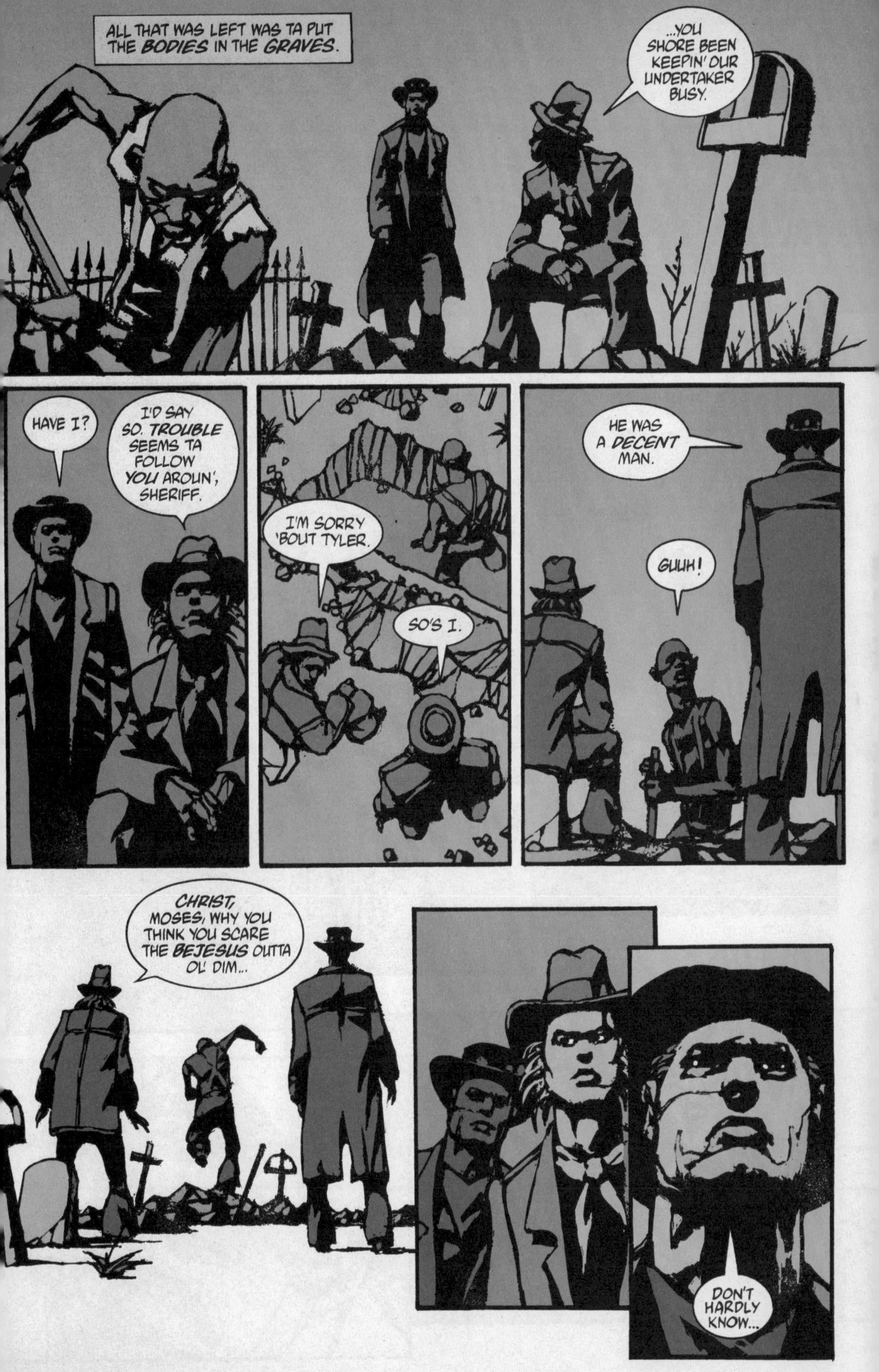
ALL THAT WAS LEFT WAS TA PUT THE BODIES IN THE GRAVES.
...YOU SHORE BEEN KEEPIN' OUR UNDERTAKER BUSY.
HAVE I?
I'D SAY SO. TROUBLE SEEMS TA FOLLOW YOU AROUN', SHERIFF.
I'M SORRY 'BOUT TYLER.
SO'S I.
HE WAS A DECENT MAN.
GUUH!
CHRIST, MOSES, WHY YOU THINK YOU SCARE THE BEJESUS OUTTA OL' DIM...
DON'T HARDLY KNOW...

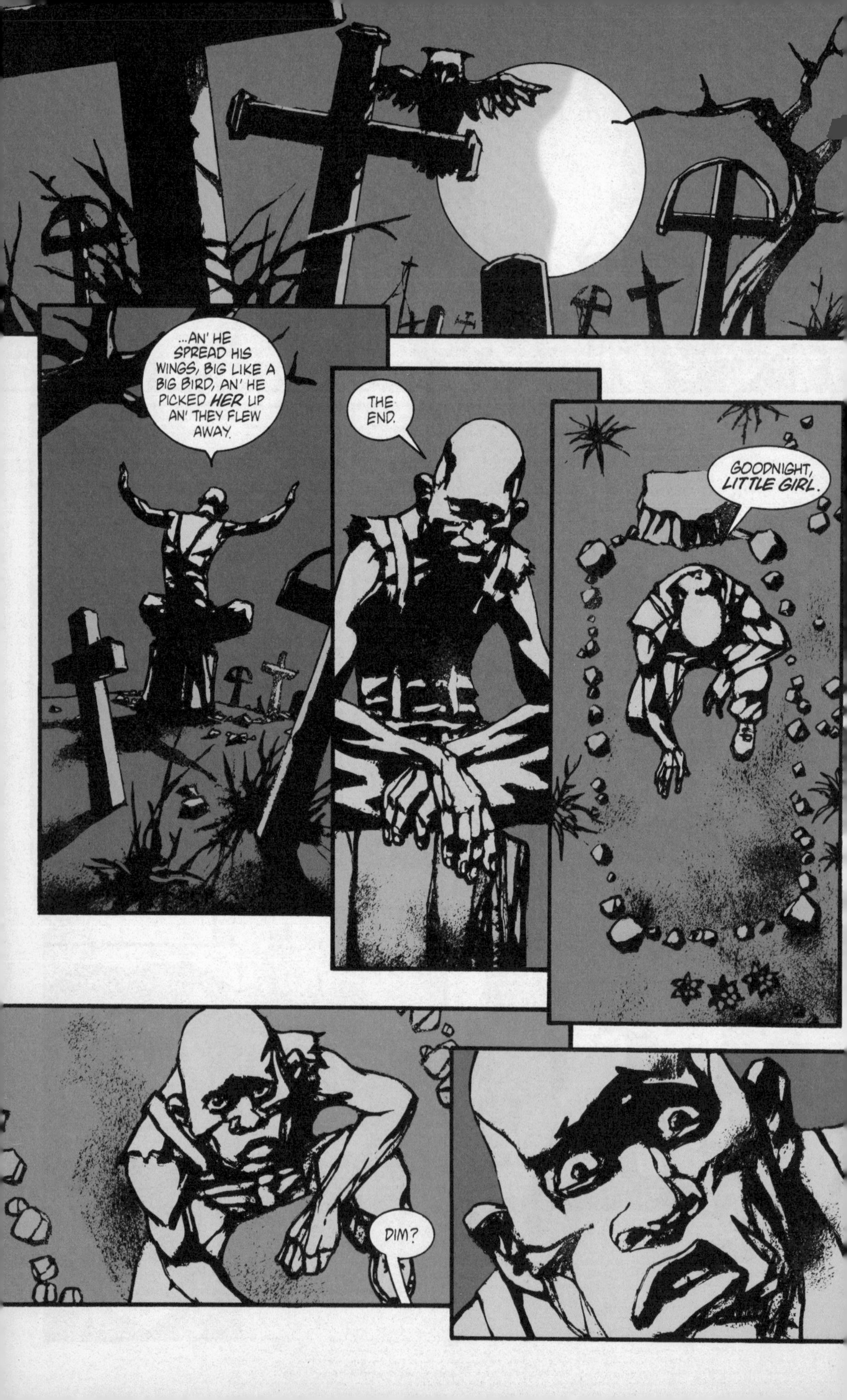
...AN' HE SPREAD HIS WINGS, BIG LIKE A BIG BIRD, AN' HE PICKED HER UP AN' THEY FLEW AWAY.
THE END.
GOODNIGHT, LITTLE GIRL.
DIM?

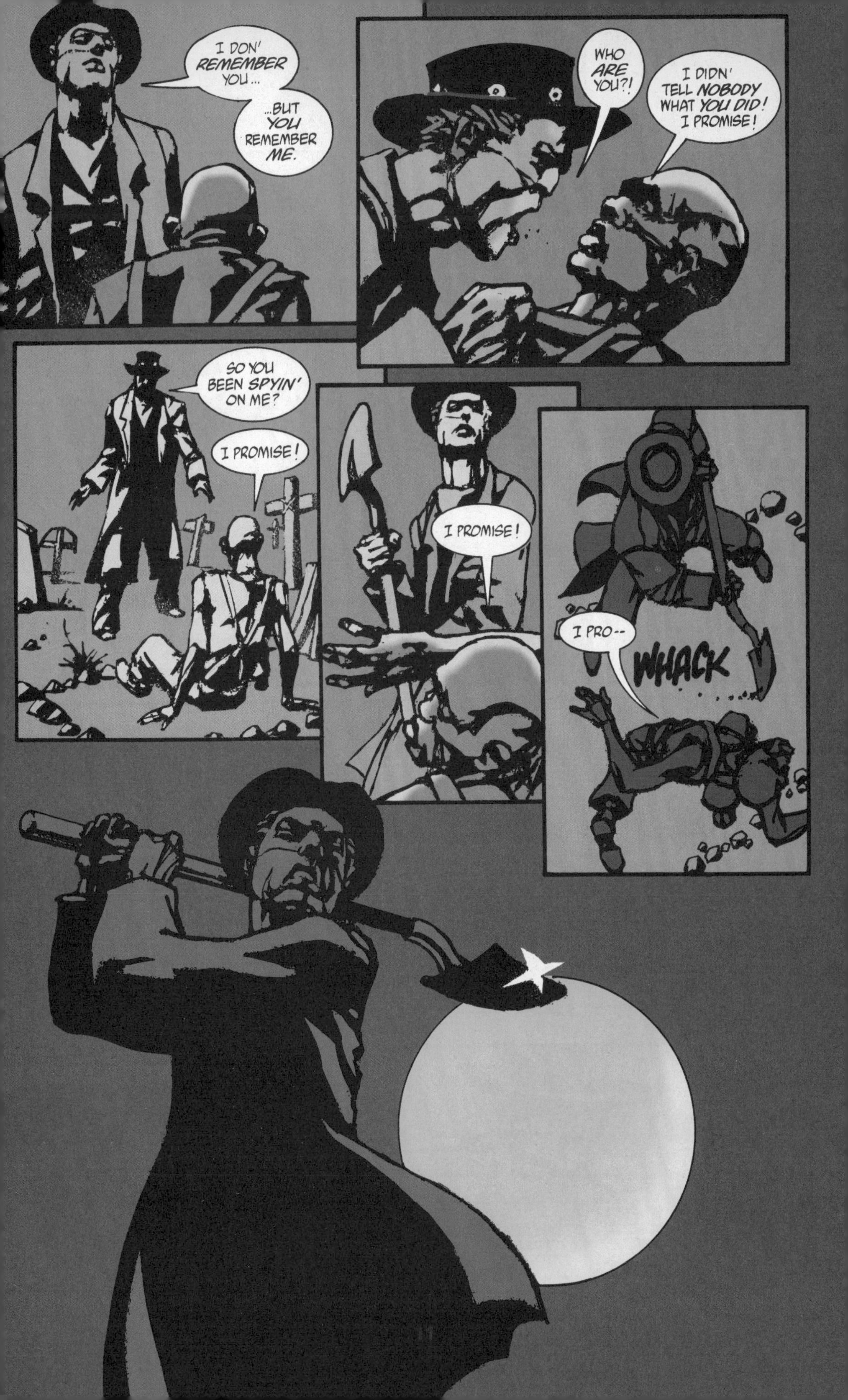
I DON' REMEMBER YOU...
...BUT YOU REMEMBER ME.
WHO ARE YOU?!
I DIDN' TELL NOBODY WHAT YOU DID! I PROMISE!
SO YOU BEEN SPYIN' ON ME?
I PROMISE!
I PROMISE!
I PRO--
WHACK

AN' THAT, THAT'S A MIGHTY FUNNY FEELIN' TA WRAP ONE'S MIND AROUN'!

SEE, I'M *NOT A KILLER.*

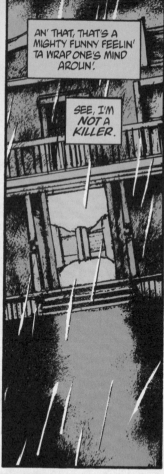

I *REGRET* WHAT I DONE TO THAT SOFT-HEADED GRAVE-DIGGER, BUT I FEEL *GOOD* ABOUT IT, TOO.

I'M NOT LIKE THAT *MURDERIN'* HORSE THIEF *ELMER HUSKEY.* I'M A LAWMAN, A SHERIFF. I HAVE A BEAUTIFUL WIFE, AN' A TOWN THAT LOOKS TA ME TA PROTECT 'EM.

SO I RECKON THAT MEANS SOMETIMES I GOTTA PROTECT *MYSELF.*

YEP, I RECKON THAT'S WHAT IT MEANS. A BODY'S GOTTA WATCH OUT FER *ITSELF,* A'FORE IT CIN WATCH OUT FER OTHERS...

SWEET LORD A MERCY...

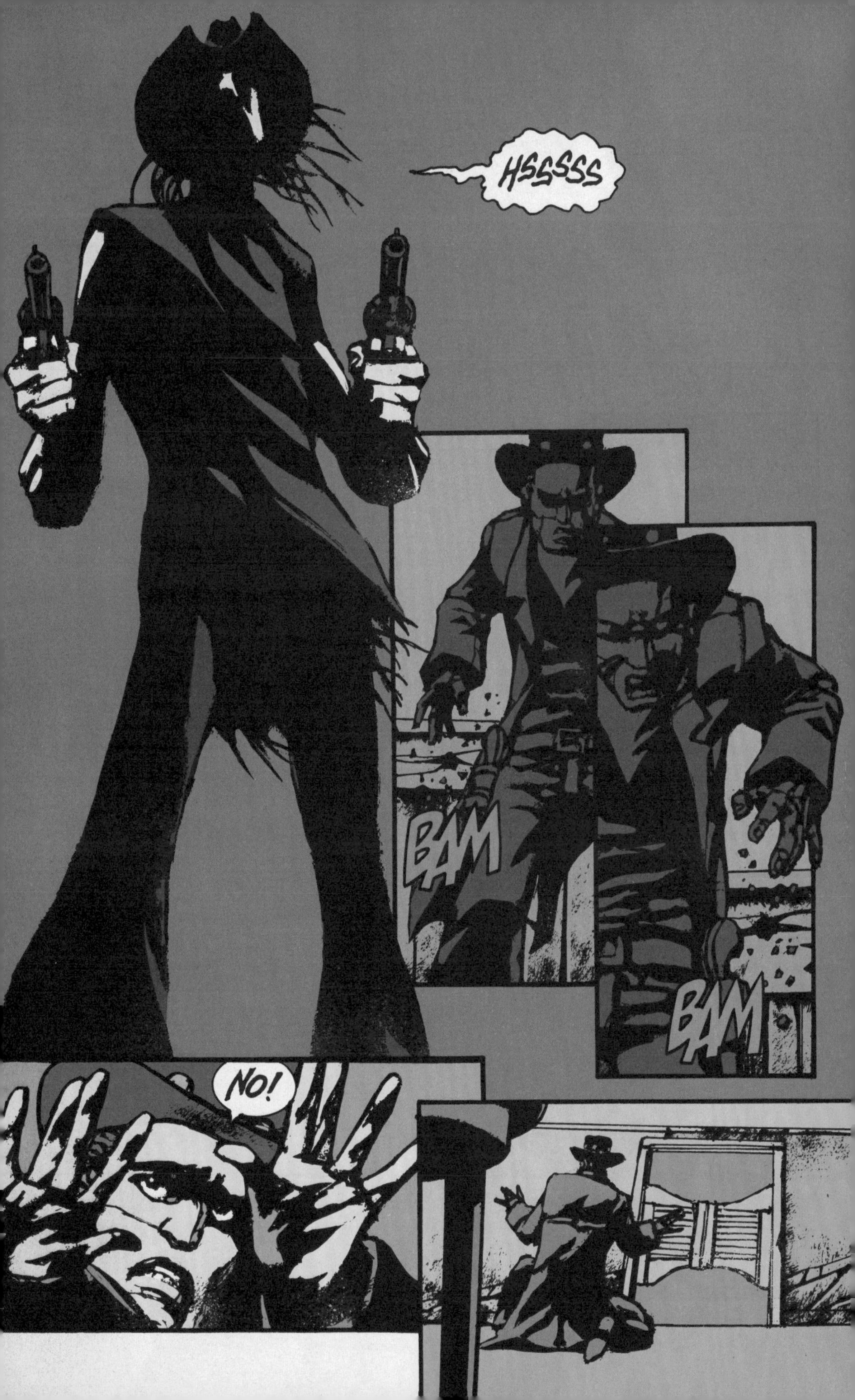
HSSSSS
BAM
BAM
NO!

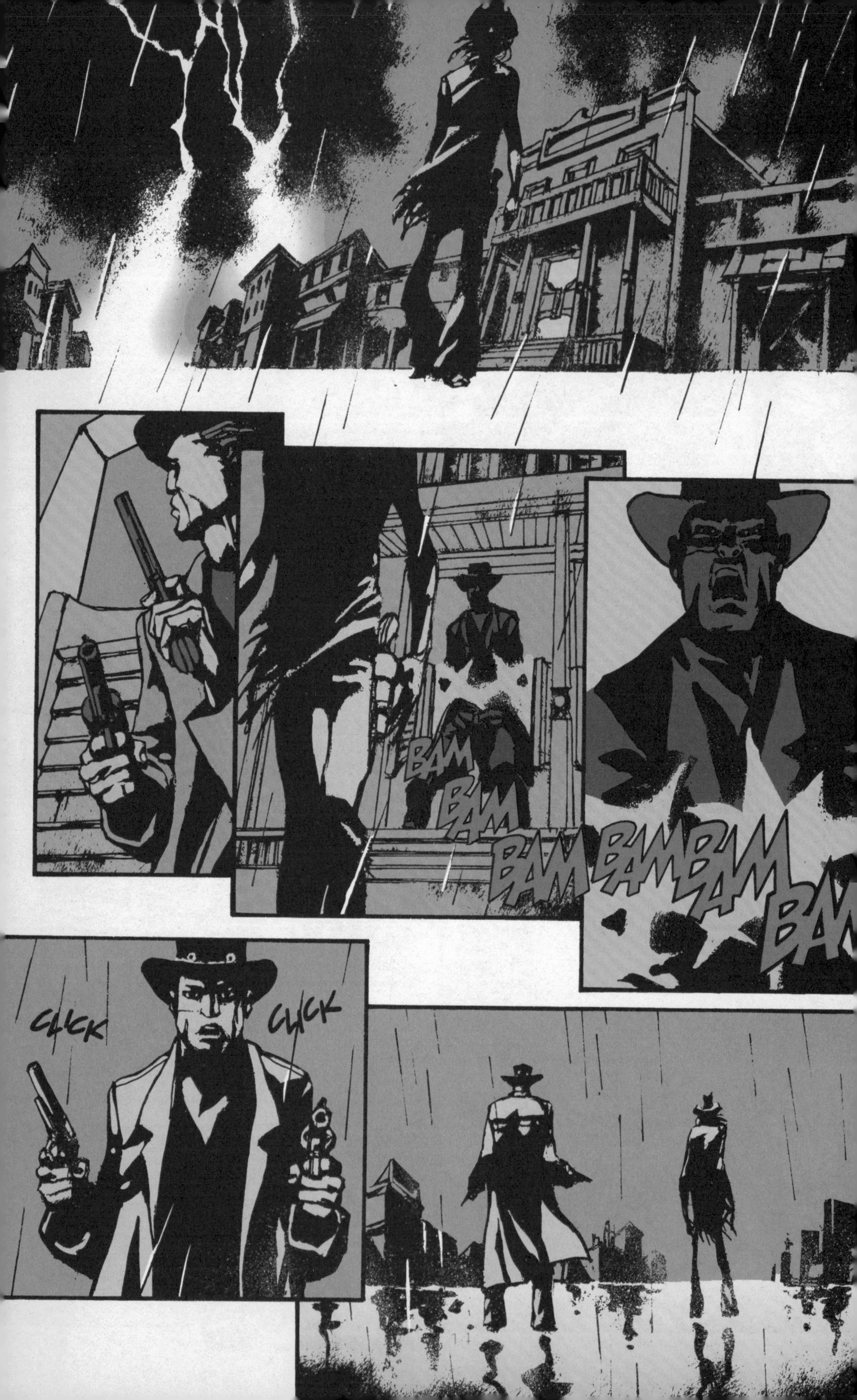
BAM
BAM
BAM BAMBAM
BAM
CLICK
CLICK

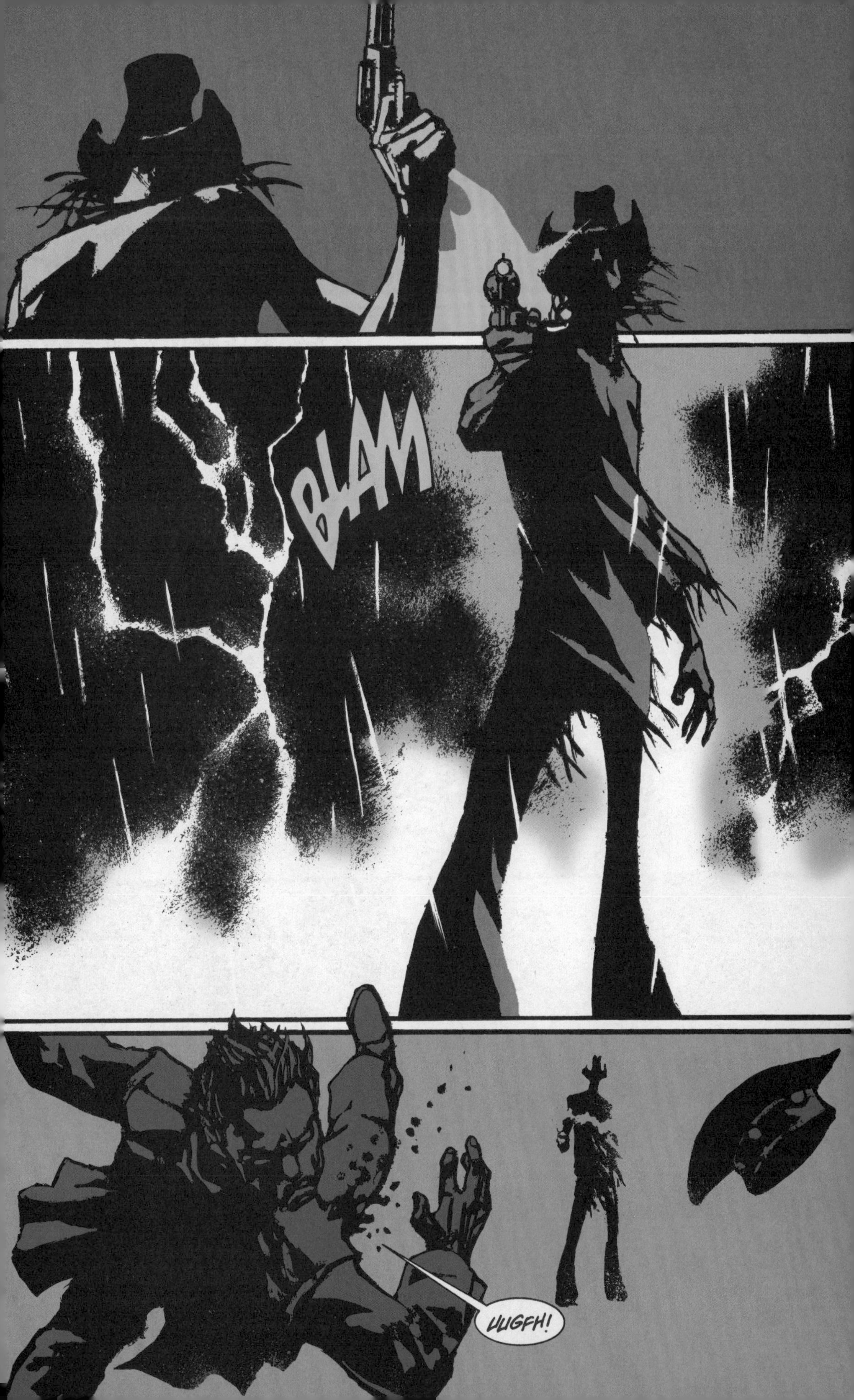
BLAM
UUGFH!

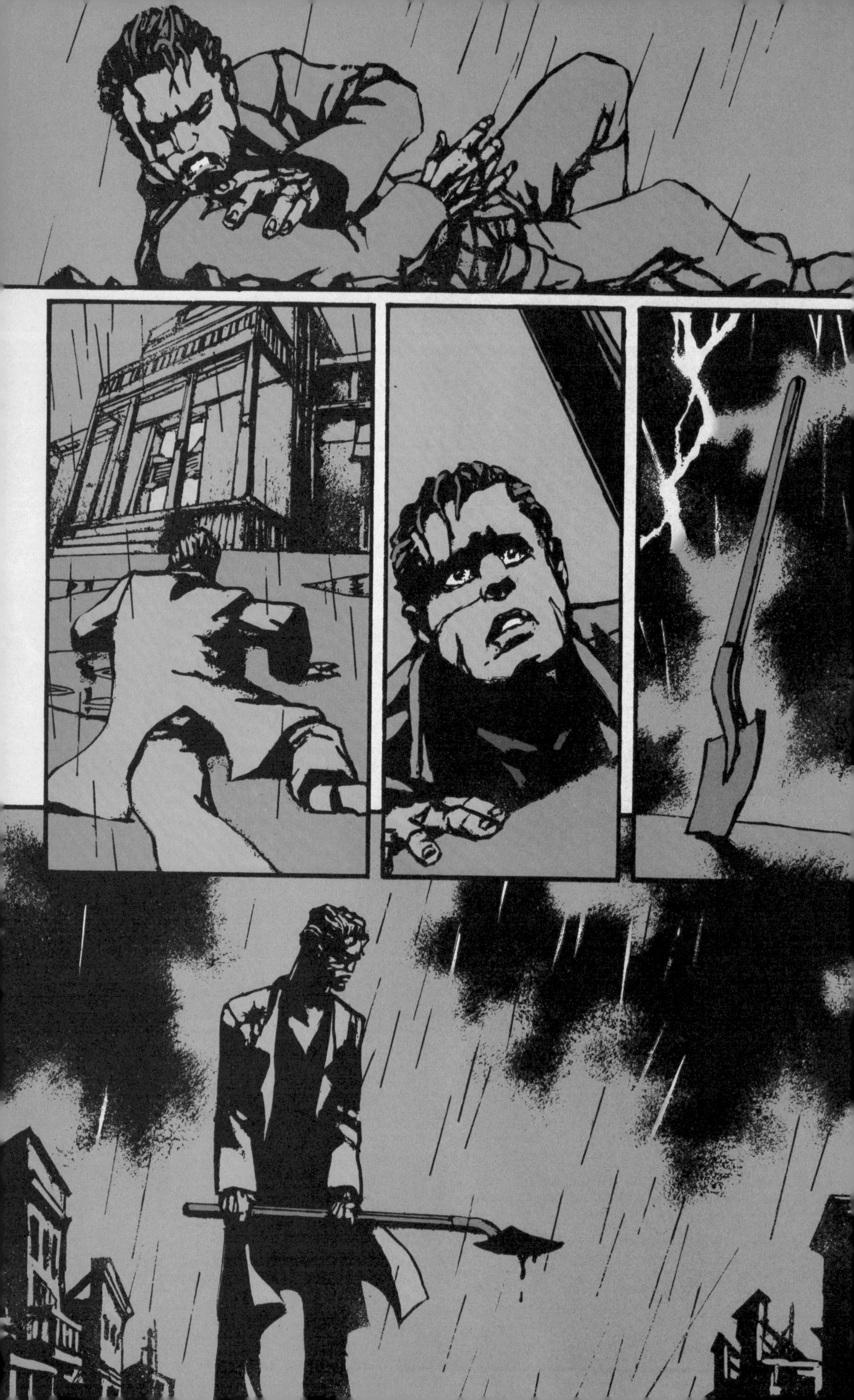

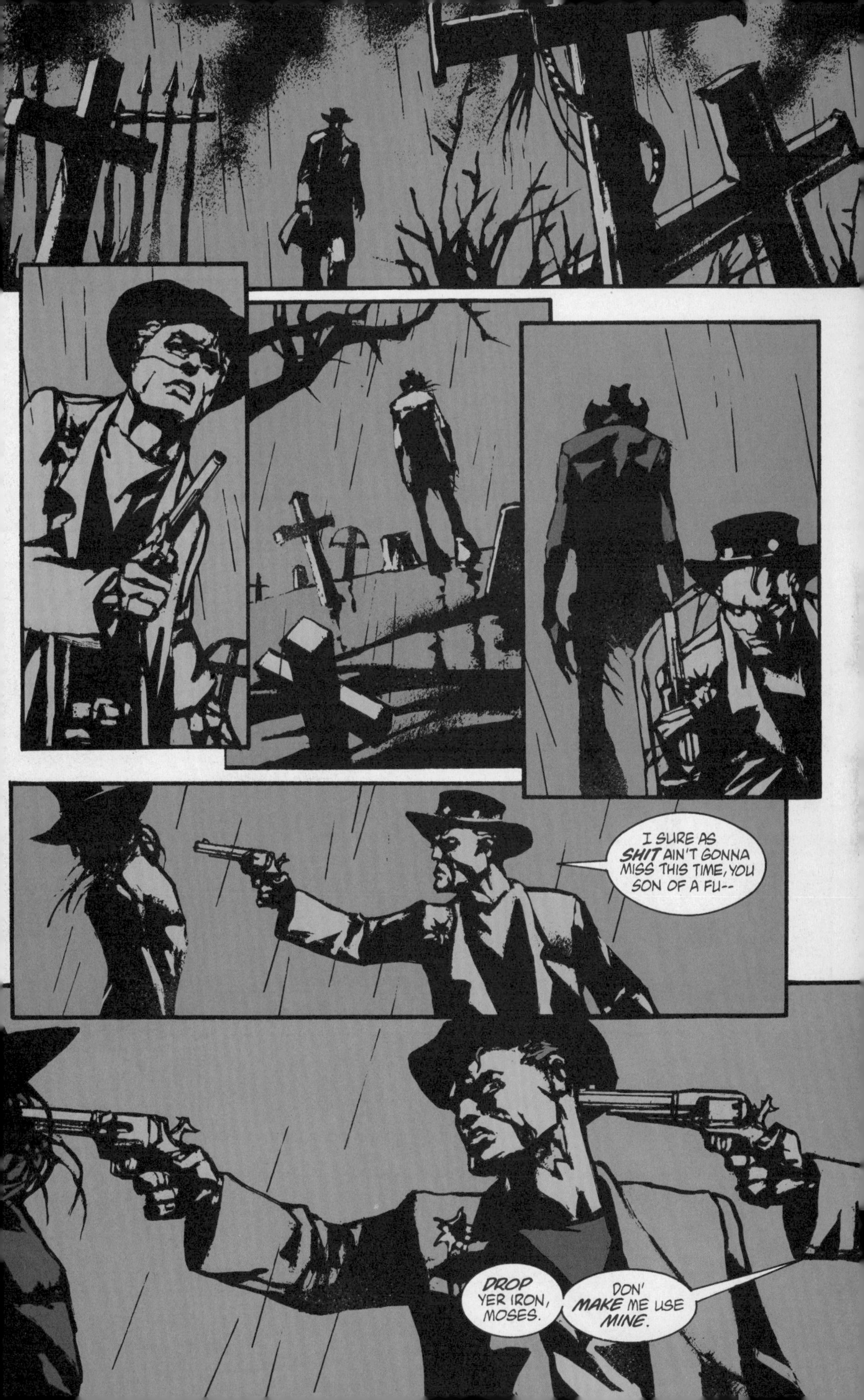
I SURE AS SHIT AIN'T GONNA MISS THIS TIME, YOU SON OF A FU--
DROP YER IRON, MOSES.
DON' MAKE ME USE MINE.

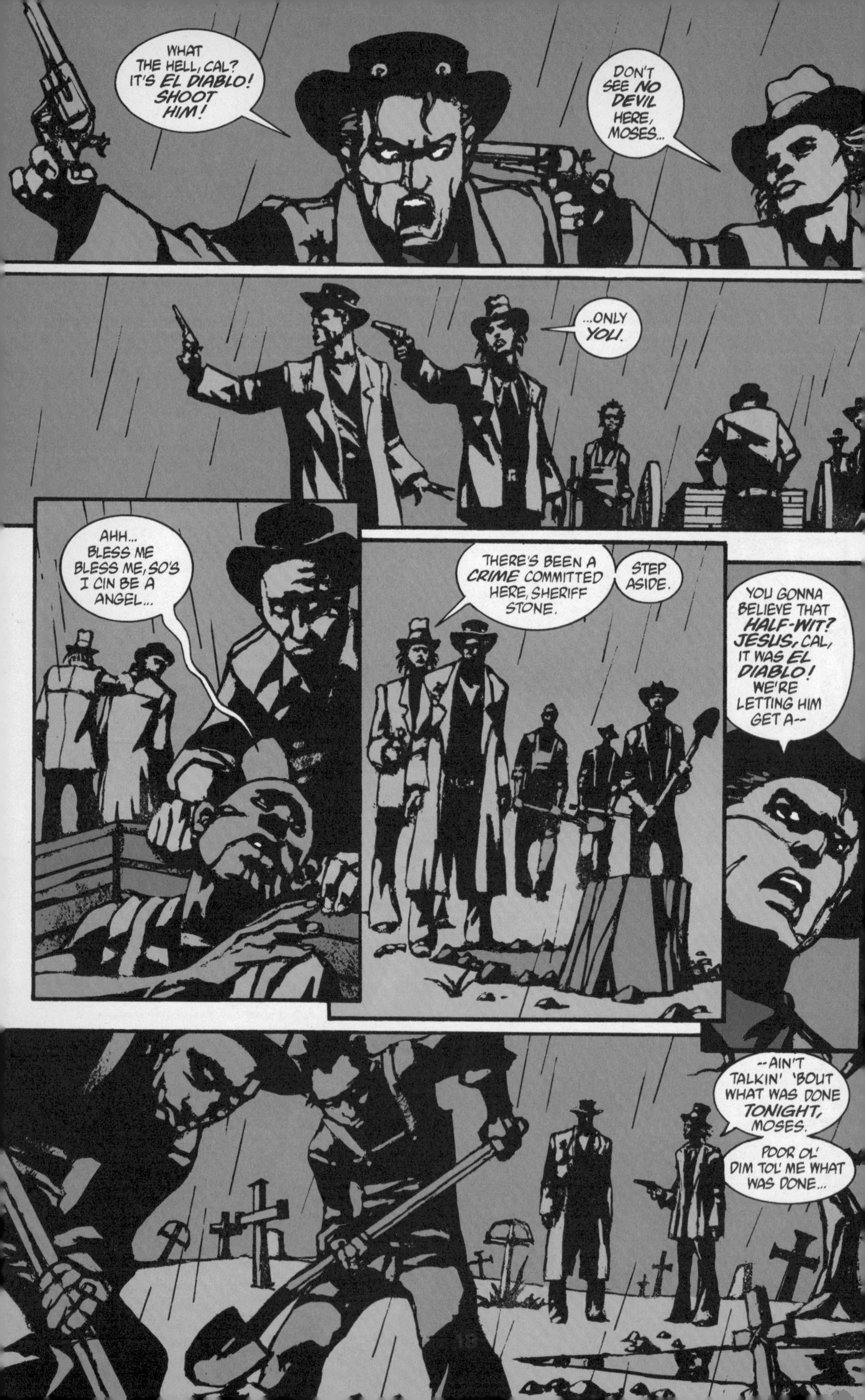
WHAT THE HELL, CAL? IT'S EL DIABLO! SHOOT HIM!
DON'T SEE NO DEVIL HERE, MOSES...
...ONLY YOU.
AHH... BLESS ME BLESS ME, SO'S I CIN BE A ANGEL...
THERE'S BEEN A CRIME COMMITTED HERE, SHERIFF STONE.
STEP ASIDE.
YOU GONNA BELIEVE THAT HALF-WIT? JESUS, CAL, IT WAS EL DIABLO! WE'RE LETTING HIM GET A--
--AIN'T TALKIN' 'BOUT WHAT WAS DONE TONIGHT, MOSES.
POOR OL' DIM TOL' ME WHAT WAS DONE...

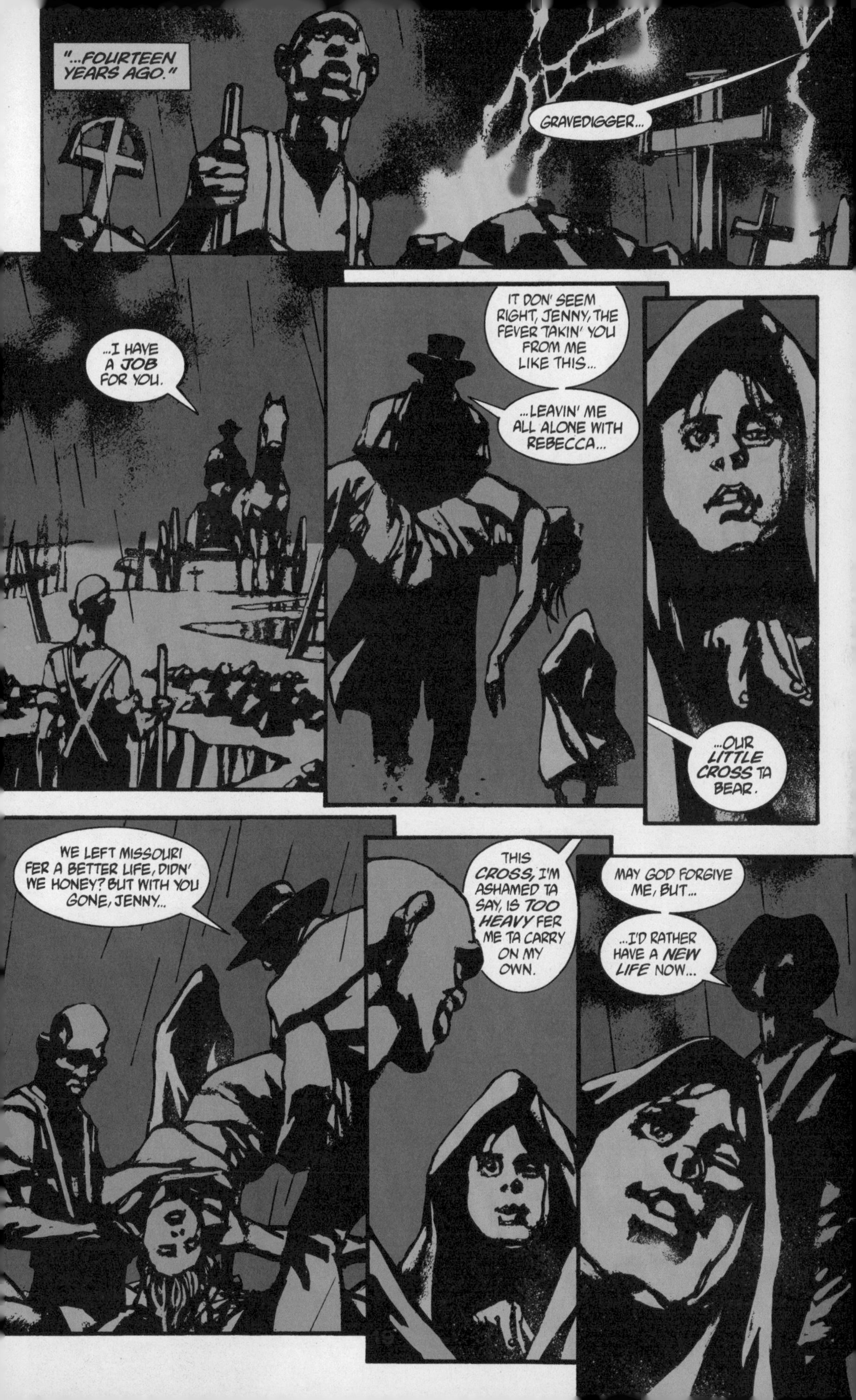
"...FOURTEEN YEARS AGO."
GRAVEDIGGER...
...I HAVE A JOB FOR YOU.
IT DON' SEEM RIGHT, JENNY, THE FEVER TAKIN' YOU FROM ME LIKE THIS...
...LEAVIN' ME ALL ALONE WITH REBECCA...
...OUR LITTLE CROSS TA BEAR.
WE LEFT MISSOURI FER A BETTER LIFE, DIDN' WE HONEY? BUT WITH YOU GONE, JENNY...
THIS CROSS, I'M ASHAMED TA SAY, IS TOO HEAVY FER ME TA CARRY ON MY OWN.
MAY GOD FORGIVE ME, BUT...
...I'D RATHER HAVE A NEW LIFE NOW...

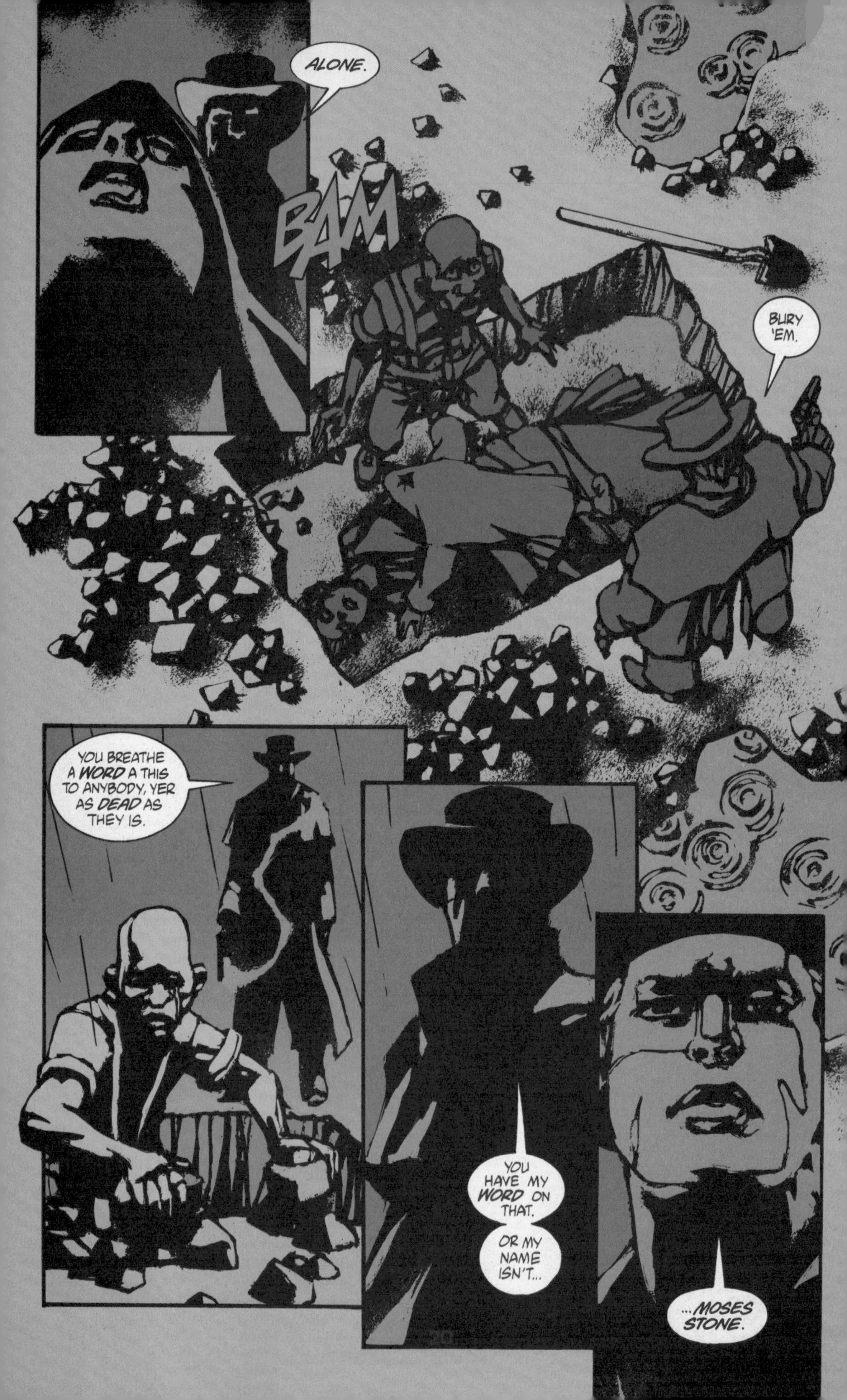
ALONE.
BAM
BURY 'EM.
YOU BREATHE A WORD A THIS TO ANYBODY, YER AS DEAD AS THEY IS.
YOU HAVE MY WORD ON THAT.
OR MY NAME ISN'T...
...MOSES STONE.

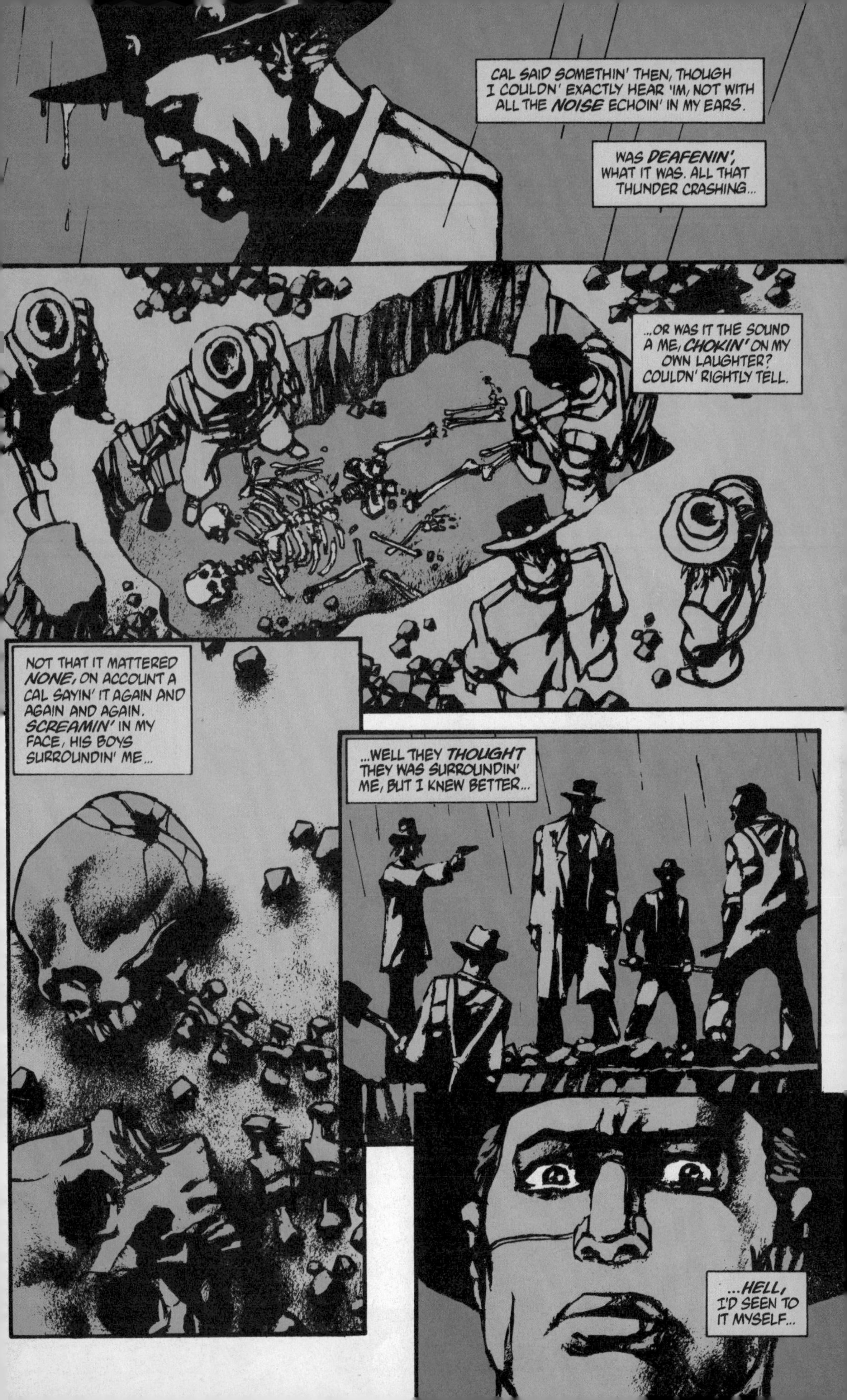
CAL SAID SOMETHIN' THEN, THOUGH I COULDN' EXACTLY HEAR 'IM, NOT WITH ALL THE NOISE ECHOIN' IN MY EARS.
WAS DEAFENIN', WHAT IT WAS. ALL THAT THUNDER CRASHING...
...OR WAS IT THE SOUND A ME, CHOKIN' ON MY OWN LAUGHTER? COULDN' RIGHTLY TELL.
NOT THAT IT MATTERED NONE, ON ACCOUNT A CAL SAYIN' IT AGAIN AND AGAIN AND AGAIN. SCREAMIN' IN MY FACE, HIS BOYS SURROUNDIN' ME...
...WELL THEY THOUGHT THEY WAS SURROUNDIN' ME, BUT I KNEW BETTER...
...HELL, I'D SEEN TO IT MYSELF...

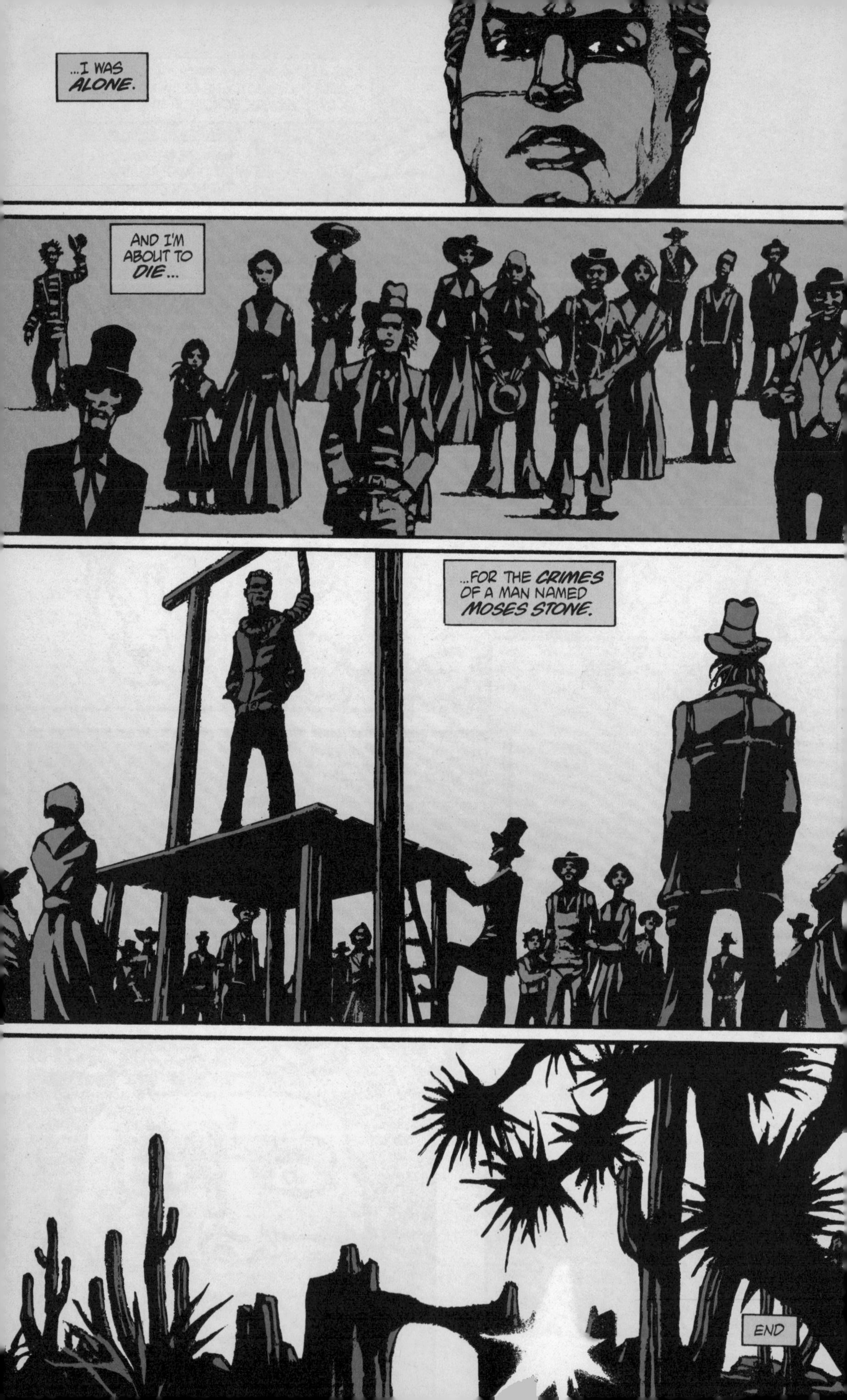
...I WAS ALONE.
AND I'M ABOUT TO DIE...
...FOR THE CRIMES OF A MAN NAMED MOSES STONE.
END

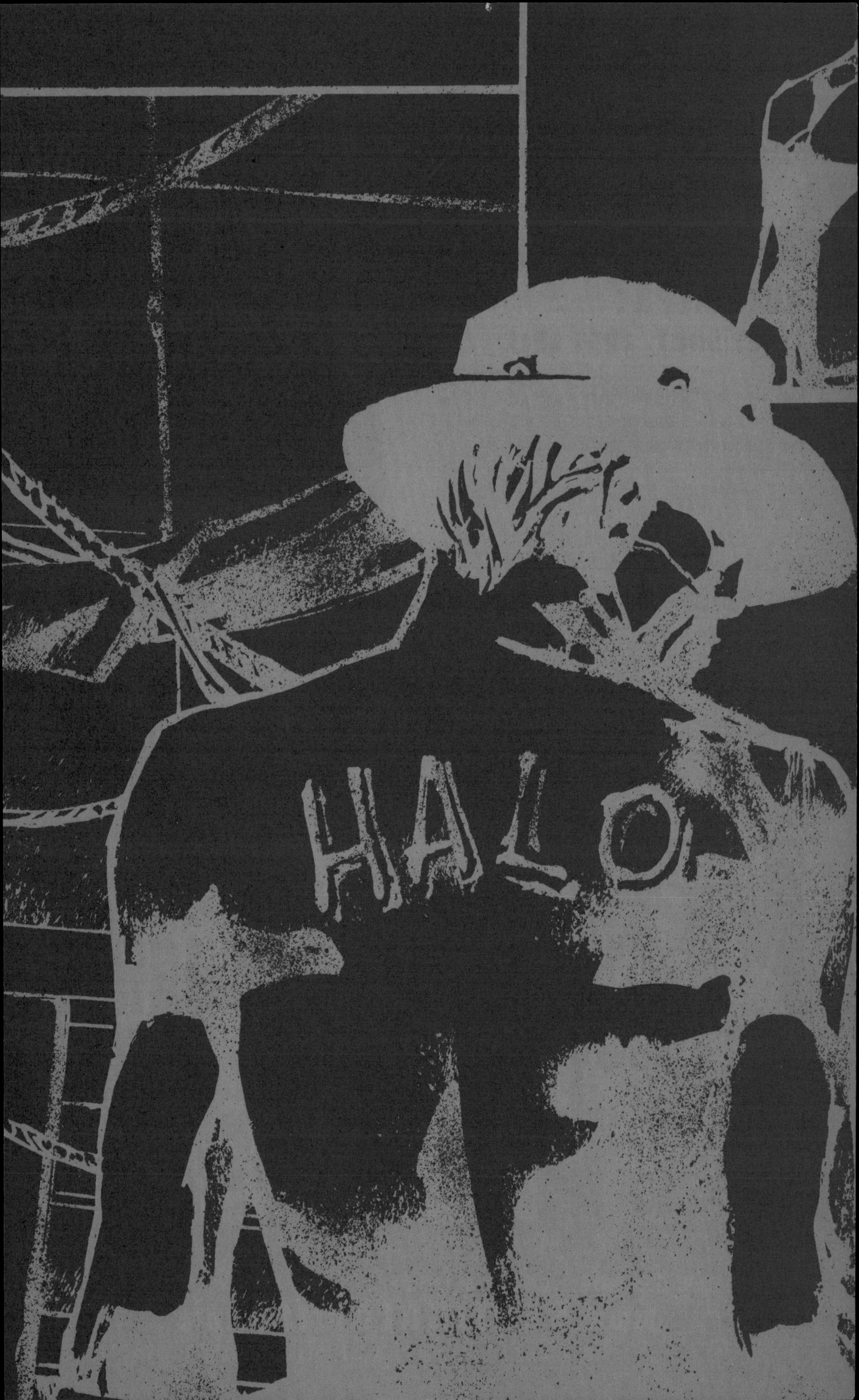
HALO

A MODERN AMERICAN EPIC OF LIFE, DEATH, GOD, LOVE AND REDEMPTION — FILLED WITH SEX, BOOZE AND BLOOD. DELIVERED BY WRITER GARTH ENNIS, ARTIST STEVE DILLON AND VERTIGO:

PREACHER

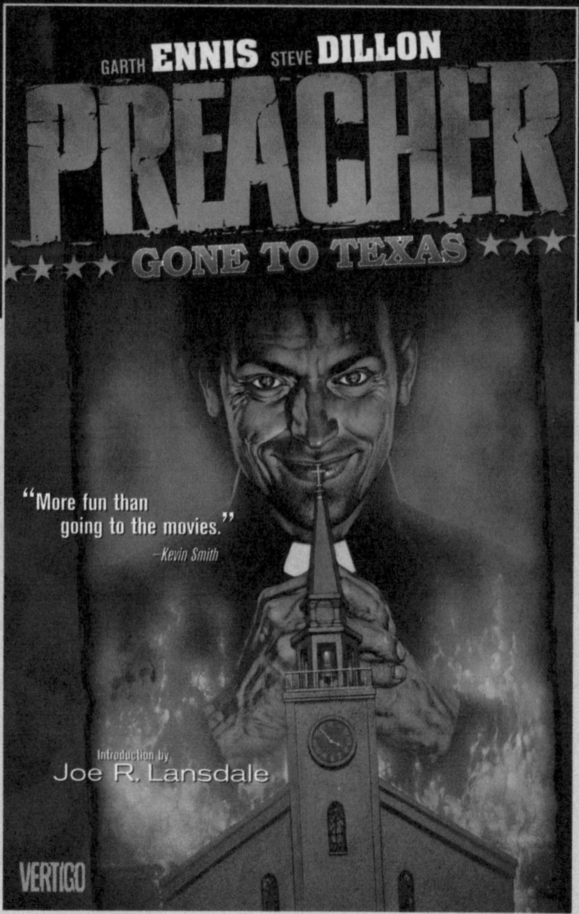
GARTH ENNIS STEVE DILLON
PREACHER
GONE TO TEXAS
"More fun than going to the movies."
—Kevin Smith
Introduction by
Joe R. Lansdale
VERTIGO

VOLUME 1:
GONE TO TEXAS

ALSO AVAILABLE:

VOL. 2: UNTIL THE END OF THE WORLD
VOL. 3: PROUD AMERICANS
VOL. 4: ANCIENT HISTORY
VOL. 5: DIXIE FRIED
VOL. 6: WAR IN THE SUN
VOL. 7: SALVATION
VOL. 8: ALL HELL'S A-COMING
VOL. 9: ALAMO

"JUST ABOUT THE BEST THING TO COME ALONG SINCE COMICS STARTED FINDING THEIR WAY INTO BOOKS."
— ***WASHINGTON POST***

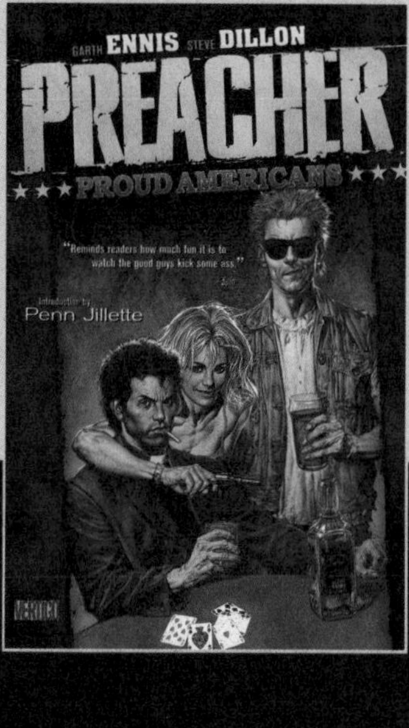
GARTH ENNIS STEVE DILLON
PREACHER
PROUD AMERICANS
"Reminds readers how much fun it is to watch the good guys kick some ass."
Introduction by
Penn Jillette

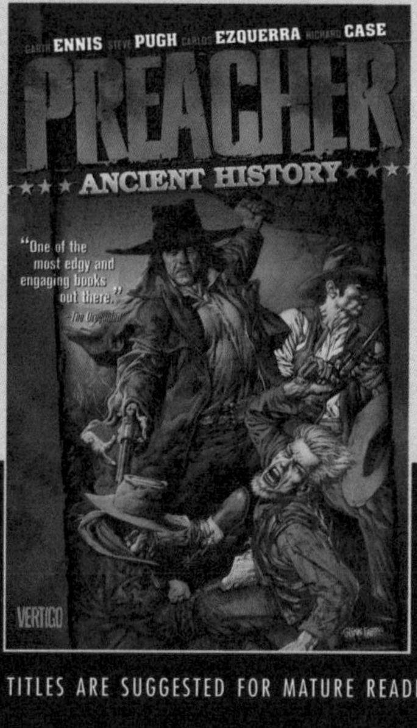
GARTH ENNIS STEVE PUGH CARLOS EZQUERRA RICHARD CASE
PREACHER
ANCIENT HISTORY
"One of the most edgy and engaging books out there."
VERTIGO

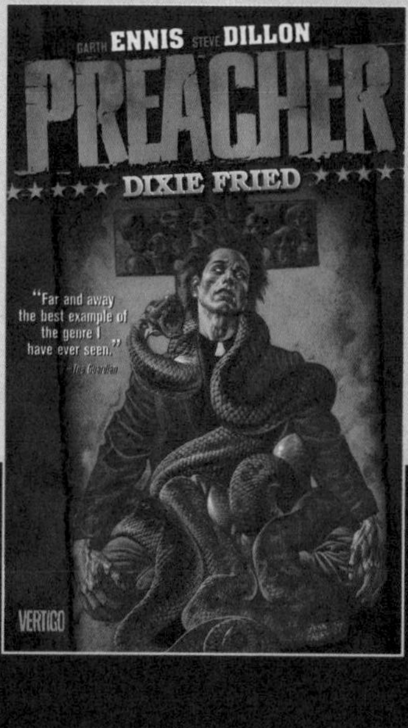
GARTH ENNIS STEVE DILLON
PREACHER
DIXIE FRIED
"Far and away the best example of the genre I have ever seen."
VERTIGO

ALL TITLES ARE SUGGESTED FOR MATURE READERS.

SEARCH THE GRAPHIC NOVELS SECTION OF

www.VERTIGOCOMICS.com

FOR ART AND INFORMATION ON ALL OF OUR BOOKS!

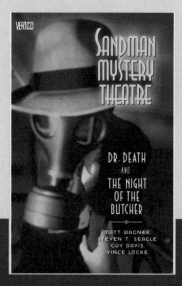